Public Corruption

Regional and National Perspectives on Procurement Fraud

Public Corruption

Regional and National Perspectives on Procurement Fraud

Edited by
Petter Gottschalk
Perry Stanislas

CRC Press
Taylor & Francis Group
Boca Raton London New York

CRC Press is an imprint of the
Taylor & Francis Group, an **informa** business

CRC Press
Taylor & Francis Group
6000 Broken Sound Parkway NW, Suite 300
Boca Raton, FL 33487-2742

First issued in paperback 2020

ISBN-13: 978-1-4987-5797-3 (hbk)
ISBN-13: 978-0-367-59546-3 (pbk)

Library of Congress Cataloging-in-Publication Data

Names: Gottschalk, Petter, 1950- editor. | Stanislas, Perry, editor.
Title: Public corruption : regional and national perspectives on procurement
fraud / edited by Petter Gottschalk, Perry Stanislas.
Description: Boca Raton : CRC Press, [2017]
Identifiers: LCCN 2016032407| ISBN 9781498757973 (hardback) | ISBN 1498757979
(hardback) | ISBN 9781351998949 (web pdf) | ISBN 1351998943 (web pdf)
Subjects: LCSH: Government purchasing--Law and legislation--Criminal
provisions. | White collar crimes--Law and legislation. | Government
purchasing--Corrupt practices.
Classification: LCC K5215 .P83 2017 | DDC 345/.0263--dc23
LC record available at https://lccn.loc.gov/2016032407

Visit the Taylor & Francis Web site at
http://www.taylorandfrancis.com

and the CRC Press Web site at
http://www.crcpress.com

Contents

Introduction

PETTER GOTTSCHALK
PERRY STANISLAS

Transparency International has estimated that the loss to the building and construction industry through corrupt practices is approximately $1 trillion in a growing industry that generates U.S. $7.2 trillion globally (Gardiner, 2013). The construction industry is not unique or alone in the level of white-collar crime that seems intrinsic to its basic operation. Recently, the governing body of the world's most popular sport, FIFA, was in the middle of a controversy that confirmed long-held suspicions about corruption at the heart of the world football administration, which linked advanced European countries and economies to those in the Caribbean, Latin America, and the Middle East inter alia (Peck and Wallace, 2015). Construction projects for major sporting events are a potentially rich source of corrupt practices (Stanislas, 2014). It appears that very few areas of commercial, civic, cultural, and political life is immune from corrupt criminal practices.

Public corruption is one form of financial crime that involves a breach of trust, or an abuse of position by federal, state, or local government officials. In 2015, the National Institute of Justice (2015) supported the research related to public corruption. FBI (2015) wrote that public corruption was their top priority among criminal investigations, and for good reason:

> Public corruption poses a fundamental threat to our national security and way of life. It impacts everything from how well our borders are secured and our neighborhoods protected . . . to verdicts handed down in courts . . . to the quality of our roads, schools, and other government services. And it takes a significant toll on our pocketbooks, wasting billions in tax dollars every year. The FBI I singularly situated to combat this corruption, with the skills and capabilities to run complex undercover operations and surveillance.

Connecticut U.S. attorney Dierdre Daly and other federal officials announced in February 2015 a new public corruption task force to investigate corrupt public officials, the misuse of public funds, and related criminal activity. It was the first time that several federal agencies were brought together in a single corruption investigation unit. The task force will focus not only on rooting out corrupt elected officials, but also federal, state, and municipal employees who use their position for personal gain (http://wtnh.com/2015/02/04/feds-announce-connecticut-public-corruption-task-force/).

The goals of the research and evaluation on white-collar crime and public corruption supported by the National Institute of Justice (2015) were to enhance scientific knowledge and to inform practice and policy related to preventing or combating white-collar crime and public corruption. The objectives of the solicitation were to fund research and evaluation projects that employ high-quality, rigorous social science methods to substantially advance knowledge in this topic area and produce results with practical implications for preventing or combating white-collar crime and public corruption.

Cordis (2014) studied public corruption in the United States. She examined the relation between corruption and the composition of state government spending. Her analysis reveals that corruption lowers the share of government spending devoted to higher education and raises the share of spending devoted to other nonallocable budget items.

Elite public criminals can use the power and apparent legitimacy of their office to extort bribes or direct procurement to entities they control or profit from. They can shape the environment by organizing procurement processes and formulating regulatory requirements. Private elites can indirectly achieve the same profitable result by suborning public officials to modify the environment to benefit the private party, for example, by going to a nonbid, sole-source market (Passas, 2007).

Financial crime can be classified into four categories: fraud, theft, manipulation, and corruption (Gottschalk, 2015). Corruption can be defined as the giving, offering, promising, requesting, receiving, taking, agreeing to taking, or accepting of an improper advantage in terms of money or other consideration related to position, office, or assignment (Boles, 2014). The improper advantage does not have to be connected to a specific action or to not doing this action. It is sufficient if the advantage can be linked to a person's position, office, or assignment. An individual or group is guilty of corruption if they accept money or money's worth for doing something that they are under a duty to do anyway or that they are under a duty not to do, or to exercise a legitimate discretion for improper reason (Ksenia, 2008). Corruption is to destroy or pervert the integrity or fidelity of a person in his discharge of duty; it is to induce to act dishonestly or unfaithfully; it is to make venal; and it is to bribe.

Transparency International (2014) defines corruption as the abuse of entrusted power for private gain. In the case of public corruption discussed later, private gain is interpreted widely to include gains accruing to the government official, his or her family members, close friends, political party, favorite charity, or hometown or a corporate or other entity in which the official or the official's family or close friends have a financial or social interest. A public official is any officer or employee of government, including legislators and judges, and any person participating as juror, advisor, consultant, or otherwise in performing a governmental function (Boles, 2014).

Cordis and Milyo (2013) do also define corruption as the abuse of entrusted power for private gain, and public corruption as the misuse of public office for private gain, or more broadly as an abuse of public trust. They include, for example, postal employees charged with theft of mail. Their definition seems to include almost all kinds of financial crime and is thus not useful in our context. In their table of U.S. Code titles for lead charge, the most relevant titles seem to be the following:

- Paragraph 201 Bribery of Public Officials and Witnesses
- Paragraph 641 Public Money, Property or Records
- Paragraph 666 Theft/Bribery in Programs Receiving Federal Funds

Corruption is a concealed abuse of a position of trust by an expectation that one will do what one is relied on to do (Boles, 2014). From an economic perspective, corruption is generally defined as the misuse of a position of authority for private or personal benefit where misuse typically constitutes a breach of legal norms. Corruption is expected to occur where (1) there is a control over economic benefits and costs and, thus, the potential for economic rents—that is, profits, and (2) persons in positions of authority have discretion over the allocation of such benefits and costs. Corruption can reflect rational, self-interested behavior by persons using their discretion to direct allocations to themselves or to other social actors who offer rewards in return for favorable discretionary treatment (Misangyi et al., 2008).

In corruption, an external opportunity can supply benefits to solve a problem. Typically, a problem is solved by providing benefits to persons in positions of authority. According to Misangyi et al. (2008), the rational choice perspective on corruption assumes that corruption is a response to situations that present opportunities for gain and the discretionary power to appropriate that gain. Corruption involves behavior on the part of officials in the public or private sectors in which they improperly and unlawfully enrich themselves and/or those close to them, or induce others to do so by misusing the position in which they are placed.

Corruption covers a wide range of illegal activities such as kickbacks, embezzlement, and extortion. Kayrak (2008) includes money laundering as well in his definition of corruption. We do not, and also we find some of the definitions referred to earlier to be too wide.

The notion of corruption may be classified as sporadic or systemic corruption, bureaucratic or political corruption, grand or petty corruption, personal or organizational corruption, and active and passive corruption. For example, Lange (2008) defines organizational corruption as the pursuit of individual interests by one or more organizational actors through the intentional misdirection of organizational resources or perversion of organizational routines, which is commonly understood to be highly undesirable for any parties holding a stake in the organization's performance. Political corruption often involves illicit collusion between states, organized criminals, and white-collar criminals (Kupatadze, 2015).

The word corruption, as originally defined, means a hidden transaction. In a study of corruption in the oil industry business in Norway, Røstvik (2015) suggests that corruption is latent in human nature. It is not about companies, it is about people, what they do, and how greed tempts them to act contrary to most people's clear ethical knowledge of where the lines are drawn. It is about ignoring the lines and crossing them.

Pinto et al. (2008) focused on two fundamental dimensions of corruption in organizations: whether the individual or the organization is the beneficiary of the corrupt activity, and whether the corrupt behavior is undertaken by an individual actor or by two or more actors. Although an organization of corrupt individuals is a scaling up of personally beneficial corrupt behaviors to the organization level, a corrupt organization consists of a group of employees carrying out corrupt behaviors on behalf of the organization. This is similar to a distinction between the bribed and the briber, where the bribed is an individual beneficiary of the corruption, whereas the briber is an organizational beneficiary of the corruption.

Bowman and Gilligan (2008) suggest that corruption may be a greater issue for the Australian public than has been assumed in the past, given the relatively low level of reported systematic corruption in Australia. Moreover, while there may be a widespread agreement that corruption in Australia is harmful and perhaps inevitable, people can find it difficult at times to differentiate between what is corrupt and what is not. In this regard, cultural differences in understanding what constitutes corrupt practices are far from straightforward. At what point do reasonable expectations around notions of duty, responsibility, and good citizenship and group belonging cross over into matters of criminal behavior is a vexed and contentious matter (Rothstein and Torsello, 2013).

Public corruption is corruption involving public officials. Section 201 of Title 18 of the U.S. Code governs the offenses of bribery and illegal gratuity. Relevant definitions are set forth in Section 201. To prove corruption, the government must generally establish that (1) a thing of value was given, offered, or promised to (or, in the case of a recipient, demanded, sought, received, or accepted by), (2) a present or future public official, (3) for an official act, and (4) with corrupt intent or intent to influence (or be influenced). Corruption requires proof of intent (Dwyer et al., 2014). Norwegian legislation emphasizes an undue, improper, and unreasonable advantage as corruption.

Recently corruption has become an issue of major political and economic significance when developing countries are trying to make their transition into becoming developed countries. In the past, bilateral donors, such as the United States and Norway, not only overlooked partisan self-enrichment on the part of developing country governments, they also supported many corrupt regimes in Africa and other parts of the world in return for bilateral relationships (Abdulai, 2009).

Public corruption is a white-collar crime (Gottschalk, 2015). A white-collar criminal is typically a member of the privileged socioeconomic classes in society (Sutherland, 1949) who is involved in illegal activities and commits nonviolent acts for a financial gain (Gottschalk, 2014). The white-collar criminal is a person of respectability who commits crime in a professional setting, where criminal activities are concealed and disguised in organizational work by law-abiding behavior (Pontell et al., 2014). The criminal has power and influence; he forms relationships with other persons or professionals, which protects him from developing a criminal identity; and he enjoys trust from others in privileged networks (Benson and Simpson, 2014). White-collar crime refers to offenses committed in an organization by those who indulge in dishonest activities—either by themselves or using agents—for a financial gain (Schoepfer et al., 2014).

Law enforcement targeted at white-collar criminals is nonaggressive and often discrete not only because of the upper-class affiliation. Another reason is white-collar defendants' ability to recruit top defense lawyers who apply symbolic defense in addition to substance defense, as well as information control, in their work for white-collar clients (Gottschalk, 2014). It is recognized that having a well-qualified and possibly famous attorney increases one's chances of a favorable outcome in any legal dispute. Some individual white-collar offenders avoid criminal prosecution because of the class bias of the courts (Tombs and Whyte, 2003).

When white-collar criminals appear before their sentencing judges, they can correctly claim to be first-time offenders. According to Slyke and Bales (2013), theory and empirical research have often agreed that white-collar offenders benefit from leniency at the sentencing stage of criminal justice system processes. Croall (2007) argues that the term *crime* is contentious, as many of the harmful activities of businesses or occupational elites are not subject to criminal law and punishment but administrative or regulatory law and penalties and sanctions. Therefore, very few white-collar criminals seem to be put on trial, and even fewer higher class criminals are sentenced to imprisonment. Another reason for the low prosecution and conviction rate for white-collar criminals is the extraordinary broadly and fuzzy defined offenses in criminal law for a white-collar crime (Hasnas et al., 2010).

References

Abdulai, A.G. (2009). Political will in combating corruption in developing and transition economies: A comparative study of Singapore, Hong Kong and Ghana, *Journal of Financial Crime*, 16 (4), 387–417.

Benson, M.L. and Simpson, S.S. (2014). *Understanding White-Collar Crime—An Opportunity Perspective*, New York: Routledge.

Boles, J. (2014). The two faces of bribery: International corruption pathways meet conflicting legislative regimes, *Michigan Journal of International Law*, 35 (4), 673–713.

Bowman, D. and Gilligan, G. (2008). Public awareness of corruption in Australia, *Journal of Financial Crime*, 14 (4), 438–452.

Cordis, A.S. (2014). Corruption and the Composition of Public Spending in the United States, *Public Finance Review*, 42 (6), 745–773.

Cordis, A. and Milyo, J. (2013). Measuring Public Corruption in the United States: Evidence from Administrative Records of Federal Prosecutions, Working Paper, University of Missouri, http://economics.missouri.edu/working-papers/2013/WP1322_milyo.pdf.

Croall, H. (2007). *Victims, Crime and Society*. Los Angeles, CA: Sage Publications.

Dwyer, L., Golden, K. and Lehman, S. (2014). Public Corruption, *American Criminal Law Review*, 51 (4), 1549–1600.

FBI (2015). *It's Our Top Priority Among Criminal Investigations—And for Good Reason*, Federal Bureau of Investigation, http://www.fbi.gov/about-us/investigate/corruption, retrieved February 4, 2015.

Gardiner, J. (2013). Construction Fraud Costs $1 Trillon Globally, www.building.co.uk, October 25, retrieved July 10, 2010.

Gottschalk, P. (2014). *Policing White-Collar Crime: Characteristics of White-Collar Criminals*. Boca Raton, FL: CRC Press Taylor & Francis Group.

Gottschalk, P. (2015). *Fraud Examiners in White-Collar Crime Investigations*. Boca Raton, FL: CRC Press Taylor & Francis Group.

Hasnas, J., Prentice, R. and Strudler, A. (2010). New directions in legal scholarship: Implications for business ethics research, theory, and practice, *Business Ethics Quarterly*, 20 (3), 503–531.

Kayrak, M. (2008). Evolving challenges for supreme audit institutions in struggling with corruption, *Journal of Financial Crime*, 15 (1), 60–70.

Ksenia, G. (2008). Can corruption and economic crime be controlled in developing countries and if so, is it cost-effective? *Journal of Financial Crime*, 15 (2), 223–233.

Kupatadze, A. (2015). Political corruption in Eurasia: Understanding collusion between states, organized crime and business, *Theoretical Criminology*, 19 (2), 198–215.

Lange, D. (2008). A multidimensional conceptualization of organizational corruption control, *Academy of Management Review*, 33 (3), 710–729.

Misangyi, V.F., Weaver, G.R. and Elms, H. (2008). Ending corruption: The interplay among institutional logics, resources, and institutional entrepreneurs, *Academy of Management Review*, 33 (3), 750–770.

National Institute of Justice (2015). *Research and Evaluation on White-Collar Crime and Public Corruption*, Office of Justice Programs, U.S. Department of Justice, https://www.ncjrs.gov/pdffiles1/nij/sl001155.pdf, retrieved February 4, 2015.

Passas, N. (1990). Anomie and corporate deviance, *Contemporary Crises*, 14, 157–178.

Peck, T. and Wallace, S. (2015). Fifa corruption scandal: Sepp blatter resigns as president of football organisation, *The Independent*, www.independent.co.uk. June 2, accessed July 2, 2015.

Pinto, J., Leana, C.R. and Pil, F.K. (2008). Corrupt organizations or organizations of corrupt individuals? Two types of organizational-level corruption, *Academy of Management Review*, 33 (3), 685–709.

Pontell, H.N., Black, W.K. and Geis, G. (2014). Too big to fail, too powerful to jail? On the absence of criminal prosecutions after the 2008 financial meltdown, *Crime, Law, and Social Change*, 61, 1–13.

Rostein, B. and Torsello, D. (2013). *Is Corruption Understood Differently in Different Cultures, Anthropology Meets Political Science*, University of Gothenburg, Working Papers 2013: 5.

Røstvik, H.N. (2015). *Corruption the Nobel Way: Dirty Fuels & The Sunshine Revolution*. Oslo, Norway: Kolofon Publishing.

Schoepfer, A., Piquero, N.L. and Langton, L. (2014). Low self-control versus the desire-for-control: An empirical test of white-collar crime and conventional crime, *Deviant Behavior*, 35 (3), 197–214.

Slyke, S.R.V. and Bales, W.D. (2013). Gender dynamics in the sentencing of white-collar offenders, *Criminal Justice Studies*, 26 (2), 168–196.

Stanislas, P. (2014). Police leadership and strategic management of mega events, policing the 2012 London olympic and paralympic games, in Albrecht, J., Dow, M., Plecas, D., and Das, D. (editors), *Policing Major Events, Perspectives from Around the World*, Boca Raton, FL: CRC Press.

Sutherland, E.H. (1949). *White Collar Crime*. New York: Holt Rinehart and Winston.

Tombs, S. and Whyte, D. (2003). Scrutinizing the powerful: Crime, contemporary political economy, and critical social research. In S. Tombs and D. Whyte (editors), *Unmasking the Crimes of the Powerful* (pp. 3–48), Lang, New York.

Transparency International (2014). *Curbing Corruption in Public Procurement—A Practical Guide*, www.transparency.org, 40 pp.

Authors

James F. Albrecht is an assistant professor of criminal justice and homeland security at Pace University, New York City. He is a retired NYPD captain and served as the police chief of criminal investigations in the EULEX Rule of Law mission in Kosovo. His research interests focus on police corruption, international terrorism and transnational crime, community policing, and effective leadership in public service. Albrecht completed his PhD in criminal justice at the University of New Haven, Connecticut, in 2016. He has conducted research and made recommendations to improve law enforcement effectiveness and legitimacy in Ukraine.

Oyesoji Aremu is a professor of counseling and criminal justice studies of an international reputation. He works at the Institute for Peace and Strategic Studies, University of Ibadan, Nigeria. Aremu is a Commonwealth fellow and visiting scholar at the Institute of Criminal Justice Studies, University of Portsmouth, the United Kingdom and has more than 100 publications in local and international serials. Oyesoji Aremu's main research areas include policing, emotional intelligence, and adolescents' non-conforming behaviors; he is currently researching on psychology of peace with an emphasis on terrorism in Nigeria.

Hasan T. Arslan is an assistant professor of criminal justice and security in the Dyson College of Arts and Sciences, Pace University, New York. Hasan holds a law degree from Marmara University, Istanbul, Turkey. He earned his PhD at the College of Criminal Justice, Sam Houston State University of Huntsville, Texas, in 2008. His doctoral dissertation involved one of the largest eco-terrorism databases in the world. Dr. Arslan worked for nine years at the Institute for the Study of Violent Groups (ISVG), where he contributed to the development of a database capable of tracking global and domestic extremist groups.

Michael L. Benson is a professor in the school of criminal justice at the University of Cincinnati, Ohio. He is a fellow of the American Society of Criminology and a former president of the white-collar crime research consortium of the National White-Collar Crime Research Center in Washington DC. He received the Outstanding Scholarship Award from the society for his book, *Combating Corporate Crime: Local Prosecutors at Work*, and has published extensively on white-collar and corporate crime. His most recent book is *The Oxford Handbook on White-Collar Crime* co-edited with Shanna R. Van Slyke and Francis T. Cullen.

Fasihuddin is a senior officer in the police service of Pakistan. He is also the president of the Pakistan Society of Criminology and the editor-in-chief of the Pakistan Journal of Criminology. Fasihuddin is also the patron-in-chief of the Utman-khel tribe, the largest tribe of Pakhtoons in Pakistan. He has contributed to criminology literature in English, Urdu, and Pashto. He has written extensively on criminology and criminal justice in Pakistan. His book titled *Expanding Criminology to Pakistan* has been widely received by the national and international audience.

Petter Gottschalk is a professor in the Department of Leadership and Organizational Behavior at BI Norwegian Business School in Oslo, Norway. He teaches knowledge management and white-collar crime investigations. He received his education at Technische Universität Berlin (MBA) in Germany, Dartmouth and MIT (MSc) in the United States, and Brunell University (DBA) in the United Kingdom. Dr. Gottschalk has published extensively on policing, law enforcement, and fraud examinations. He has been the CEO, president, and managing director in several business corporations.

Karen Lancaster-Ellis holds an MSc in criminology and criminal justice and is currently a doctoral student of criminology and criminal justice at the University of the West Indies, St. Augustine, Trinidad Campus. Karen's PhD explores the emotional impact of crime on offenders. Her research interests include policing, security planning, white-collar crime, punishment, and corrections. Karen has been a member of the Trinidad and Tobago Police Service for more than 22 years. She is currently working as an assistant superintendent in the Crime and Problem Analysis Branch, responsible for leading a team of 160 police and civilian staff.

Evangelos Mantzaris is an extraordinary professor and senior researcher at the University of Stellenbosch, South Africa. Prof. Mantzaris was born in Lemnos, Greece. After graduating from Panteios University, Athens, he came to South Africa where he obtained a master degree in Social Science and PhD from the Sociology Department at the University of Cape Town. He has published widely in English, Greek, and Yiddish on ethnic and class relations, industrial sociology, and corruption.

Kennedy Mkutu Agade is an associate professor of international relations and peace studies at United States International University (USIU), Nairobi.

He is currently on a sabbatical, working as a senior conflict and violence sensitivity consultant for the World Bank, Kenya. His published work includes *Guns and Governance in the Rift Valley: Pastoral Conflict and Small Arms* (published by James Currey, 2008); "'Ungoverned Space' and the Oil Find in Turkana, Kenya" (*The Round Table Journal of Commonwealth Affairs*, 2014) and "Changes and Challenges of the Kenya Police Reserve: The Case of Turkana County, Kenya" (*African Studies Review*, 2015).

Pregala Pillay is a professor and the head of School of Public Administration and Development Management in the Faculty of Management Studies at Stellenbosch University, South Africa. She has worked with the Anti-corruption Centre for Education and Research at the university on integrity leadership. Dr. Pillay has published on contemporary issues in public administration and management, local government, leadership, ethics, and service delivery in local and international journals. She has mentored several postgraduate students to present their research at international conferences.

Harald N. Røstvik is a professor of urbanism specialized in sustainability at the University of Stavanger, Norway, and professor of architecture at Bergen School of Architecture, Norway. He was educated as an architect at The University of Manchester, the United Kingdom, and he has been running his own practice in Norway since 1977. He has lectured widely and internationally and written eight books on architecture, urbanism, ethics, and energy, and has cowritten many more. His latest book is *Corruption the Nobel Way* in 2015. His interest in corruption stems from the fact that the building industry is among the most fraud and corruption exposed sectors.

Imran Ahmad Sajid is a PhD in social work. His PhD was on juvenile justice in Pakistan. He is the assistant editor of *Pakistan Journal of Criminology* and general secretary of the Pakistan Society of Criminology. He exclusively edited two issues of *Pakistan Journal of Criminology* (volume 5/2 July–December 2013 and volume 6/1 January–June 2014). Dr. Imran is working as a lecturer in the Department of Social Work, University of Peshawar, Pakistan. He has contributed many research papers on criminological issues including juvenile justice, kidnapping, police, and suicide bombing.

Perry Stanislas has more than 36 years of policing experience, starting his career for a nongovernment security and intelligence agency supporting pan-African political movements, leaders, and emerging governments. He was the senior policy advisor for Bedfordshire Police, the United Kingdom, for 12 years and taught at Bramshill Staff College, Hampshire, the United Kingdom. Perry is a senior lecturer at De Montfort University and specializes in international policing and organizational change, and security planning.

Farhat Ullah is working as a lecturer in the Department of Social Work in Kohat University of Science and Technology (KUST), Kohat, Pakistan. His PhD research is focused on police training and practices in Pakistan. He has recently become assistant editor of *Pakistan Journal of Criminology*. He exclusively edited an issue of *Pakistan Journal of Criminology* (volume 6/2/July–December 2014). Ullah teaches qualitative social research, quantitative social research, and sociological theory. He has published on motivational aspects in police basic training to counter terrorism in Khyber Pakhtunkhwa.

Aydoğan Vatandaş is an investigative journalist from Turkey, specializing in political science and international relations. He is the author of 13 books, many of which have become bestsellers in Turkey. *Reporting from the Bridge* and *Hungry for Power: Erdogans Witch Hunt and the Abuse of State Power* are the first two books published in the United States. The latter book, apart from delving into complex issues such as violence in the Middle East, serves as a collection of significant articles that shed light on President Recep Tayyip Erdoğan's transition from a Muslim democrat to an authoritarian leader.

Theoretical Perspectives

I

Convenience Theory of White-Collar Crime

1

PETTER GOTTSCHALK

Contents

Introduction

Public procurement corruption is a typical case of white-collar crime. In this chapter, we present a general theory of white-collar crime in terms of three dimensions: economical dimension of crime, organizational dimension of crime, and behavioral dimension of crime. This chapter is a summary of my previous publications on a general theory of white-collar crime (Gottschalk, 2016).

In this chapter, we study white-collar crime at the microlevel. At the macrolevel, we find conflict theory suggesting that capitalism leads to a more crime intensive society (Lanier and Henry, 2009b). Capitalism is a system of economic production in which power is concentrated in the hands of a few, with the majority existing in a dependency relationship to the powerful. This class-based economic order finds its existence through a criminal justice apparatus that serves the interest of the wealthy at the expense of the poor (Lanier and Henry, 2009a). To limit the exploitation of the poor, governments have passed some laws that set some limits to what the powerful can do (Haines, 2014). When the powerful break these laws, they commit white-collar crime.

This theoretical chapter is an attempt to provide systematic clarity to the debate around the issue of defining white-collar crime. The theory provides a reference point for further debate and development. This chapter should provide a useful summary and processing, what constitute the main elements of the crime situation.

The theory proposed is concerned with the *what* and *how* and *why* of crime. The why part is a general theory of the etiology of crime, that is, what causes crime. It is a gathering together of ideas around why a certain thing is happening. The theory is based on what should be included in the definition of white-collar crime that is mainly all kinds of financial crime carried out by individuals who qualify as white-collar criminals. We define the concept and explain why it occurs.

The approach here is to delineate the general boundaries of the definition of white-collar crime by looking at *how* and *why* the crime in terms of economical, organizational as well as behavioral dimensions, and then to organize extant theories as subtheories of those types of dimensions into a system of categories that may together generate a detailed definitional boundary. This sort of approach, which may appear as *back to front* to some readers, is justified by moving in reasoning from the general back to the detailed front of the phenomenon of white-collar crime. In doing so, there is a joint discussion of defining and explaining the phenomenon. This is the method of theorizing in the following.

Extracting the concept from marketing theory (Farquhar and Rowley, 2009), convenience in white-collar crime relates to savings in time and effort by privileged and trusted individuals to reach a goal. Convenience is an attribute of an illegal action. Convenience comes at a potential cost to the offender in terms of the likelihood of detection and punishment. In other words, reducing time and effort now entails a greater potential for future cost. *Paying for convenience* is a way of phrasing this proposition.

Convenience is the perceived savings in time and effort required to find and to facilitate the use of a solution to a problem. Convenience directly relates to the amount of time and effort that is required to accomplish a task. Convenience addresses the time and effort exerted before, during, and after a transaction. Convenience represents a time and effort component related to the complete illegal transaction process or processes (Collier and Kimes, 2012).

People differ in their temporal orientation, including perceived time scarcity, the degree to which they value time, and their sensitivity to time-related issues. Facing strain, greed, or other situations, an illegal activity can represent a convenient solution to a problem that the individual or the organization otherwise find difficult or even impossible to solve. The desire for convenience varies among people. Convenience orientation is a term that refers to a person's general preference for convenient solutions to problems. A convenience-oriented individual is one who seeks to accomplish a task in the shortest time with the least expenditure of human energy (Farquhar and Rowley, 2009).

Three main dimensions to explain white-collar crime have emerged (Gottschalk, 2016). All of them link to convenience. The first dimension is concerned with economic aspects, where convenience implies that the illegal financial gain is a convenient option for the decision-maker to cover needs. The second dimension is concerned with organizational aspects, where convenience implies that the offender has convenient access to premises, and convenient ability to hide illegal transactions among legal transactions. The third dimension is concerned with behavioral aspects where convenience implies that the offender has convenient access to and accept of his or her own deviant behavior.

This article reviews the state of the art relating to white-collar crime and criminals by applying the economic, organizational, and behavioral dimensions. By combining these dimensions, an integrated explanation of white-collar crime emerges, which we label as convenience theory. White-collar criminals have convenient access, and financial crime saves them time, and effort to solve a problem related to making a profit. Convenience is a relative concept, where the ease of problem solving can cause future costs for the offender. Crime is committed if found suitable by the offender, and especially when no alternative is in sight.

General Theory Construction

Whetten (1989) suggests that a theoretical contribution starts by identifying factors (variables, construct, and concepts) that we may consider as part of the explanation of the phenomenon. He then suggest the how part, which is how these concepts are related to each other. He also suggests that a theory has to explain the underlying psychological, economic, or social dynamics that justify the selection of factors and the proposed causal relationships. This rationale constitutes the theory's assumptions—the theoretical glue that welds the model together.

Sutton and Staw (1995) argue that a theory has to meet some minimum standards. They argue that references, data, lists of variables or constructs, diagrams, and hypotheses, or predictions are not theory. They assert that theory is the answer to queries of *why*. Theory is about the connections among phenomena, a story about why acts, events, incidents, and reactions occur. They argue that theory emphasizes the nature of causal relationships, identifying what comes first as well as the timing of such events. Strong theory, in their view, delves into underlying processes to understand the systematic reasons for a particular occurrence or nonoccurrence.

Weick (1995) commented on Sutton and Staw's (1995) definition of theory by stating that what theory is not, theorizing is. Products of the theorizing process seldom emerge as full-blown theories. Data, lists, diagrams, and hypotheses can be part of a theorizing process. The process of theorizing consists of activities like abstracting, generalizing, relating, selecting, explaining, synthesizing, and idealizing. Although theorizing is a process, theory is a product.

DiMaggio (1995) as well commented on Sutton and Staw's (1995) definition of theory by stating that there are more than one kind of good theory. They mentioned theory as covering laws, theory as enlightenment, and theory as narrative. He argues that good theory splits the difference, and that theory construction is social construction, often after the fact.

A few years later, Weick (1999) argued that theorizing in organizational studies has taken on a life of its own. He found that researchers seem more preoccupied with intellectual fashions than with advancement of knowledge. He argues that so much research is irrelevant to practice.

Colquitt and Zapata-Phelan (2007) found that many academics support Sutton and Staw's (1995) definition of a theory in terms of relationships between independent and dependent variables. Theory is then a collection of assertions that identifies how they are interrelated and why, and identifies the conditions under which relationships exist or do not exist. From this perspective, a theory is primarily useful to the extent that it has the ability to explain variance in a criterion of interest. Other scholars support DiMaggio's (1995) suggestion that theory is an account of a social process, with emphasis on empirical tests of the plausibility of the narrative as well as careful attention to the scope conditions of the account.

Michailova et al. (2014) support Weick's view that theory cannot improve until we improve the theorizing process, and we cannot improve the theorizing process until we describe it more explicitly. They challenge the view that interesting theorizing would be an outcome only of high-quality, sustained relationships in the field, as suggested by the why-only perspective on theory.

In the following, general theory of white-collar crime—consisting of economical, organizational, and behavioral dimensions—the emphasis is on theory as an explanation. An explanation is a set of statements constructed to describe a set of facts, which clarifies contexts, modes, causes, and consequences of those facts. This is in line with Whetten (1989) who argues that a theory is an explanation of a phenomenon. He suggests that a theory has to explain the underlying economic, social, and psychological dynamics that justify the selection of factors. This is also in line with Weick (1995) who argued that the process of theorizing consists of several activities including explanations. It is as well in line with Colquitt and Zapata-Pelan (2007) who emphasize a theory's ability to explain variance in criteria of interest. Strong theory, in Sutton and Staw's (1995) view, delves into underlying processes in order to understand the systematic reasons for a particular occurrence or nonoccurrence, which the following theoretical descriptions intend to do.

Explanation for understanding is thus at the core of the following theory. We search for a better understanding of white-collar crime. We are certainly not the only ones (Benson and Simpson, 2005: 71):

> Just as with conventional crime, many theoretical approaches have been tried in the search for a better understanding of white-collar crime. The process of applying standard criminological theories to white-collar crime often involves "conceptual acrobatics." Theorists have to take ideas and concepts that were originally developed to apply to traditional forms of crime and tweak them to account for the special features of white-collar crime and the distinguishing characteristics of white-collar offenders.

An example of a theorist who takes ideas and theorize them is Jacques (2014), who defines an idea as a statement about the nature of reality that people have said, written, or otherwise communicated. This is in line with Williams (2008), who argues that we must devote more attention to considerations of knowledge and knowledgeability in the study of white-collar crime. He suggests that we need to be concerned with the extent to which the power of organizations maintains and reproduces itself, and that we need theory to help document white-collar offending in society impeded by a crisis of knowledge.

Economical Dimension of Crime

White-collar crime is profit-driven crime based on economic opportunities and threats. As argued by Naylor (2003), transfers of property occur by free-market exchange or fraud; and these transfers involve redistribution of wealth and distribution of income. Fraud is illegal procurement of a private asset or means of advantage through deception, or through the neglect of care for the interests of an asset required by duty. In particular, fraud includes heterogeneous forms such as misappropriation, balance manipulation, insolvency, and capital investment abuse (Füss and Hecker, 2008). Opportunity is a distinct characteristic of white-collar crime and varies depending on the kinds of criminals involved (Michel, 2008). An opportunity is attractive as a means of responding to desires (Bucy et al., 2008).

Threats can come from loss-making business and special market structure and forces. Economic power available only to certain corporations in concentrated industries, but not to others, may generate criminal conduct. The threat of losing in a bankruptcy, what owners already had created can cause executives to rescue, and save the company by illegal means. An entrepreneur, who has spent all his time building the enterprise, might be unable to let it disappear. The intention is to protect economic interests of the corporation (Blickle et al., 2006). Threats can come from a monopoly, where potential competitors have the choice of either committing crime or joining the monopoly (Chang et al., 2005). A financial gain is a requirement for survival in all markets (Brightman, 2009).

The economic model of rational self-interest considers incentives and probability of detection (Welsh et al., 2014). The rational choice model finds support in an empirical study by Bucy et al. (2008), who identified a number of motives for white-collar crime. According to their study, greed is the most common reason for white-collar criminal acts (Hamilton and Micklethwait, 2006). Money and other forms of financial gain is a frequent motivator documented in many studies. Criminals pursue desired goals, weigh-up likely consequences, and make selections from various options. When criminal opportunity is attractive as a means to fulfill one's desires, rational actors will choose it. Goldstraw-White (2012) defines greed as socially constructed needs and desires that can never be completely satisfied. As we move up the social class ladder, need is replaced by greed as the motivating factor behind crime. Greed is a very strong wish, continuously to get more of something; it is a strong preference for maximizing wealth.

As participating in crime is a rational choice, crime rates will be lower where levels of punishment are more certain and/or more severe (Pratt and Cullen, 2005). Rational choice theorists have generally adopted the position of standard economic theory's notion of revealed preferences. However, Kamerdze et al. (2014) argue that affects and individual affective states play a role in one's utility functions and are thus relevant for rational choice theory because they have an impact on mediating cognitive processes.

Aguilera and Vadera (2008: 434) describe a criminal opportunity as *the presence of a favorable combination of circumstances that renders a possible course of action relevant*. Opportunity arises when individuals or groups can engage in illegal and unethical behavior and expect, with reasonable confidence (Haines, 2014), to avoid detection and punishment. Opportunity to commit crime may include macro and microlevel factors. Macrolevel factors encompass the characteristics of the industries in which the business finds itself embedded, such as market structure, business sets of an industry, that is, companies whose actions are visible to one another, and variations in the regulatory environment (Aguilera and Vadera, 2008).

If the criminal considers the criminal opportunity convenient in terms of current gain (profit) relative to future cost (punishment), and the criminal would like to avoid additional time and effort to solve the problem, then convenience theory suggests that white-collar crime will be committed. White-collar crime incidents are not offenses of passion; they are not spontaneous or emotional, but calculated risks for a convenient solution to a challenge or problem by rational actors.

Organizational Dimension of Crime

Agency theory is a management theory often applied to crime, where normally the agent, rather than the principal, is in danger of committing crime. Problems arise in the relationship because of diverging preferences and conflicting values, asymmetry in knowledge about activities, and different attitudes toward risk. Agency theory describes the relationship between the two parties using the concept of work-based interactions. The agent carries out work on behalf of the principal in an organizational arrangement. Principal-agent theory holds that owners (principals) have different interests from administrators (agents), such that principals must always suspect agents of making decisions that benefit themselves, to the cost of the principals. For example, chief executive officers (CEOs) are suspects for cheating the owners (Williams, 2008), and purchasing managers are suspects of cheating their CEOs (Chrisman et al., 2007).

In general, agency models view corruption and other kinds of financial crime, a consequence of the principal's inability effectively to prevent the agent from abusing power for his or her personal gain (Li and Ouyang, 2007). However, the principal can just as well commit financial crime in the principal-agent relationship. For example, the chief financial officer (CFO) as an agent provides a board member with inside information, on which the principal acts illegally.

An organization is a system of coordinated actions among individuals and groups with boundaries and goals (Puranam et al., 2014). An organization can be a hierarchy, a matrix, a network, or any other kind of relationships between people in a professional work environment. Dysfunctional network theory suggests that corporate crime emerges as consequence of the dysfunction of value networks (Dion, 2008).

The organizational setting may prevent some white-collar criminals from prosecution. The company may be too big to fall, and the criminal too powerful to jail. For example, after the 2008 financial meltdown in the United States, people expected that the government would prosecute fraud in large financial institutions. Pontell et al. (2014: 10) assessed the reasons why there have been no major prosecutions to date:

> From a criminological standpoint, the current financial meltdown points to the need to unpack the concept of status when examining white-collar and corporate offenses. The high standing of those involved in the current scandal has acted as a significant shield to accusations of criminal wrongdoing in at least three ways. First, the legal resources that offenders can bring to bear on any case made against them are significant. This would give pause to any prosecutor, regardless of the evidence that exists. Second, their place in the organization assures that the many below them will be held more directly

responsible for the more readily detected offenses. The downward focus on white-collar and corporate crimes is partly a function of the visibility of the offense and the ease with which it can be officially pursued. Third, the political power of large financial institutions allow for effective lobbying that both distances them from the criminal law and prevents the government from restricting them from receiving taxpayer money when they get into trouble.

Similarly, Valukas (2010) found no wrongdoing at Lehman Brothers, which went bankrupt because of mismanagement in decision-making.

Benson and Simpson (2015) argue that many white-collar offenses manifest the following opportunity properties: (1) the offender has legitimate access to the location in which the crime is committed, (2) the offender is spatially separate from the victim, and (3) the offender's actions have a superficial appearance of legitimacy. Opportunity occurs in terms of those three properties that are typically the case for executives and other individuals in the elite. In terms of convenience, these three properties may be attractive and convenient when considering white-collar crime to solve a financial problem. It is convenient for the offender to conceal the crime and give it an appearance of outward respectability (Pickett and Pickett, 2002).

The organizational dimension of white-collar crime becomes particularly evident when financial crime is committed to benefit the organization rather than the individual (Trahan, 2011). Hansen (2009) argues that the problem with occupational crime is that it is committed within the confines of positions of trust and in organizations, which prohibit surveillance and accountability. Heath (2008) found that individuals who are further up the chain of command in the firm tend to commit bigger and more severe occupational crime. Corporate crime, on the other hand, is resulting from offenses by collectivities or aggregates of discrete individuals. If a corporate official violates the law in acting for the corporation, we still define it as corporate crime. However, if he or she gains personal benefit in the commission of a crime against the corporation, we regard it as occupational crime. A corporation cannot be subject to imprisonment, and therefore, the majority of penalties to control individual violators are not available for corporations and corporate crime (Bookman, 2008).

Behavioral Dimension of Crime

Most theories of white-collar crime develop along the behavioral dimension. Researchers introduce numerous suggestions to explain white-collar individuals such as Madoff, Rajaratman, and Schilling. Along the behavioral dimension we find a number of theories—such as strain theory (Langton and Piquero, 2007), deterrence theory (Comey, 2009; Holtfreter et al., 2008), self-control theory (Holtfreter et al., 2010; Piquero et al., 2010), obedience theory (Baird and Zelin, 2009), fear of falling (Piquero, 2012), negative life events (Engdahl, 2014), slippery slope (Welsh et al., 2014), and the American dream of economic success (Pratt and Cullen, 2005; Schoepfer and Piquero, 2006)—just to name a few. These theories suggest motives for committing white-collar crime, and they make crime a convenient option according to convenience theory. It is convenient for the criminal to be deceitful and breach trust to cause losses to others and gain for one self (Pickett and Pickett, 2002).

In recent years, neutralization theory seems to increase in importance as a source of explanation. By applying neutralization techniques, white-collar criminals think they are doing nothing wrong. They deny responsibility, injury, and victim. They condemn the condemners. They claim appeal to higher loyalties and normality of action. They claim entitlement, and they argue the case of legal mistake. They find their own mistakes acceptable. They argue a dilemma arose, whereby they made a reasonable trade-off before committing the act (Siponen and Vance, 2010). The idea of neutralization techniques (Sykes and Matza, 1957) resulted from work on Sutherland's (1949) differential association theory. According to this theory, people are always aware of their moral obligation to abide by the law, and they are aware that they have the same moral obligation within themselves to avoid illegitimate acts. The theory postulates that criminal behavior learning occurs in association with those who find such criminal behavior favorable and in isolation from those who find it unfavorable (Benson and Simpson, 2015). Crime is relatively convenient when there is no guilt feeling for doing something learned from others.

Another important source of explanation is strain theory, ever since Gottfredson and Hirschi (1990) in their classic book on the general theory of crime wrote about pressure crime. Strain may involve the removal of positively valued stimuli (Johnson and Graff, 2014). Agnew (2005) identified three categories of strain: failure to achieve positive goals, the removal of positive stimuli, and the presentation of negative stimuli. Strain theory posits that each type of strain ultimately lead to deviance for slightly different reasons. All three types tend to increase the likelihood that an individual will experience negative emotions in proportion to the magnitude, duration, and closeness of the stress. Strain characterizes a condition that individuals dislike. The theory argues that structural strain weakens the ability of normative standards to regulate behavior (Pratt and Cullen, 2005). Strain creates the need for a convenient solution to the problem.

Research by Ragatz et al. (2012) is an example of work that explores psychological traits among white-collar offenders. Their research results suggest that white-collar offenders have lower scores on lifestyle criminality, but higher score on some measures of psychopathology and psychopathic traits compared to nonwhite-collar offenders. Similarly, McKay et al. (2010)

examined the psychopathology of the white-collar criminal acting as a corporate leader. They looked at the impact of a leader's behavior on other employees and the organizational culture developed during his or her tenure. Narcissistic behavior is suggested often to be observed among white-collar offenders (Arnulf and Gottschalk, 2013; Ouimet, 2009, 2010).

Some theorists believe that authorities can reduce crime by means of deterrents. Crime prevention (the goal of deterrence) assumes that criminals or potential criminals will think carefully before committing a crime if the likelihood of detection and/or the fear of swift and severe punishment are present. According to Comey (2009), deterrence works best when punishment is swift and certain.

Scholars apply self-control theory in two different directions. First, the theory proposes that individuals commit crime because of low self-control. The theory contends that individuals who lack self-control are more likely to engage in problematic behavior—such as criminal behavior—over their life course because of its time-stable nature (Gottfredson and Hirshi, 1990). Second, the desire to control and the general wish to be in control of everything and everybody might be a characteristic of some white-collar criminals, meaning that low self-control can lead to heavy control of others. Desire for control is the general wish to be in control over everyday life events. Desire for control is similar to low self-control in terms of behavioral manifestations and influence on the decision-making power of individuals (Piquero et al., 2005, 2008, 2010).

Low self-control finds support in anomie theory. Anomie refers to a sense of normlessness, which can occur when there is a strong emphasis on the desirability of material success and individual achievement (Schoepfer and Piquero, 2006). Benson and Simpson (2015) suggest that coupled with the cultural themes of success and endless striving, are a cultural uncertainty and confusion about where the line between acceptable and unacceptable business behavior is developing.

Slippery slope means that a person slides over time from legal to illegal activities. Arjoon (2008: 78) explains slippery slope in the following way:

> As commonsense experience tells us, it is the small infractions that can lead to the larger ones. An organization that overlooks the small infractions of its employees creates a culture of acceptance that may lead to its own demise. This phenomenon is captured by the metaphor of the slippery slope. Many unethical acts occur without the conscience awareness of the person who engaged in the misconduct. Specifically, unethical behavior is most likely to follow the path of a slippery slope, defined as a gradual decline in which no one event makes one aware that he or she is acting unethically. The majority of unethical behaviors are unintentional and ordinary, thus affecting everyone and providing support for unethical behavior when people unconsciously lower the bar over time through small changes in their ethical behavior.

Welsh et al. (2014) argue that many recent scandals result from a slippery slope, in which a series of small infractions gradually increase over time. Committing small indiscretions over time may gradually lead people to complete larger unethical acts that they otherwise would have judged to be impermissible.

The slippery slope theory thus suggests an incremental progression toward serious white-collar crime. The sliding individual experiences no resistance or reaction, although at the same time starting to gain benefits. An offender first moves and subsequently removes the borderline between right and wrong from his or her mind. This state of mind finds its coupling to self-deception where the person deliberately refuses to gather all available evidence because he or she strongly fears that it will tell against some established beliefs. In incidents of slippery slope there are no single turning point that separates the inception stage from the escalation.

Benson and Simpson (2015: 145) found that white-collar criminals seldom think of injury or victims:

> Many white-collar offenses fail to match this common-sense stereotype because the offenders do not set out intentionally to harm any specific individual. Rather, the consequences of their illegal acts fall upon impersonal organizations or a diffuse and unseen mass of people.

An Integrated Approach

The behavioral dimension of crime interacts with the organizational dimension of crime. For example, antisocial executives may search for opportunities to commit crime, although conforming that executives will probably not see opportunities to commit financial crime.

The behavioral dimension of crime interacts with the economic dimension of crime as well. For example, the fear of falling (Piquero, 2012) finds causality in situations such as an acute liquidity problem, where executives perceive financial crime as the only way out of the crises. Profit-driven crime is thus not only an issue of making even more money. Rather, it is an issue of survival, and it may be to rescue a sinking ship.

As suggested by Whetten (1989), a theoretical contribution starts by identifying factors (variables, construct, and concepts) that are parts of the explanation of the phenomenon. The phenomenon of white-collar crime finds explanation in the concepts of economics, organization, and behavior. This is the what part of our theory.

Whetten (1989) suggests that a theory has to explain the underlying psychological, economic, or social dynamics that justify the selection of factors and the proposed causal relationships. This rationale constitutes the theory's assumptions—the theoretical glue that welds the model together. In the proposed theory, causal relationships exist both within each dimension and between the three dimensions.

The integrated explanation of white-collar crime as a convenient option when facing challenges portrays the path of least resistance. Offenders are responding to an event or a situation (Langton and Piquero, 2007). There are no safeguards to stop them from choosing the path of least resistance. Especially heroic white-collar criminals as described by Arnulf and Gottschalk (2013) are uninterrupted and no glass ceiling exists.

The motivation for white-collar crime can range from greed to panic. Someone afraid of losing his job may panic and bribe a customer to get a large order for his firm to save his job. An entrepreneur and founder may panic to save his lifework and commit tax evasion to save his firm and to continue to be successful in his business venture. Crime represents a convenient option to cope with problems, as failure is not an option. People on the other end of the scale, driven by greed, will be looking for opportunities to commit white-collar crime independent of real need as long as they find a suitable target. Between these two extremes, we find people who find themselves coerced by others, obeying orders from superiors, or just following normal business practices of their profession (Langton and Piquero, 2007). If detected, they do not expect others to scrutinize them. Those revealed express surprise by being prosecuted like *regular criminals* (Kerik, 2015).

Convenience is a term also found in crime studies. For example, Petrossian and Clarke (2014) studied ports of convenience for illegal commercial fishing. They found that countries in close proximity to the ten ports of convenience were more vulnerable to illegal fishing than those that were farther away. McGloin and Stickle (2011) phrased the question—influence or convenience? They were studying peer influence versus co-offending for chronic offenders, and found that it is convenient for chronic offenders to involve themselves in co-offending.

Criminology reminds us of the meaning of the term convenience when we study convenience store crime. A convenience store usually charges significantly higher prices than conventional grocery stores or supermarkets. Nevertheless, customers choose to buy there anyway because of closer location, longer opening hours, and shorter cashier lines (White and Katz, 2013). Similarly, white-collar criminals are willing to commit crime, because it is convenient and the calculated costs are low.

The proposition of a new theory, convenience theory, takes into accounts why, where, who, what, when, and how as suggested by the literature on theory discussed earlier.

Limits to a General Theory

Sutherland (1940, 1949) introduced the term white-collar crime, and Gottfredson and Hirschi (1990) presented a general theory of crime. The term white-collar crime has soon survived for almost a century and has been subject to much research, making an updated general theory of white-collar crime a necessity and requirement to strengthen future research. Too much struggle has occurred in numerous recent articles to apply the concept of white-collar crime. Reviewers may argue that the sample is not of white-collar crime, although authors say it is.

Of course, three suggestions here—economical, organizational, and behavioral dimensions of such a theory—will not survive for long. The contribution of this section lies more in an initiative, rather than a conclusion. It is an initiative to take a step back to reflect on the concept, rather than determine in specific terms and cases what is or what is not white-collar crime.

The purpose is to present a systematic view of the phenomenon of white-collar crime. We illustrate this phenomenon by the white-collar crime triangle. White-collar crime is (1) based on an opportunity for illegal profit, (2) carried out in the arena of an organization, and (3) where the decision of criminal acts is causing deviant behavior.

The systematic view is an argument to explain phenomena of white-collar crime. If the profit is both available and desirable, if the arena is both accessible and secret, and if deviant behavior is both acceptable and defendable, then white-collar crime is likely to occur. The theory represents both the conditions under which crime occurs, as well as the sequence of factors. Potential criminals base a decision of deviant behavior on availability and desirability of profit that is secretly accessible in a legally perceived organizational setting.

The more famous fraud triangle of opportunity, pressure, and rationalization (Baird and Zelin, 2009) is implicit in the white-collar crime triangle. Opportunity can be found in desirable profit in accessible arena, although pressure and rationalization leads to the decision to commit crime. Pressure and rationalization are criteria in decision-making. Pressures exist in the organization as well as in its competitive environment (Dodge, 2009).

One problem with only three elements in the triangle is the treatment of risk and risk willingness versus risk aversion. Risk is an element included in motivation as well as opportunity and indeed in justification. However, risk deserves an equal place at the level of opportunity, motivation, and rationalization. Here we thus propose an alternative to the crime triangle in terms of a crime star. As in the triangle, the elements in the star are indeed dependent on each other. For example, opportunity without motivation leads to no crime, and opportunity with too great a risk, leads to no crime.

Despite McGurrin et al.'s (2013) finding that few educational criminology programs include white-collar crime, research on white-collar crime is currently growing. There is research on how white-collar criminals are sentenced differently and possibly milder (Maddan et al., 2012; Schoepfer et al., 2007; Stadler et al., 2013), on gender gap (Robb, 2006; Simpson et al., 2012; Steffensmeier et al., 2013), occupational versus corporate crime (Bookman, 2008; Heath, 2008; Perri and Brody, 2011), criminal leaders versus criminal followers (Bucy et al., 2008; McKay et al., 2010), criminal profiles (Onna et al., 2014), white-collar defense in court (Weissmann and Block, 2010), and many other interesting perspectives. Such specific perspectives will of course challenge a general theory of white-collar crime.

The white-collar crime triangle covers both offense-based as well as offender-based perspectives. The offense is economic in nature, and it occurs in an organizational setting. The offender makes a decision to commit the crime. Crime arises out of a criminal opportunity with the following five characteristics (Huisman and Erp, 2013): (1) the effort required to carry out the offense, (2) the perceived risks of detection, (3) the rewards gained from the offense, (4) the situational conditions that may encourage criminal action, and (5) the excuse and neutralizations of the offense.

Pratt and Cullen (2005) distinguished between microlevel and macrolevel perspectives on crime. Issues of strain, self-control, and other behavioral indicators belong to the individual explanations of crime at the microlevel. Issues of organizational setting, inequality and availability of illegal profits belong to the people's explanations of crime at the macrolevel. Thus, our proposed theory covers both micro and macrolevel predictors of crime.

White-collar crime involves some form of social deviance by individuals and represents a breakdown in social order (Heath, 2008). Many scholars emphasize the nonphysical and nonviolent act committed for financial gain as a key characteristic of white-collar crime (Bookman, 2008; Brightman, 2009). Although it is included as a characteristic in the proposed general theory here, it is relevant to notice that Perri and Brody (2011) document that even white-collar criminals may resort to violence including murder to cover up their crime. By examining several criminology theories that offer explanations regarding why this type of crime is so prevalent among seemingly respectable individuals, we can explore and then summarize the origins of elite crime.

Maybe future research on a general theory of white-collar crime should focus on theorizing rather than theory. As argued by Weick and cited in Michailova et al. (2014), theory cannot be improved until we improve the theorizing process, and we cannot improve the theorizing process until we describe it more explicitly. Theorizing involves a mixture of observing something, penetrating something, and finding something out, where there is not necessarily a linear process at all. Weick (1995) argued that the process of theorizing consists of activities like abstracting, generalizing, relating, selecting, explaining, synthesizing, and idealizing. These ongoing products summarize progress, give direction, and serve as place makers.

The activities that make up theorizing—observing, choosing something interesting, formulating the central concept, building the theory, and completing the tentative theory—can happen in a very different order or in no order at all. Observing white-collar criminals is not easy; it will always be in retrospect a story told by newspapers, police, prosecutors, defendants, defense lawyers, witnesses, victims, and court documents. Penetrating the crime is difficult, but penetrating the criminal as an inmate in prison might be easier. Some white-collar inmates may be reluctant to participate in interviews, although others would like to tell their stories. For those of us who have had the opportunity to interview white-collar inmates, we observe interesting individuals who have the ability to present themselves and their actions in fascinating ways.

Compared to research on members of Hells Angels in organized crime (Gottschalk, 2013) and research on pedophiles who have groomed children on the Internet (Davidson and Gottschalk, 2015), research on white-collar criminals is in so many respects different. A white-collar criminal is simply one of us. Maybe that is why Sutherland's (1940, 1949) analysis of white-collar criminality serves as the catalyst for an area of research that continues and grows today.

Michailova et al. (2014) argue that theorizing is inherently personal. Some even argue that there is no theory that is not a fragment carefully prepared of some autobiography, and that all scholarship is self-revelatory. Michailova et al. (2014) suggest that since it is impossible to make sense of a situation without a personal identity, it is important for theorists to decide and declare who they think they are. Without going too far in this direction, I as the author of this chapter, am certainly willing to testify that I have never committed white-collar crime, that I have observed white-collar crime as a business executive, that I have interviewed and done statistical research on a large sample of convicted white-collar criminals as a professor, and that I have done empirical research on other convicted criminals as well. My background has led me to the belief that people with wealth and power who commit crime against other people's property deserve punishment at least as severely as drug barons and murderers. This is not the case in Norway today, where drug barons and murderers receive a jail sentence of 10 years on average, while white-collar criminals receive a sentence of only two years on average. Let me add that pedophiles that destroy lives of young children also get only two years sentence. Maybe white-collar criminals and offending pedophiles should receive 10 years on average, while drug barons may serve two years in prison, as long as we do not want the prison population to grow as a whole. This is not in support of deterrence theory, but about relative seriousness of criminal actions as perceived by society. It is just a thought to tell who I am.

In recent years, most published research work on white-collar crime seems to struggle to define what is and what is not to be included in the concept. This section represents an initiative to debate and clarify the concept, so that future research will have an easier avenue to follow when developing a sample. Specifically, to identify financial crime as white-collar offense, there has to be an economical dimension, an organizational dimension, as well as a behavioral dimension (Gottschalk, 2016).

It is the organizational dimension that probably will create most debate, as a computer hacker sitting in his home alone to commit bank fraud is not a white-collar criminal. Similarly, a fake bank on the Internet is not white-collar crime, as criminal activities are not hiding behind and among legal activities, and it is not a breach of trust. Some will find the organizational requirement too restrictive in the definition of white-collar crime.

For example, Bookman (2008) avoids the organizational dimension by defining white-collar crime as an illegal act committed by nonphysical means and by concealment, to obtain money or property, to avoid payment or loss of money or property, or to obtain business or personal advantage. The organizational dimension requires that white-collar crime is committed in a setting of legal and organized work, where people relate to each other in a professional environment. However, to open up at the end of this section, it is important to emphasize that the term organization itself can be many things, as long as it can be portrayed as (1) a multiagent system with (2) identifiable boundaries, and (3) system-level goals (purpose) toward which (4) the constituent agent's efforts are expected to make a contribution (Puranam et al., 2014).

Ahrne and Brunsson (2011) argue that organizational characteristics include membership, hierarchy, monitor, and sanctions. Organizations decide about membership, about who they will allow to join the organization as employees. Membership brings a certain identity with it, an identity that differs from that of nonmembers. Organizations include a hierarchy, a duty to oblige others to comply with decisions. Hierarchy entails a form of organized power. Organizations can issue commands, and can decide on rules that its members are expected to follow in their actions. An organization has the right to monitor compliance with its commands and rules. Organizations have the right to decide about sanctions, both positive and negative. They can decide to change a member's status by using promotions, grading systems, awards, diplomas, and medals.

In the process undertaken here, if we unduly exclude some things from the types of cases on which the definition is based, then if the definition is accepted, this will subsequently affect things like, which motivations are considered important in white-collar offenders as we analyze them going forward. Including and excluding particular types of crime and theories that seek to explain aspects of what people other than the author may currently consider to be white-collar crime is therefore a key and critical decision-making process in this sort of work. Maybe exclusion needs to more care and thoroughness. For example, excluding environment and safety crime needs more explanation. Does environment crime include pollution? If so, that may seem within current conceptions of profit-driven crime (McGurrin et al., 2013) and would certainly need some further discussion before we excluded it permanently. Occupational health and safety crime are what is meant by the second part, but these are usually financially motivated as well (Tombs and Whyte, 2007), at least in the cost cutting approach that may involve casual negligence. In fact, McGurrin et al. (2013: 12) in their discussion of white-collar crime argue that if greater attention was paid to "occupational and environmentally related deaths like air, land, and water pollution, or preventable medical errors and hospital acquired infectious diseases, as well as occupational diseases contracted on the job, public health would be significantly less relevant than it is today."

The choice at the outset to exclude certain areas from the ambit of white-collar crime is thus probably questionable to many scholars. It is certainly not a sufficient justification to argue by the inconvenience generated by an overly capacious conceptualization of the object of study. Rather, the justification so far is that there are indirect financial effects of environment and safety crime.

Conclusion

This chapter was set out with an ambitious goal, namely to establish an avenue toward a general theory of white-collar crime, thereby resolving long-standing tensions, ambiguities, and disagreements about how such offending behavior is to be conceptualized and explained. Some readers may find that the chapter failed, and that it amounts to a literature review of existing work that focuses variously on the economical, organizational, and behavioral dimensions of analysis, as represented in the work of others. However, the chapter proposes dimensions drawn from extant studies that find their use in tandem, and thereby offer a new theoretical framework for the analysis of white-collar crime.

The claim in this article that convenience theory is new is potentially contentious. The key components of the theory are very similar to Marcus Felson's problem triangle analysis in the area of crime prevention, which posits the three conditions for crime as: (1) a motivated offender, (2) an opportunity, and (3) the absence of a capable guardian. Although the first two factors find explicit coverage in this chapter's explanations and critique of conventional theories, this chapter made little mention of the existence of moral guardian as a facilitator or inhibitor for crime. This may give the impression that the omission serves to give more weight to the claims of originality of convenience theory. Therefore, it is important to emphasize the work on guardians by Felson (1994). Felson may not have used the term convenience explicitly in his theory on crime and crime prevention, but there is no doubt it shaped much of his thinking.

The originality of convenience theory is that it throws new light on a previously unappreciated conceptual lens of convenience in theorizing and practically understanding white-collar crime such as public procurement corruption. The theory addresses the important areas of financial and economic crime, who carries out these offenses and under what conditions, and how we understand these activities. Equally relevant, the theory enables exploration of how to detect and prevent these kinds of crime. Therefore, it should be a welcomed contribution to the growing literature on these issues. The theory engages with the current literature to be up to date. It makes a useful contribution to scholarship in the areas related to financial crime and the teaching of these subjects.

The strengths of this chapter are its critical examination of theories around financial or white-collar crime, and the section that addressed theory building. This chapter provided a comprehensive summary that is useful for students or other types of readers when gaining insights into public procurement corruption.

References

Agnew, R. (2005). *Pressured into Crime—An Overview of General Strain Theory*, Oxford, UK: Oxford University Press.

Agnew, R. (2012). Reflection on "A revised strain theory of delinquency," *Social Forces*, 91 (1), 33–38.

Agnew, R. (2014). Social concern and crime: Moving beyond the assumption of simple self-interest, *Criminology*, 52 (1), 1–32.

Aguilera, R.V. and Vadera, A.K. (2008). The dark side of authority: Antecedents, mechanisms, and outcomes of organizational corruption, *Journal of Business Ethics*, 77, 431–449.

Ahrne, G. and Brunsson, N. (2011). Organization outside organizations: the significance of partial organization, *Organization*, 18 (1), 83–104.

Arjoon, S. (2008). Slippery when wet: The real risk in business, *Journal of Markets & Morality*, Spring, 11 (1), 77–91.

Arnulf, J.K. and Gottschalk, P. (2013). Heroic leaders as white-collar criminals: An empirical study, *Journal of Investigative Psychology and Offender Profiling*, 10, 96–113.

Baird, J.E. and Zelin, R.C. (2009). An examination of the impact of obedience pressure on perceptions of fraudulent acts and the likelihood of committing occupational fraud, *Journal of Forensic Studies in Accounting and Business*, Winter, 1–14.

Benson, M.L. and Simpson, S.S. (2015). *Understanding White-Collar Crime—An Opportunity Perspective*, New York: Routledge.

Blickle, G., Schlegel, A., Fassbender, P. and Klein, U. (2006). Some personality correlates of business white-collar crime, *Applied Psychology: An International Review*, 55 (2), 220–233.

Bookman, Z. (2008). Convergences and omissions in reporting corporate and white collar crime, *DePaul Business & Commercial Law Journal*, 6, 347–392.

Brightman, H.J. (2009). *Today's White-Collar Crime: Legal, Investigative, and Theoretical Perspectives*, New York: Routledge.

Bucy, P.H., Formby, E.P., Raspanti, M.S. and Rooney, K.E. (2008). Why do they do it?: The motives, mores, and character of white collar criminals, *St. John's Law Review*, 82, 401–571.

Chang, J.J., Lu, H.C. and Chen, M. (2005). Organized crime or individual crime? Endogeneous size of a criminal organization and the optimal law enforcement. *Economic Inquiry*, 43 (3), 661–675.

Chrisman, J.J., Chua, J.H., Kellermanns, F.W. and Chang, E.P.C. (2007). Are family managers agents or stewards? An exploratory study in privately held family firms, *Journal of Business Research*, 60 (10), 1030–1038.

Collier, J.E. and Kimes, S.E. (2012). Only if it is convenient: Understanding how convenience influences self-service technology evaluation, *Journal of Service Research*, 16 (1), 39–51.

Colquitt, J.A. and Zapata-Phelan, C.P. (2007). Trends in theory building and theory testing: A five-decade study of the Academy of Management Journal, *Academy of Management Journal*, 50 (6), 1281–1303.

Comey, J.B. (2009). Go directly to prison: White collar sentencing after the Sarbanes-Oxley act, *Harvard Law Review*, 122, 1728–1749.

Davidson, J. and Gottschalk, P. (2015). The context of online abuse: policy and legislation, in: Webster, S., Davidson, J. and Bifulco, A. (editors), *Online Offending Behaviour and Child Victimisation*, Palgrave Macmillan, London, 1–20.

DiMaggio, P.J. (1995). Comments on "What theory is not," *Administrative Science Quarterly*, 40, 391–397.

Dion, M. (2008). Ethical leadership and crime prevention in the organizational setting, *Journal of Financial Crime*, 15 (3), 308–319.

Dodge, M. (2009). *Women and White-Collar Crime*, Upper Saddle River, NJ: Prentice Hall.

Engdahl, O. (2014). White-collar crime and first-time adult-onset offending: Explorations in the concept of negative life events as turning points, *International Journal of Law, Crime and Justice*, doi:10.1016/j.ijlcj.2014.06.001.

Farquhar, J.D. and Rowley, J. (2009). Convenience: A services perspective, *Marketing Theory*, 9 (4), 425–438.

Felson, M. (1994). *Crime and Everyday Life: Insight and Implications for Society*, Thousand Oaks, CA: Pine Forge Press.

Füss, R. and Hecker, A. (2008). Profiling white-collar crime: Evidence from German-speaking countries, *Corporate Ownership & Control*, 5 (4), 149–161.

Goldstraw-White, J. (2012). *White-Collar Crime: Accounts of Offending Behaviour*, London: Palgrave Macmillan.

Gottfredson, M.R. and Hirschi, T. (1990). *A General Theory of Crime*, Stanford, CA: Stanford University Press.

Gottschalk, P. (2016). *Understanding White-Collar Crime. A Convenience Perspective*, Boca Raton, FL: CRC Press.

Haines, F. (2014). Corporate fraud as misplaced confidence? Exploring ambiguity in the accuracy of accounts and the materiality of money, *Theoretical Criminology*, 18 (1), 20–37.

Hamilton, S. and Micklethwait, A. (2006). *Greed and Corporate Failure: The Lessons from Recent Disasters*, Basingstoke, UK: Palgrave Macmillan.

Hansen, L.L. (2009). Corporate financial crime: Social diagnosis and treatment, *Journal of Financial Crime*, 16 (1), 28–40.

Heath, J. (2008). Business ethics and moral motivation: A criminological perspective, *Journal of Business Ethics*, 83, 595–614.

Holtfreter, K., Beaver, K.M., Reisig, M.D. and Pratt, T.C. (2010). Low self-control and fraud offending, *Journal of Financial Crime*, 17 (3), 295–307.

Holtfreter, K., Slyke, S.V., Bratton, J. and Gertz, M. (2008). Public perceptions of white-collar crime and punishment, *Journal of Criminal Justice*, 36, 50–60.

Huisman, W. and Erp, J. (2013). Opportunities for environmental crime, *British Journal of Criminology*, 53, 1178–1200.

Jacques, S. (2014). The quantitative-qualitative divide in criminology: A theory of ideas' importance, attractiveness, and publication, *Theoretical Criminology*, 18 (3), 317–334.

Johnson, S.D. and Groff, E.R. (2014). Strengthening theoretical testing in criminology using agent-based modeling, *Journal of Research in Crime and Delinquency*, 51 (4), 509–525.

Kamerdze, S., Loughran, T., Paternoster, R. and Sohoni, T. (2014). The role of affect in intended rule breaking: Extending the rational choice perspective, *Journal of Research in Crime and Delinquency*, 51 (5), 620–654.

Kerik, B.B. (2005). *From Jailer to Jailed—My Journey From Correction and Police Commissioner to Inmate #84888-054*, New York: Threshold Editions.

Langton, L. and Piquero, N.L. (2007). Can general strain theory explain white-collar crime? A preliminary investigation of the relationship between strain and select white-collar offenses, *Journal of Criminal Justice*, 35, 1–15.

Lanier, M.M. and Henry, S. (2009a). Chapter 3: Conflict and radical theories, in Lanier, M.M., Henry, S., Anastasia, D.J.M. (editors), *Essential Criminology*, 3rd Edition, Boulder, CO: Westview, Member of the Perseus Books Group, 63–92.

Lanier, M.M. and Henry, S. (2009b). Chapter 10: Capitalism as a criminogenic society—Conflict, marxist, and radical theories of crime, in Lanier, M.M., Henry, S., Anastasia, D.J.M. (editors), *Essential Criminology*, 3rd Edition, Boulder, CO: Westview, Member of the Perseus Books Group, 210–237.

Li, S. and Ouyang, M. (2007). A dynamic model to explain the bribery behavior of firms, *International Journal of Management*, 24 (3), 605–618.

Maddan, S., Hartley, R.D., Walker, J.T. and Miller, J.M. (2012). Sympathy for the devil: An exploration of federal judicial discretion in the processing of white collar offenders, *American Journal of Criminal Justice*, 37, 4–18.

McGloin, J.M. and Stickle, W.P. (2011). Influence or convenience? Disentangling peer influence and co-offending for chronic offenders, *Journal of Research in Crime and Delinquency*, 48 (3), 419–447.

McGurrin, D., Jarrell, M., Jahn, A. and Cochrane, B. (2013). White collar crime representation in the criminological literature revisited, 2001–2010, *Western Criminology Review*, 14 (2), 3–19.

McKay, R., Stevens, C. and Fratzi, J. (2010). A 12-step process of white-collar crime, *International Journal of Business Governance and Ethics*, 5 (1), 14–25.

Michailova, S., Piekkari, R., Plakoyiannaki, E., Ritvala, T., Mihailova, I. and Salmi, A. (2014). Breaking the silence about exiting fieldwork: A relational approach and its implications for theorizing, *Academy of Management Review*, 39 (2), 138–161.

Michel, P. (2008). Financial crimes: the constant challenge of seeking effective prevention solutions, *Journal of Financial Crime*, 15 (4), 383–397.

Naylor, R.T. (2003). Towards a general theory of profit-driven crimes, *British Journal of Criminology*, 43, 81–101.

Onna, J.H.R., Geest, V.R., Huisman, W. and Denkers, J.M. (2014). Criminal trajectories of white-collar offenders, *Journal of Research in Crime and Delinquency*, 51, 759–784.

Ouimet, G. (2009). Psychology of white-collar criminal: In search of personality, *Psychologie Du Travail Et Des Organisations*, 15 (3), 297–320.

Ouimet, G. (2010). Dynamics of narcissistic leadership in organizations, *Journal of Managerial Psychology*, 25 (7), 713–726.

Perri, F.S. and Brody, R.G. (2011). The Sallie Rohrbach story: Lessons for auditors and fraud examiners, *Journal of Financial Crime*, 18 (1), 93–104.

Petrossian, G.A. and Clarke, R.V. (2013). Explaining and controlling illegal commercial fishing, *British Journal of Criminology*, 54, 73–90.

Pickett, K.H.S. and Pickett, J.M. (2002). *Financial Crime Investigation and Control*, New York: John Wiley & Sons.

Piquero, N.L. (2012). The only thing we have to fear is fear itself: Investigating the relationship between fear of falling and white collar crime, *Crime and Delinquency*, 58 (3), 362–379.

Piquero, N.L., Carmichael, S. and Piquero, A.R. (2008). Assessing the perceived seriousness of white collar and street crimes, *Crime & Delinquency*, 54 (2), 291–312.

Piquero, N.L., Schoepfer, A. and Langton, L. (2010). Completely out of control or the desire to be in complete control? How low self-control and the desire for control relate to corporate offending, *Crime & Delinquency*, 56 (4), 627–647.

Piquero, N.L., Tibbetts, S.G. and Blankenship, M.B. (2005). Examining the role of differential association and techniques of neutralization in explaining corporate crime, *Deviant Behavior*, 26 (2), 159–188.

Pontell, H.N., Black, W.K. and Geis, G. (2014). Too big to fail, too powerful to jail? On the absence of criminal prosecutions after the 2008 financial meltdown, *Crime, Law and Social Change*, 61 (1), 1–13.

Pratt, T.C. and Cullen, F.T. (2005). Assessing macro-level predictors and theories of crime: A meta-analysis, *Crime and Justice*, 32, 373–450.

Puranam, P., Alexy, O. and Reitzig, M. (2014). What's "new" about new forms of organizing? *Academy of Management Review*, 39 (2), 162–180.

Ragatz, L.L., Fremouw, W. and Baker, E. (2012). The psychological profile of white-collar offenders: Demographics, criminal thinking, psychopathic traits, and psychopathology, *Criminal Justice and Behavior*, 39 (7), 978–997.

Robb, G. (2006). Women and white-collar crime, *British Journal of Criminology*, 46, 1058–1072.

Schoepfer, A. and Piquero, N.L. (2006). Exploring white-collar crime and the American dream: A partial test of institutional anomie theory, *Journal of Criminal Justice*, 34, 227–235.

Schoepfer, A., Carmichael, S. and Piquero, N.L. (2007). Do perceptions of punishment vary between white-collar and street crimes? *Journal of Criminal Justice*, 35, 151–163.

Schoepfer, A., Piquero, N.L. and Langton, L. (2014). Low self-control versus the desire-for-control: An empirical test of white-collar crime and conventional crime, *Deviant Behavior*, 35 (3), 197–214.

Simpson, S.S., Alper, M. and Benson, M.L. (2012). *Gender and White-Collar Crime in the 21st Century*. Paper presented at the American Society of Criminology, Chicago, IL.

Siponen, M. and Vance, A. (2010). Neutralization: New insights into the problem of employee information security policy violations, *MIS Quarterly*, 34 (3), 487–502.

Stadler, W.A. and Benson, M.L. (2012). Revisiting the guilty mind: The neutralization of white-collar crime, *Criminal Justice Review*, 37 (4), 494–511.

Stadler, W.A., Benson, M.L. and Cullen, F.T. (2013). Revisiting the special sensitivity hypothesis: The prison experience of white-collar inmates, *Justice Quarterly*, iFirst, 1–25.

Steffensmeier, D. and Allan, E. (1996). Gender and crime: Toward a gendered theory of female offending, *Annual Review of Sociology*, 22, 459–487.

Steffensmeier, D., Schwartz, J. and Roche, M. (2013). Gender and twenty-first-century corporate crime: Female involvement and the gender gap in enron-era corporate frauds, *American Sociological Review*, 78 (3), 448–476.

Sutherland, E.H. (1940). White-collar criminality, *American Sociological Review*, 5, 1–12.

Sutherland, E.H. (1949). *White Collar Crime*, New York: Holt Rinehart and Winston.

Sutherland, E.H. (1983). *White Collar Crime—The Uncut Version*, New Haven, CT: Yale University Press.

Sutton, R.I. and Staw, B.M. (1995). What theory is not, *Administrative Science Quarterly*, 40, 371–384.

Sykes, G. and Matza, D. (1957). Techniques of neutralization: A theory of delinquency, *American Sociological Review*, 22 (6), 664–670.

Tombs, S. and Whyte, D. (2003). Scrutinizing the powerful: Crime, contemporary political economy, and critical social research, in: Tombs, S. and Whyte, D. (editors), *Unmasking the Crimes of the Powerful*, Lang, New York, 3–48.

Trahan, A. (2011). Filling in the gaps in culture-based theories of organizational crime, *Journal of Theoretical and Philosophical Criminology*, 3 (1), 89–109.

Valukas, A.R. (2010). *In regard Lehman Brothers Holdings Inc. to United States Bankruptcy Court in Southern District of New York*, Jenner & Block, March 11, 239 pages, http://www.nysb.uscourts.gov/sites/default/files/opinions/188162_61_opinion.pdf.

Valukas, A.R. (2014). *Report to Board of Directors of General Motors Company Regarding Ignition Switch Recalls*, law firm Jenner & Block, May 29, 325 pages, http://www.beasleyallen.com/webfiles/valukas-report-on-gm-redacted.pdf.

Weick, K.E. (1995). What theory is not, theorizing is, *Administrative Science Quarterly*, 40, 385–390.

Weick, K.E. (1999). Theory construction as disciplined reflexivity: Trade-offs in the 90s, *Academy of Management Review*, 24 (4), 797–806.

Weissmann, A. and Block, J.A. (2010). White-collar defendants and white-collar crimes, *Yale Law Journal*, 116, 286–291.

Welsh, D.T., Oronez, L.D., Snyder, D.G. and Christian, M.S. (2014). The slippery slope: How small ethical transgressions pave the way for larger future transgressions, *Journal of Applied Psychology*, http://dx.doi.org/10.1037/a0036950.

Whetten, D.A. (1989). What constitutes a theoretical contribution? *Academy of Management Review*, 14 (4), 490–495.

White, M.D. and Katz, C.M. (2013). Policing convenience store crime: Lessons from the glendale, Arizona smart policing initiative, *Police Quarterly*, 16 (3), 305–322.

Williams, J.W. (2008). The lessons of "Enron"—Media accounts, corporate crimes, and financial markets, *Theoretical Criminology*, 12 (4), 471–499.

Neutralization Theory of Public Corruption

2

PETTER GOTTSCHALK

Contents

Introduction

Criminals apply techniques in order to make them feel as though they have not done any wrong. These techniques represent neutralization techniques, whereby the feeling of guilt decreases and possibly disappears (Gottschalk, 2016). In convenience theory, a supporting theory in the behavioral dimension of crime is neutralization theory. The briber and bribed both may think they do nothing wrong by public procurement corruption.

As mentioned in the previous chapter on convenience theory, neutralization theory seems to increase in importance as a source of explanation in recent years. By applying neutralization techniques, white-collar criminals think they are doing nothing wrong. They deny responsibility, injury, and victim. They condemn the condemners. They claim appeal to higher loyalties and normality of action. They claim entitlement, and they argue the case of legal mistake. They find their own mistakes acceptable. They argue a dilemma arose, whereby they made a reasonable trade-off before committing the act (Siponen and Vance, 2010). The idea of neutralization techniques (Sykes and Matza, 1957) resulted from work on Sutherland's (1949) differential association theory. According to this theory, people are always aware of their moral obligation to abide by the law, and they are aware that they have the same moral obligations within themselves to avoid illegitimate acts. The theory postulates that criminal behavior learning occurs in association with those who find such criminal behavior favorable, and in isolation from those who find it unfavorable (Benson and Simpson, 2015). Crime is relatively convenient when there is no guilt feeling for doing something learned from others.

Five Original Neutralization Techniques

Sykes and Matza (1957) proposed neutralization techniques in its original formulation to explain how the desire to conform, coexists with deviance. Neutralization theory encompasses all these techniques, whereby offenders neutralize their feelings of guilt. In their original formulation of neutralization theory, Sykes and Matza (1957) proposed five techniques of neutralization: denial of responsibility, denial of injury, denial of the victim, condemnation of the condemners, and appeal to the higher loyalties. Sykes and Matza (1957) proposed the following five techniques of neutralization that found application in a number of later research studies (e.g., Benson and Simpson, 2015; Bock and Kenhove, 2011; Gottschalk and Smith, 2011; Heath, 2008; Moore and McMullan, 2009; Siponen and Vance, 2010):

1. *Denial of responsibility.* It is the belief by an individual that the person is not blameworthy because responsibility for his or her criminal behavior lies elsewhere. The offender here claims that one or more of the conditions of responsible agency were not present. The person committing the deviant act defines himself or herself as lacking responsibility for his or her actions. In this technique, the person rationalizes, that the action in question is beyond his or her control. The offender views himself or herself as a billiard ball, helplessly propelled through different situations. Offenders will propose that they were victims of circumstances, or others forced them into situations beyond their control. Corporate leaders can avoid taking on responsibility by claiming that laws regulating practices in many industries are enormously complex and difficult to interpret. They can avoid responsibility for their actions by maintaining ignorance about the risks that they are imposing on others. They can avoid knowing what their subordinates are doing.

2. *Denial of injury.* The offender seeks to minimize or deny the harm done. Denial of injury involves justifying an action by explaining that harm was minimal. The offender does not consider this misbehavior as serious because no party apparently suffers directly as result of the action. Offenders insist that their actions did not cause any harm or damage. There is no relationship between wrongfulness and possible harm. Denying that actions are injurious is relatively easy for white-collar criminals because they seldom witness the harm they cause firsthand.

3. *Denial of victim.* The offender may acknowledge the injury, but claims that the victim is unworthy of concern. Any blame for illegal actions

are unjustified because the violated party deserves whatever injury it receives. Offenders believe that victims deserved whatever action offenders committed. In some types of securities offenses, such as insider trading, it may be difficult to identify victims in the traditional sense at all. Offenders blame their victims for their own suffering.

4. *Condemnation of the condemners.* The offender tries to accuse his or her critics of questionable motives for criticizing him. According to this technique, the offender neutralizes his or her actions by blaming those who are the target of the action. The offender deflects moral condemnation onto the ridiculing parties by pointing out that they engage in similar disapproved behavior. Offenders maintain that those who condemn their offenses are doing so purely out of spite, or are shifting the blame away from themselves unfairly. If the law itself is not legitimate or necessary and if those who enforce it are not competent or trustworthy, then offenders' moral obligation to obey the law is seriously undermined. Offenders express denial of the legitimacy of those who enforce the law. Some criminals condemn their condemners by developing and presenting conspiracy theories. A conspiracy theory is an explanatory hypothesis that accuses two or more persons, a group, or an organization of having caused or covered up, through secret planning and deliberate action, the investigation, prosecution, and conviction of the white-collar criminal.

5. *Appeal to higher loyalties.* Violating the law is a necessary component of the pursuit of broader, more important goals. The offender denies the act was motivated by self-interest, claiming that it was instead done out of obedience to some moral obligation. Those who feel they are in a dilemma that the offenders must resolve at the cost of violating a law or policy employ this technique. In the context of an organization, an employee may appeal to organizational values or hierarchies. For example, an employee could argue that he or she has to violate a policy in order to get his or her work done. Offenders suggest that their offenses were for the greater good, with long-term consequences that will justify their actions. Employees who experience requests to do something illegal may recognize that their behavior is wrong, but argue to themselves that being loyal to their employer or organization is more important. Offenders can also make a distinction between morality and the technical requirements of the law and claim that it is more important to do what they consider the right thing than the legal thing.

Five More Neutralization Techniques

After Sykes and Matza (1957) proposed their five techniques of neutralization, researchers have later added the following five more neutralization techniques (Gottschalk and Smith, 2011; Moore and McMullan, 2009; Siponen and Vance, 2010):

1. *Normality of action.* The offender argues that everyone else is doing it, thus he or she has done nothing wrong. It is simply quite normal what the offender did. The criminal has recognized that it is so common to have no respect for the law that the person claims no wrongdoing on his or her part. The offender can argue that it is consensus in the population to ignore the law at this point. Rather than abnormal, the action is normal, meaning conforming to common standards.

2. *Claim to entitlement.* The offender claims he or she was in his right to do what he or she did, perhaps because of a very stressful situation or because of some misdeed perpetrated by the victim. This is defense of necessity, which people base on the justification that if the offender views the rule breaking as necessary, one should feel no guilt when committing the action. The entitlement to the action can follow from position and responsibility.

3. *Legal mistake.* The offender argues that the law is wrong, and what he or she did, others should indeed consider quite acceptable. Therefore, one may violate the law because the law is unreasonable. There is something wrong with the law, since the offender perceives his or her own act as sensible and correct. It may seem that the law is there to enable law enforcement on a general basis, although it is wrong to apply the law to this specific situation.

4. *Acceptable mistake.* The offender argues that what he or she did is acceptable, given the situation and given his or her position. The person feels he or she has been doing so much good for the organization, that others should excuse them for their wrongdoing. He or she feels that that their crime is a relatively minor matter when compared to the good they have done and thus, others should ignore the matter. This is in line with the metaphor of the ledger, which uses the idea of compensating bad acts with good acts, that is, an individual believes that he or she has previously performed a number of good acts and has accrued a surplus of good will, and as the result of all good deeds can afford to commit some bad actions. Executives in corporate environments neutralize their actions through the metaphor of the ledger by rationalizing that their overall past good behavior justifies occasional rule breaking.

5. *Dilemma tradeoff.* The offender argues that a dilemma arose, whereby he or she made a reasonable trade-off before committing the act. Trade-off between many interests, therefore resulted in the offense. Dilemma represents a state of mind, where the difference between right and wrong is not obvious. For example, the offender might have carried out the offense to prevent a more serious offense from happening.

Two More Neutralization Techniques

After having studied 369 white-collar criminals in Norway, we suggest two more neutralization techniques:

1. *Victim of crime.* The criminal is convinced that rather than being the offender, he or she is a victim of the crime. The situation and other actors turned the person involuntarily into a criminal. The offender is a victim of the crime, and the offender perceives being a victim of poor treatment after disclosure and arrest. The offender continues to be a victim of the criminal justice system through investigation, prosecution, sentence, and imprisonment. The offender may be a victim because of conspiracy created by others to hurt him or her. Rather than taking on responsibility for the crime, and rather than neutralizing by denial of responsibility, the offender has a completely opposite view of the incident, where the offender suffered injury and became a victim of crime.
2. *Role in society.* Because of the person's prominent role in society, the offender is convinced that other rules and procedures apply to the person's case. The role might have connections to political responsibility, responsibility for employees, and personal attention to society as a whole. The offender may have supported local sports clubs and activities for children. The offender may have donated sums of money to universities and other institutions. The role in society is different from claim to entitlement, because the role includes and requires actions that others may define as crime.

Differential Association Theory

Justifications are socially constructed accounts that individuals who engage in criminal acts adopt to legitimate their behavior. They are beliefs that counteract negative interpretations, by articulating why the acts are justifiable, or excusable exceptions to the norms (Aguilera and Vadera, 2008).

The idea of neutralization techniques resulted from work on Sutherland's (1949) differential association theory. According to this theory, people are always aware of their moral obligation to abide by the law, and they are aware that they have the same moral obligation within themselves to avoid illegitimate acts. Thus, when persons commit illegitimate acts, they must employ some sort of mechanism to silence the urge to follow these moral obligations. Implicitly, neutralization theory thus rejects suggestions that groups containing delinquents have set up their own permanent moral code, which completely replaces moral obligations.

Differential association is a theory proposing that through interaction with others, individuals learn the values, attitudes, techniques, and motives for criminal behavior. When criminal behavior is learned, the learning includes techniques of committing the crime, motives and drives for the crime, and rationalizations for the crime. It is the rationalization for the crime, which implies that offenders know it is wrong what they are doing, but they apply neutralization techniques to justify their behavior.

Personal neutralization of misconduct and crime is not limited to white-collar criminals. However, it seems that such criminals apply these techniques extensively both before and after committing offenses (Benson and Simpson, 2015; Gottschalk and Smith, 2011; Piquero et al., 2005). The role that the criminal or potential criminal occupies makes him or her adopt these techniques.

Stadler and Benson (2012: 494) argue that the feeling of innocence is indeed a characteristic of many white-collar criminals:

> Indeed, a distinguishing feature of the psychological makeup of white-collar offenders is thought to be their ability to neutralize the moral bind of the law and rationalize their criminal behavior.

Stadler and Benson (2012) base their argument on an empirical study that they conducted among prison inmates. Almost without exception, white-collar inmates denied responsibility for crime. Other inmates felt to a much larger extent responsibility for crime. That the feeling of innocence is a characteristic of white-collar criminals is also a result of a study by Dhami (2007), who interviewed inmates in a prison in the United Kingdom.

Politically exposed persons exemplify this role theory. A politically exposed person (PEP) is an individual who enjoys the trust to attend prominent public functions. Gilligan (2009) argues that as such individuals pose a potential reputation risk to regulated entities, financial institutions must track them. Most of the high-profile media PEP-related coverage in recent years relates to persons such as the former president of the Philippines, Ferdinand Marcos, and former president of Nigeria, Sani Abacha, who others accused of fostering corruption within their countries and transferring millions of dollars of public funds out of their home countries into bank accounts overseas.

Neutralization theory connects to attribution theory, where criminals have a tendency to attribute causes of crime to everyone else but themselves.

Attribution theory is about identifying causality predicated on internal and external circumstances (Eberly et al., 2011: 731):

> Identifying the locus of causality has been at the core of attribution theory since its inception and has generated an extensive research stream in the field of organizational behavior. But the question emerges whether the "internal" and "external" categories capture the entire conceptual space of this phenomenon.

Based on this argument, Eberly et al. (2011) suggest that there is a third category in addition to internal explanation and external explanation, which they label *relational explanation*. Exploring these three categories of attributes helps seek causal explanations on how persons react in criminal situations.

Attribution theory is a part of social psychology that studies how humans spontaneously attribute reasons, guilt, and responsibility in situations that arise. The fundamental attribution error is a term used to designate overemphasis on person factors rather than situational factors in order to explain behavior.

Conclusion

Neutralization theory represents an insightful perspective to shed light on deviant and criminal behavior that is justified or rationalized by the person who commits the offense (Harris and Dumas, 2009). If there obviously is nothing wrong with the actions, there is no need for neutralization (Moore and McMullan, 2009).

Kvalnes and Iyer (2011) link neutralization theory to moral dissonance and moral neutralization. Moral neutralization implies rinsing criminal actions of moral content and meaning, preferably in advance of actions. The moral neutralization lowers the threshold for committing the crime and makes potential moral doubts disappear.

Kvalnes and Iyer (2011: 41) state that the conflict between a person's moral values and alternatives for action create dissonance. If a person perceives no dissonance, it means either that the person finds white-collar crime completely unacceptable, or that the person finds white-collar crime completely acceptable. People who are in between these two extremes will have a greater tendency to apply neutralization techniques.

References

Aguilera, R.V. and Vadera, A.K. (2008). The dark side of authority: Antecedents, mechanisms, and outcomes of organizational corruption, *Journal of Business Ethics*, 77, 431–449.

Benson, M.L. and Simpson, S.S. (2015). *Understanding White-collar Crime—An Opportunity Perspective*, New York: Routledge.

Bock, T.D. and Kenhove, P.V. (2011). Double standards: The role of techniques of neutralization, *Journal of Business Ethics*, 99, 283–296.

Dhami, M.K. (2007). White-collar prisoners' perceptions of audience reaction, *Deviant Behavior*, 28, 57–77.

Eberly, M.B., Holley, E.C., Johnson, M.D. and Mitchell, T.R. (2011). Beyond internal and external: A dyadic theory of relational attributions, *Academy of Management Review*, 36 (4), 731–753.

Gilligan, G. (2009). PEEPing at PEPs, *Journal of Financial Crime*, 16 (2), 137–143.

Gottschalk, P. (2016). *Understanding White-Collar Crime. A Convenience Perspective*, Boca Raton, FL: CRC Press.

Gottschalk, P. and Smith, R. (2015). Gender and white-collar crime: Examining representations of women in media, *Journal of Gender Studies*, 24 (3), 310–325.

Harris, L.C. and Dumas, A. (2009). Online consumer misbehaviour: An application of neutralization theory, *Marketing Theory*, 9 (4), 379–402.

Heath, J. (2008). Business ethics and moral motivation: A criminological perspective, *Journal of Business Ethics*, 83, 595–614.

Kvalnes, Ø. and Iyer, N.K. (2011). Skal vi danse? Om korrupsjon og moralsk ansvar (Shall we dance? About corruption and moral responsibility), *Praktisk Økonomi og Finans*, 27 (4), 39–46.

Moore, R. and McMullan, E.C. (2009). Neutralizations and rationalizations of digital piracy: A qualitative analysis of university students, *International Journal of Cyber Criminology*, 3 (1), 441–451.

Piquero, N.L., Tibbetts, S.G. and Blankenship, M.B. (2005). Examining the role of differential association and techniques of neutralization in explaining corporate crime, *Deviant Behavior*, 26 (2), 159–188.

Siponen, M. and Vance, A. (2010). Neutralization: New insights into the problem of employee information security policy violations, *MIS Quarterly*, 34 (3), 487–502.

Stadler, W.A. and Benson, M.L. (2012). Revisiting the guilty mind: The neutralization of white-collar crime, *Criminal Justice Review*, 37 (4), 494–511.

Sutherland, E.H. (1949). *White Collar Crime*, New York: Holt Rinehart and Winston.

Sykes, G. and Matza, D. (1957). Techniques of neutralization: A theory of delinquency, *American Sociological Review*, 22 (6), 664–670.

Public Service Motivation Theory

3

MICHAEL L. BENSON
PETTER GOTTSCHALK

Contents

Introduction

White-collar criminals are individuals who commit occupationally related financial crimes in a professional or organizational setting, where they have legal access and can hide misconduct in legitimate transactions (Benson and Simpson, 2014). White-collar crime is a global problem of enormous dimensions. Fraud, financial manipulation, and corruption occur to varying degrees in every economy and society in the world. White-collar criminals are present in both the private and the public sectors of an economy. Public service motivation theory seeks to explain why individuals choose public service over work in the private sector, given the perceived disparity in pay scale, advancement opportunities, and overall work environment (Kjeldsen and Jacobsen, 2013). We apply this theory to answer the following research question (Benson and Gottschalk, 2015a, 2015b): *What differences can be found in the prevalence and characteristics of white-collar criminals in the public versus the private sector?*

White-Collar Criminals

A white-collar criminal is typically a member of the privileged socioeconomic classes in society (Sutherland, 1949), who is involved in illegal activities, and commits nonviolent acts for financial gain (Gottschalk, 2014).

The white-collar criminal is a person of respectability who commits crime in a professional setting, where he or she conceals and disguises criminal activities in organizational work as law-abiding behavior (Pontell et al., 2014). The criminal has power and influence; he forms relationships with other persons or professionals, who protect him from developing a criminal identity, and he enjoys trust from others in privileged networks (Benson and Simpson, 2014). White-collar crime refers to offenses committed in an organization by those who indulge in dishonest activities. They do it either by themselves or using agents, for financial gain (Schoepfer et al., 2014).

Law enforcement targeted at white-collar criminals tends to be nonaggressive and often defensive not only because of the upper-class affiliation. Another reason is the white-collar defendants' ability to recruit top defense lawyers who conduct both symbolic defense and substantive defenses, as well as information control, in their work for white-collar clients (Gottschalk, 2014). Most people recognize that having a well-qualified and possibly famous attorney increases one's chances of a favorable outcome in any legal dispute. Some individual white-collar offenders avoid criminal prosecution because of the class bias of the courts (Tombs and Whyte, 2003).

When white-collar criminals appear before their sentencing judges, they can correctly claim to be first-time offenders. According to Slyke and Bales (2013), theory and empirical research often have agreed that white-collar offenders benefit from leniency at the sentencing stage of criminal justice system processing. Croall (2007) argues that the term *crime* is contentious, as many of the harmful activities of businesses or occupational elites are not subject to criminal law and punishment, but administrative or regulatory law, and penalties and sanctions. Therefore, very few white-collar criminals seem to become defendants in legal trials, and even fewer higher-class criminals seem to end up with a sentence of imprisonment. Another reason for the low prosecution and conviction rate for white-collar criminals is the extraordinary broad and fuzzily defined offenses in criminal law for white-collar crime (Hasnas et al., 2010).

Public Service Motivation Theory

Public service motivation theory suggests that some individuals work in the public sector based on their values. These values include a desire to contribute to the well-being of society in general through their work (Nalbandian and Edwards, 1983; Wright, 2007). The theory attempts to explain why individuals choose public service or private service (Kjeldsen and Jacobsen, 2013; Perry et al., 2010; Wittmer, 1991). Researchers have studied this question in terms of how the work environment can create and facilitate public service motivation (Moynihan and Pandey, 2007), and how to secure empirical measurement validity and reliability (Coursey and Pandey, 2007; Kim and Vandenabeele, 2010).

The concept of public service motivation is a theorized attribute of government employees that provides them with a desire to serve the public. It has been defined as "an individual's predisposition to respond to motives grounded primarily or uniquely in public institutions or organizations" (Perry and Wise, 1990). The theory attempts to explain why some people choose careers in the government and nonprofit sectors despite the potential for more financially lucrative careers in the private sector. Although job positions in the private sector can be more financially lucrative, they also tend to be very limited in scope with little or no impact on society. Conversely, job positions in the public sector can be less financially lucrative but tend to have a wider scope with a greater potential impact on society. Research into such correlates reveals that public service motivation varies among employees, and it is difficult to generalize regarding the motivations of everyone who works in the public sector. Research has been done to identify antecedents to public service motivation, exploring the impacts of political and religious socialization, professionalism, political ideology, and individual demographic characteristics on preference for public service employment (Perry, 1997). The findings suggest that childhood, religious, and professional experiences all contribute to the development of public service motivation. Similarly, Perry et al. (2008) found that religion and volunteer experiences have relationships to public service motivation. Because of this positive relationship between volunteering and public service motivation, some of the determinants of volunteering are useful in our study; Because higher educational attainment and being female have been shown to positively influence propensity for volunteering (Perry et al., 2008), we could expect education and gender to influence whether or not an individual takes part in white-collar crime. An interesting note in the Perry et al. study (2008) is that while they were investigating public service motivation, their sample consisted of volunteers that were not public sector employees, meaning that education level and gender could be important to our study, irrespective of whether the crime was in the public or private sector.

Many of the general theories that explain white-collar crime in the private sector are also relevant in the public sector. A first example is rational choice theory, which postulates that government officials may take calculated risks when benefits seem to outweigh costs (Paternoster and Simpson, 1996; Shover and Hochstetler, 2006). A second example is opportunity theory, which suggests that attractive criminal opportunities may arise in the public sector because of weak controls and absence of credible oversight (Benson and Simpson, 2014; Benson et al., 2009). A third example is strain theory, which argues that individual level strains sometimes is alleviated via financial crime, such as low pay or threats to employment status (Messner and

Rosenfeld, 2013; Passas, 1990). A fourth and final example is social learning theory suggesting at local and organizational based attitudes, value orientations, and rationalizations that are conducive to involvement in white-collar crime (Braithwaite, 1989; Sutherland, 1949).

As we are framing this chapter as a test or exploration of public service motivation theory, it might be helpful to draw out a specific implication or prediction from the theory. As we understand public service motivation theory, it will predict that the rate of white-collar crime in the public sector should be lower than the rate in the private sector because the values that push people to work in the public sector are not compatible with white-collar crime. Therefore, the rate of crime per opportunity should be lower in the public sector.

Research Method

Our data come from a content analysis of reports about white-collar crime in the two main financial newspapers in Norway: *Dagens Næringsliv* and *Finansavisen*. Both of these papers are conservative-leaning business newspapers. In addition, the business-friendly national daily newspaper *Aftenposten* regularly reports news of white-collar criminals and so was included in the study. Left-wing newspapers such as *Klassekampen* very seldom cover specific white-collar criminal cases, although they do report on the problem of white-collar crime in general.

The use of newspaper reports to assess involvement in white-collar crime is, of course, not without potential problems. As a data source, newspaper stories are not at all independent of the issue under investigation. Williams (2008) found that media coverage of white-collar crime cases tries to make sense of stories by selectively coding and communicating information to a variety of audiences.

Dagens Næringsliv, Finansavisen, and Aftenposten were read on a daily basis from 2009 to 2013 (five years) to identify stories reporting on white-collar cases and the people involved in them. A person was defined as a white-collar criminal if he or she satisfied the following criteria: (1) he or she committed an offense in a deliberate and purposeful manner as part of professional activity linked to regular business activities; (2) the offense involved large sums of money or large losses for others; (3) the offender was portrayed in the paper as being successful and having high social status, and a position of some power, and access to organizational resources. In short, our approach to defining white-collar crime is consistent with the approach championed by Sutherland (1940) and other well-known white-collar crime scholars (Braithwaite, 1989). We focus on offenses committed by people of high social status and respectability in the course of their occupations. All of the offenses involved individuals working in organizational settings (Benson and Gottschalk, 2015a).

We carried out verification of facts in newspaper accounts by obtaining court documents in terms of final verdicts. After registering newspaper accounts as an important indication of a white-collar offender, the contents in newspaper articles, we compared the contents to and corrected it by court sentencing documents, which typically range from five to 50 pages in Norwegian district courts, courts of appeal, and the Supreme Court. Thus, we reduce the effects of counter measures by firms and individuals to cover up for their wrongdoings (Zavyalova et al., 2012).

Because our study includes only cases that were of sufficient notoriety or newsworthiness as to garner newspaper coverage, our sample is similar (but not identical) to the high profile white-collar cases investigated by Steffensmeier et al. (2013). Because our study is limited to cases that law enforcement successfully prosecuted, our findings may not be generalizable to the broader population of undetected or unprosecuted white-collar cases. A number of data on each case found relevant codes in this research, including age of offender, amount of money involved in financial crime, and the length of prison sentence.

Research Results

We reviewed the three newspapers noted above from 2009 to 2013 to identify stories reporting on cases of white-collar crime. We registered 369 criminals in this five-year period in Norway (Gottschalk, 2015). There were 344 convicts in the private sector and 25 convicts in the public sector as listed in Table 3.1. Thus, the public sector fraction of the sample is 7%.

In 2013, Norway had a population of 5 million people. Public sector employees make up approximately 29% of the Norwegian work force, whereas the private sector employs 71% of Norwegian workers. However, as noted above, only 7% of the reported cases of white-collar crime between 2009 and 2013 involved public sector employees. This figure is substantially lower than would be expected, if the prevalence rate for public sector white-collar crime approximated the proportion of public sector employees.

This finding lends support to public service motivation theory concerning white-collar crime.

Besides the low prevalence rate, there are other differences between public and private sector white-collar criminals. White-collar criminals in the public sector are significantly older than criminals found in the private sector. Detected public sector criminals are 50 years old on average when they commit crime, and they are 55 years when they are sentenced to prison in a Norwegian court. They are older than private sector offenders, as listed in the table.

Table 3.1   Comparison of Private Sector Criminals Versus Public Sector Criminals

Total 369 White-Collar Criminals	344 Criminals in Private Sector	25 Criminals in Public Sector	T-Statistic Difference	Significance of t-Statistic
Age convicted	48 years	55 years	−3.111	0.002
Age at time of crime	43 years	50 years	−3.386	0.001
Years in prison	2.3 years	2.5 years	−0.683	0.495
Crime amount	50 m NOK	15 m NOK	1.119	0.264
Personal income	388,000 NOK	329,000 NOK	0.409	0.683
Personal tax	182,000 NOK	118,000 NOK	0.903	0.367
Personal wealth	3.0 m NOK	0.6 m NOK	0.885	0.376
Involved persons	3.4 persons	2.7 persons	1.447	0.149
Business revenue	208 m NOK	379 m NOK	−1.885	0.060
Business employees	123 persons	266 persons	−1.918	0.056

Public sector criminals receive a prison sentence of 2.5 years on average, which is slightly higher than private sector criminals. This is surprising, since the sum of money involved in crime is lower, only 15 million as compared to 50 million Norwegian kroner.

Private sector criminals are somewhat wealthier and work in smaller organizations, but these differences are statistically not significant. There are more people involved in a crime case in the private sector, but again, this difference is not significant.

Discussion

Public service motivation theory predicts that the rate of white-collar crime in the public sector should be lower than in the private sector because of the values typically held by people who work in the public sector. These values promote the ideas of community service and the importance of the overall welfare of society in general. People who hold such values should be less inclined, therefore, to harm the public welfare by engaging in financial fraud or embezzlement in their work places. Although the low fraction of white-collar criminals in the public sector (7%) as compared to the fraction of the workforce in the public sector (29%) is consistent with public service motivation theory, there are other possible explanations. For example, opportunity theory can be introduced as a source of explanation. Opportunities may be more limited in the public sector, where rules rather than goals dominate the culture. Rules imply that adherence to rules is both desired and controlled. Deviant behavior is difficult, because norms and guidelines are explicit and known. Focus is on how you do your work, rather than what you achieve in your work. Rules limit opportunities and demotivates from exploiting opportunities (Gottschalk, 2015).

Furthermore, the public sector is dominated by a security culture. For example, information systems security is taken much more seriously, often at the expense of user access and ease of use (Chekwa et al., 2013). Increased IT security reduces opportunities for fraud. In the area of procurement, public procurement may be less efficient and more bureaucratic, but at the same time provide fewer opportunities for fraud (Hawkins et al., 2011).

Opportunity theory suggests that criminal opportunities are an important cause of white-collar crime. Without an opportunity, there cannot be a crime. Opportunity manifests itself by legitimate access, spatial separation, and appearance of legitimacy (Benson and Simpson, 2014). We argue that the extent to which the offender has legitimate access, is spatially separated, and appears to be acting legally is dependent on the position. Public sector executives seem to have less opportunity to commit crime when compared to their colleagues in the private sector.

Opportunities to commit financial crime by white-collar people are more available in the private sector. The private sector is dominated by goals. Rules can be bent and possibly broken to achieve goals. Focus is on what you achieve in your work, rather than how you do your work. Dodge (2009: 15) argued that it is tough rivalry that makes people in an organization commit crime:

> The competitive environment generates pressures on the organization to violate the law in order to attain goals.

The private sector is driven by goals, whereas the public sector is driven by following rules. Goals cause strain. Agnew (2005) identified three categories of strain: failure to achieve positively valued goals, the removal of positively valued stimuli, and the presentation of negative or noxious stimuli. Strain theory posits that each type of strain ultimately lead to deviance for slightly different reasons.

The American dream suggests that everyone in America has an opportunity to become monetarily successful. High white-collar crime rates can be attributed to the commitment to the goal of material success as experienced in the American dream. It is caused by an overemphasis on success in exposed assets (Schoepfer and Piquero, 2006), and it is not matched by a concurrent normative emphasis on what means are legitimate for reaching desired goals (Pratt and Cullen, 2005).

In addition to difference in opportunities and rules versus goals, other possible factors to explain the difference in the fraction of convicted white-collar criminals include detection rate, recruitment profile, and perceived compensation.

Difference in detection rates between public sector and private sector is possible, in that detection in the private sector is more likely than detection in the public sector. However, it is difficult to find theoretical arguments for such a difference in detection rates.

Next, there is the issue of whether or not different people are attracted to work in the public versus the private sector. Maybe job security and stability attracts more risk-averse individuals to the public sector, who are less likely to practice deviant behavior. Pedersen (2013) found that public interest is positively associated with attraction to public sector employment and negatively associated with attraction to private sector employment. This is in line with the public services motivation theory.

Reilly (2013) compared public versus private sector pay and benefits in terms of lifetime compensation. Competitive compensation is a key factor in ensuring that the public sector can recruit and retain a high-quality workforce (Sakellariou, 2012). In Norway, there is a general impression that employees on average are compensated well in the private sector compared to the public sector. However, employees in a sector tend to compare their salary with others in the same sector, and compensation variation is smaller in the public sector than in the private sector.

Conclusion

This article has explored differences between the public and private sector, in terms of the frequency and characteristics of white-collar criminals. Based on a sample of 369 convicted white-collar criminals in Norway from 2009 to 2013, this study showed that the frequency of convicted white-collar criminals in the public sector is substantially lower than in the private sector. Furthermore, white-collar criminals in the public sector are significantly older, and they work in significantly larger organizations.

References

Agnew, R. (2005). *Pressured into Crime—An Overview of General Strain Theory*, Oxford, UK: Oxford University Press.

Benson, M.L. and Gottschalk, P. (2015a). Gender and white-collar crime in Norway: An empirical study of media reports, *International Journal of Law, Crime and Justice*, 43, 535–552.

Benson, M.L. and Gottschalk, P. (2015b). Public service motivation theory: Differences between white-collar criminals in the public and private sectors, *Journal of International Doctoral Research*, 4 (1), 56–68.

Benson, M.L., Madensen, T.D. and Eck, J. (2009). White-collar crime from an opportunity perspective, in: Simpson, S. and Weisburd, D. (editors), *The Criminology of White-Collar Crime*, Springer, New York, pages 175–193.

Benson, M.L. and Simpson, S.S. (2014). *Understanding White-Collar Crime—An Opportunity Perspective*, New York: Routledge.

Braithwaite, J. (1989). Criminological theory and organizational crime. *Justice Quarterly*, 6 (3), 333–358.

Chekwa, C., Ogungbure, A., Mmutakaego, C.T. and Thomas, E. (2013). Information security threats: What is public versus private sector's perception? *Journal of Business & Public Administration*, 10 (1), 87–97.

Coursey, D. and Pandey, S. (2007). Public service motivation measurement, *Administration & Society*, 39 (5), 547–568.

Croall, H. (2007). *Victims, Crime and Society*, Los Angeles, CA: Sage Publications.

Dodge, M. (2009). *Women and White-Collar Crime*, Upper Saddle River, NJ: Prentice Hall.

Gottschalk, P. (2014). *Policing White-Collar Crime: Characteristics of White-Collar Criminals*, Boca Raton, FL: CRC Press.

Gottschalk, P. (2015). *Fraud Examiners in White-Collar Crime Investigations*, Boca Raton, FL: CRC Press.

Hasnas, J., Prentice, R. and Strudler, A. (2010). New directions in legal scholarship: Implications for business ethics research, theory, and practice, *Business Ethics Quarterly*, 20 (3), 503–531.

Hawkins, T., Gravier, M. and Powley, E. (2011). Public versus private sector procurement ethics and strategy: What each sector can learn from the other, *Journal of Business Ethics*, 103 (4), 567–586.

Kim, S. and Vandenabeele, W. (2010). A strategy for building public service motivation research internationally, *Public Administration Review*, September/October, 701–709.

Kjeldsen, A.M. and Jacobsen, C.B. (2013). Public service motivation and employment sector: Attraction or socialization? *Journal of Public Administration Research and Theory*, 23 (4), 899–926.

Messner, S. and Rosenfeld, R. (2013). *Crime and the American Dream*, 4th edition, Belmont, CA: Wadsworth.

Moynihan, D.P. and Pandey, S.K. (2007). The role of organizations in fostering public service motivation, *Public Administration Review*, January/February, 40–53.

Nalbandian, J. and Edwards, J.T. (1983). The professional values of public administrators: A comparison with lawyers, social workers, and business administrators. *Review of Public Personnel Administration*, 4, 114–127.

Passas, N. (2007). *Corruption in the Procurement Process/Outsourcing Government Functions: Issues, Case Studies, Implications*, Report to the Institute for Fraud Prevention, shortened version by W. Black, 33 pages, http://www.theifp.org/research-grants/procurement_final_edited.pdf.

Paternoster, R. and Simpson, S. (1996). Sanction threats and appeals to morality: Testing a rational choice model of corporate crime. *Law and Society Review*, 30 (3), 549–583.

Pedersen, M.J. (2013). Public service motivation and attraction to public versus private sector employment: Academic field of study as moderator? *International Public Management Journal*, 16 (3), 357–385.

Perry, J.L. (1997). Antecedents of public service motivation, *Journal of Public Administration Research and Theory*. 10 (2), 181–197.

Perry, J.L., Brudney, J.L., Coursey, D. and Littlepage, L. (2008). What drives morally committed citizens? A study of the antecedents of public service motivation, *Public Administration Review*, 68 (3), 445–458.

Perry, J., Hondeghem, A. and Wise, L. (2010). Revisiting the motivational bases of public service, *Public Administration Review*, September/October, 681–690.

Perry, J.L. and Wise, L.R. (1990). The motivational bases of public service. *Public Administration Review*. 50 (3), 367–373.

Pontell, H.N., Black, W.K. and Geis, G. (2014). Too big to fail, too powerful to jail? On the absence of criminal prosecutions after the 2008 financial meltdown, *Crime, Law and Social Change*, 61, 1–13.

Pratt, T.C. and Cullen, F.T. (2005). Assessing macro-level predictors and theories of crime: A meta-analysis, *Crime and Justice*, 32, 373–450.

Reilly, T. (2013). Comparing public-versus-private sector pay and benefits: Examining lifetime compensation, *Public Personnel Management*, 42 (4), 521–544.

Sakellariou, C. (2012). Central Government versus private sector wages and cognitive skills: Evidence using endogenous switching regression, *Applied Economics*, 44 (25), 3275–3289.

Schoepfer, A. and Piquero, N.L. (2006). Exploring white-collar crime and the American dream: A partial test of institutional anomie theory, *Journal of Criminal Justice*, 34, 227–235.

Schoepfer, A., Piquero, N.L. and Langton, L. (2014). Low self-control versus the desire-for-control: An empirical test of white-collar crime and conventional crime, *Deviant Behavior*, 35 (3), 197–214.

Shover, N. and Hochstetler, A. (2006). *Choosing White-Collar Crime*, New York: Cambridge University Press.

Slyke, S.R.V. and Bales, W.D. (2013). Gender dynamics in the sentencing of white-collar offenders, *Criminal Justice Studies*, 26 (2), 168–196.

Steffensmeier, D., Schwartz, J. and Roche, M. (2013). Gender and twenty-first-century corporate crime: Female involvement and the gender gap in enron-era corporate frauds, *American Sociological Review*, 78 (3), 448–476.

Sutherland, E.H. (1940). White-collar criminality, *American Sociological Review*, 5, 1–12.

Sutherland, E.H. (1949). *White Collar Crime*, New York: Holt Rinehart and Winston.

Tombs, S. and Whyte, D. (2003). Scrutinizing the powerful: Crime, contemporary political economy, and critical social research, in: Tombs, S. and Whyte, D. (editors), *Unmasking the Crimes of the Powerful*, Lang, New York, pages 3–48.

Williams, J.W. (2008). The lessons of "Enron"—Media accounts, corporate crimes, and financial markets, *Theoretical Criminology*, 12 (4), 471–499.

Wittmer, D. (1991). Serving the people or serving for pay: Reward preference among government, hybrid sector, and business managers, *Public Productivity and Management Review*, 14 (4), 369–383.

Wright, B.E. (2007). Public service and motivation: Does mission matter? *Public Administration Review*, 67 (1), 54–64.

Zavyalova, A., Pfarrer, M.D., Reger, R.K. and Shapiro, D.L. (2012). Managing the message: The effects of firm actions and industry spillovers on media coverage following wrongdoing, *Academy of Management Journal*, 55 (5), 1079–1101.

Europe

II

Public and Police Corruption in Eastern Europe

4

JAMES F. ALBRECHT

Contents

Introduction

Most of the states that fell under the Soviet Union or Soviet influence prior to the end of the cold war, from Hungary on the west, across to the eastern Russian coastal border, down south through the Balkan states, often generically referred to as *Eastern Europe*, have been chronically plagued by corruption that permeates both public and private organizations. To many, paying a bribe to obtain a service continues to be a routine practice in all daily activities. In order to better understand these phenomena, two nations, the independent Republic of Kosovo, which has been under international supervision since the end of the conflict with Serbia in 1999, and Ukraine, presently undergoing political and constitutional reform since the *Euromaidan Revolution* in 2014, will be compared, contrasted, and analyzed in order to better comprehend the underlying causes of the criminality, misconduct and fraud that pervade Eastern European society. Criminological explanations will be examined, and the impact of efforts at political and sociological reform by international organization and nations will be evaluated.

"Eastern Europe"

The geographical region often referred to as *Eastern Europe* has often been considered to include many of the nations that were member states of the Soviet Union or that fell under the influence of the Soviet umbrella. This area could be said to include Poland on the east and stretch all the way to Russia, even with her Asian coastal border. Although not directly under the influence of the Soviet Union, the former Yugoslavian nations, stretching south along the Balkan peninsula, continue to be referred to as *Southeast Europe*. Unfortunately one of the common practices throughout both Eastern and Southeastern Europe continues to involve corruption and fraud when dealing with both public agencies and private organizations. The payment of a bribe or a *proactive tip* is often the only means for individuals to get necessary tasks, from procurement to medical services, accomplished.

Kosovo

The Republic of Kosovo

Kosovo is a region that is located in the southernmost area of the former People's Republic of Serbia that had previously been under the political control of the former Federal Republic of Yugoslavia. It encompasses around 4,200 square miles (or 11,000 square kilometers) with a population of approximately 2 million, which presently consists of a majority (+90%) ethnic Albanian population who had moved into the region during the 500 year Ottoman occupation. Kosovo originally was designated an autonomous province in 1945, but did not gain actual political autonomy until 1946 (Mertus, 1999). After the fall of Yugoslavia, autonomy came to an end under the direction of Serbian President Slobodan Milosevic in 1989. Milosevic ordered that all government positions could only be filled by ethnic Serbians. The ethnic Albanian population formed a parallel society and declared their independence in 1990. This was not recognized by Serbia, nor by other countries, and Milosevic flooded Kosovo with Serbian paramilitary and law enforcement officials. The Albanian population countered by forming the Kosovo Liberation Army (KLA) and engaging in guerilla conflict with Serbian authorities. Originally the KLA was designated a terrorist organization by the international community, but the widespread ethnic cleansing perpetrated under Milosevic's guidance later resulted in repeated efforts by the international community to end the armed conflict. Milosevic and Serbian officials repeatedly participated in peace negotiations, but refused to sign any treaties. As such, the North Atlantic Treaty Organization (NATO) in March 1999 engaged in an 11-week bombing campaign that crippled Serbia's infrastructure and military operations in Kosovo (Hagan, 1999; Solana, 1999).

In June 1999, NATO and Serbia signed a technical agreement that led to the withdrawal of Serbian troops from Kosovo. The United Nations Security Council (UNSC) in 1999 also ratified resolution 1244, that designated the region of Kosovo as United Nations administered territory. As such, the United Nations took over political control of this area. More than 700,000 ethnic Albanians, who had mainly fled to neighboring Albania and Macedonia during the NATO conflict, quickly returned, but many found their homes, businesses, and neighborhood mosques had been destroyed by Serbian forces or their ethnic Serbian neighbors (Sklias and Roukanas, 2007). With a power and security vacuum in existence, the leadership of the KLA took control and advantage, engaging in organized crime to gain financial resources, and also took revenge by killing ethnic Serbs and destroying their homes, and by killing other Albanians that either were accused of collaboration with Serbian authorities, or were not considered to be in line with KLA endeavors.

The United Nations Administered Kosovo

Once Serbia capitulated at the conclusion of the NATO bombing raids, the UNSC adopted Resolution 1244 on June 10, 1999, which established the United Nations Interim Administration in Kosovo (UNMIK). The first UN officials arrived three days later to observe a devastated and destroyed region with a limited population. However, by July 1999, it is estimated that more than 650,000 refugees, predominantly ethnic Albanians, had returned. Initial criminality commonly involved the looting and destruction of Serbian residences and intimidation against the Serbian population. The previous law enforcement and judicial system had collapsed and the majority population took advantage of the crime control vacuum. Criminal gangs, mainly headed by former KLA leaders, engaged in rampant organized crime that included smuggling, drug, and human trafficking among other illicit activities (Strohmeyer, 2001). The suppression of violence, interethnic criminality, and organized crime became the responsibility of the Kosovo Force (KFOR), which was an international military mission, staffed by UN member nations. However, their responsibilities ended after apprehension and detention. The overwhelming challenge involved the creation of a justice system, specifically the hiring and training of prosecutors and judges to move the cases along. However, the task proved to be difficult, as the quest to develop a pool of prosecutors and judges from the different ethnic groups often led to intimidation and violence. Quite quickly a prosecutorial and judicial backlog developed that still exists to this day.

One of the daunting tasks was the development of a legal framework. The majority ethnic Albanian population refused to accept legislation that had been imposed by the oppressive Serbian regime, so former Yugoslavian law was instituted. On December 12, 1999, UNMIK promulgated a regulation that provided the legal framework in place prior to March 22, 1989 would serve as the provisional legislation within Kosovo. However, this proved to cause difficulties as some of the provisions were in violation of accepted human rights practices (Strohmeyer, 2001). In May 2001, UNMIK implemented the constitutional framework for provisional self government in Kosovo, which resulted in the subsequent elections in November 2001, and later the development of provisional legislation for criminal justice administration (Yannis, 2004). Thereafter, local political, government, and criminal justice actors have remained under the supervision and guidance of United Nations personnel.

As for law enforcement, the primary responsibility fell on the international community under the supervision and coordination of the United Nations (i.e., United Nations Civilian Policing or *CIVPOL* program). The 1,800 international police officers in 1999 rapidly increased to 4,450 in the year 2000. All were professional law enforcement practitioners from United Nations member countries. Their two primary tasks were to immediately establish law and order, and to develop law enforcement capabilities at the local level. Although UN CIVPOL was rapidly deployed throughout Kosovo, the responsibility of developing, training, and deploying a new Kosovo Police Service (KPS) was predominantly accomplished through the United States Department of Justice ICITAP (International Criminal Investigative Training Assistance Program) program, and through the support of the

OSCE (the Organization for Security Cooperation in Europe). The KPS commenced recruitment in June 1999, and the KPS School in Vushtri became fully operational in March 2000. In the year 2000, there were 2,516 KPS officers working across Kosovo and this increased to 5,704 in 2004 (Wilson, 2006), and finally to the present level that exceeds 7,000.

In addition to, the establishment of rule of law and the development of the criminal justice agencies (i.e., police, prosecutors, judges, and correctional system), the United Nations has also been responsible for the administration and coordination of: humanitarian assistance, civil administration, democratization and institution building, and reconstruction and economic development (Wilson, 2006). What this resulted in was the distribution of funds from many donor nations and organizations, which eventually supported the corrupt atmosphere endemic in Kosovo.

Planned European Union Involvement

As part of the *Ahtisaari Plan* (Ki-moon, 2007), there was to be a 120-day transition period allowing transfer from United Nations administration to supervision under the European Security and Defense Policy (ESDP) program. In April 2006, the European Union in conjunction with the United States of America and Norway deployed the European Union Planning Team (EUPT) in Pristina, Kosovo to prepare for this development. The ESDP initiative was called the European Union Rule of Law Mission in Kosovo (or EULEX—Kosovo). EULEX would be primarily deployed to support the Kosovo institutions responsible for law enforcement, customs and justice, and act in a monitoring, mentoring, and advisory (MMA). The EULEX mission would also retain limited executive authority and would be responsible for conducting criminal investigations involving war crimes, corruption, organized crime, and financial crimes. The total complement of EULEX was planned for approximately 1,950 international staff with more than 75% of this cadre dealing with policing and customs control.

The "Russian Roadblock" and Kosovo's "Independence"

The 120-day transition from United Nations administration to supervised independence under the guidance of the European Union was to commence on February 17, 2008, with the United Nations supported declaration of independence and formation of the new Republic of Kosovo. The plan called for the end of United Nations administration on April 9, 2008. Only days prior to the declaration of independence and the implementation of that stage of the Ahtisaari Plan, Russia, as a permanent member of the UNSC, in mid-February 2008, obstructed the initiation of the process. This created chaos and an atmosphere of indecision. In February 2008, the Republic of Kosovo declared her independence, but there was no coinciding transition from the United Nations to the European control. In reality, the past hour ploy by the Russian government, consistently a Serbian ally, created overwhelming confusion and the abrupt end to international rule of law participation across Kosovo. Many United Nations member states had commenced the withdrawal of personnel, and those involved in criminal justice functions that had remained, undertook a *wait and see* position, leaving arrests and case prosecutions in limbo. Since the European Union and the EULEX mission had not been granted executive authority, the staff maintained their planning mode. In the interim, this uncertainty ultimately hampered many United Nations member states from recognizing Kosovo as an independent country.

The European Union Rule of Law Mission in Kosovo

Even given the ambiguity, the European Union and other cooperating nations commenced the large-scale deployment of justice, customs, and law enforcement personnel to Kosovo in the spring of 2008. Eventually in November 2008, the UNSC, with overwhelming pressure from the United States, Germany, the United Kingdom, France, and other key nations, approved a resolution that called for the one-day transition of authority from the United Nations to the European Union. The date designated for the application of executive authority to the EULEX mission was December 9, 2008. Although compounded by chronic logistical and planning difficulties, the Head of the EULEX mission announced full operational capability in April 2009. The Republic of Kosovo, although now recognized as being independent by a majority of the United Nations member states, is still considered by many countries to be under *international supervision.*

Criminality and Safety within Kosovo

The development of a relatively professional and effective Kosovo Police agency, supported by international advisors and colleagues has resulted in continuing crime reduction, since the conflict officially concluded in 1999. Although the rates for most crime categories are relatively low when compared to European Union and the United States averages, the most accurate measure of violence affecting the estimated population of two million could be assessed through the analysis of murder incidents. The reported murder rate in Kosovo for the year 2000 was 12 per 100,000 residents; for 2005 was three per capita (United Nations Office on Drugs and Crime, 2008); and for 2010 was 2.5 per capita (International Crisis Group, 2010). Murder statistics have disclosed a continuous downward trend that reflects the reduction in overall crime recorded within Kosovo Police annual reports from 2000 through 2010.

Kosovo is not noted for overwhelming danger and violence, and most murders and assaults can be said to be the result of property, family, or personal disputes. On the other hand, the United Nations and other international organizations estimate that there are more than 350,000 unaccounted for small arms present throughout Kosovo (United Nations Development Programme [UNDP], 2010). Given this potential threat, it is quite surprising that firearm related incidents are limited. However, the greatest safety hazard within Kosovo involves the general lack of traffic safety. In 2007, there were 127 vehicle fatalities and 17,006 vehicle accidents; in 2008, 114 fatalities and 15,939 accidents; in 2009, 176 fatalities and 19,212 accidents; and in 2010, 175 fatalities and 18,030 accidents (Bislimi, 2011). Police traffic enforcement, other than speed control is negligible. The vast majority of drivers within Kosovo operate defective vehicles, do not wear seat belts, and drive in a reckless and haphazard fashion. Traffic accident statistical evaluations were not conducted by the Kosovo Police, and traffic intersection engineering assessments were clearly not supervised by international experts. Quite amazingly, the command staff of the Kosovo Police was repeatedly unresponsive to proposals by international law enforcement experts to enhance vehicular, pedestrian, and traffic safety.

Organized Crime Activity within Kosovo

Although crime in general is relatively low, Kosovo is a notorious smuggling hub between Asia, Africa, South America, North America, and Europe. Two main smuggling routes are used for smuggling drugs, humans, contraband, and other goods from Asia to the European Union. Goods from the east enter Turkey and exit either into Bulgaria, continuing through Romania into Hungary, or exit Turkey into Greece, traveling through Macedonia, and ending up in Kosovo. Afghanistan heroin is smuggled in this fashion. Although farmers in Kosovo have been known to grow marijuana, both cocaine and marijuana normally arrive in Kosovo after arriving at Albanian and Montenegrin ports. Ethnic Albanian crime groups then repackage the material into small parcels for transit to European nations, normally in private vehicles, tour buses, and commercial trucks.

Due to the large number of illegal small arms and explosives still remaining from the conflict, the smuggling of weapons between ethnic Albanian groups in Kosovo to ethnic Albanian communities in southern Serbia and Macedonia is routine. Most of the illegal weapons are under the control of former KLA fighters (or Serbian radicals in North Mitrovica).

Human smuggling mainly takes three forms. There are very small number of females smuggled from Ukraine or Moldova into Kosovo for sex trade purposes, but prostitution routinely involves ethnic Albanian females to avoid the attention of the international community or United Nations/European law enforcement. Organized crime groups are active in offering stolen, counterfeit, or duplicate travel documents (i.e., passports and visas) to the local population in order for them to gain entry into the European Union. And finally, due to the presence of the United Nations and other human rights organizations, and due to lax passport and border control, Kosovo has become a location where people from China, Afghanistan, Iraq, Somalia, Pakistan, Algeria, and other countries enter, request asylum, and then continue their illegal journey to Europe.

Both ethnic Serbian and ethnic Albanian organized crime groups are known to engage in regular fuel smuggling, in order to avoid paying related customs fees and taxes. Coffee, tobacco, and other goods routinely enter Kosovo in similar illegal fashion, normally through unguarded mountainous border areas. In addition, Kosovo is recognized for the open sale of pirated and counterfeit products (United States Department of State, 2011a). Finally, due to the lack of cooperation and information exchange with other law enforcement agencies, it is common to observe vehicles stolen from the United States and European Union nations being operated on the streets of Kosovo with their original license plates.

Corruption within Kosovo

Corruption within Southeast Europe has normally taken three general forms. Government employees routinely demand bribes from the citizens and business persons in order to engage in official misconduct, thereafter either performing, or failing to perform the responsibilities of their job. The second type of corruption involves direct political interference into the justice process. The third version of corruption involves the participation of government representatives overseeing or taking part in organized crime activity. Because these factors are common within Kosovo, Kosovo is often referred to as *Europe's mafia state* (Filiminova, 2010), since government leaders consistently have engaged in all three activities with little to no reaction from the United Nations, European Union, American, and other international supporters. And many of the local criminal justice actors within Kosovo are under the control and influence of key political leaders, so no investigative or enforcement action, from their side has occurred or is anticipated.

A survey of the residents of Kosovo has revealed that corruption is a highly perceived occurrence among government actors. Findings revealed that corruption was present in all government sectors, including political party leaders (33.7%); municipal government (28.2%); the judiciary (27.7%); prosecutors (25.2%); the Kosovo President (16.4%); Parliament (15.6%); and Kosovo government (14.3%); but was viewed as being limited within the Kosovo Police (9.4%). Almost 39% of Kosovo residents rated corruption as the second most relevant problem facing Kosovo (following unemployment), and 40% of the public believed that all government officials are involved in corrupt practices. Over 16% of all residents report being asked for unofficial cash by a municipal employee to deal with an official issue, as compared to 10% who were coerced to pay a bribe to a federal government official over the past 12 months (Spector et al., 2003). A more recent survey that has measured the perception of corruption across the globe reported that Kosovo presently ranks at 110 out of the 175 countries, and received a notably low score of 3.3 out of 10 in corruption perception (Transparency International, 2014) by Kosovo citizens.

The political leadership of Kosovo, at the request of the international community, has developed a number of official mechanisms to address the issue of corruption. The Kosovo Anti-Corruption Agency was introduced in 2007 and the Prime Minister established the Task Force against Corruption in 2010. However, both have proven to be ineffective. Both are staffed by relatives or party members from the Prime Minister's ruling Democratic Party of Kosovo (PDK), who clearly have been appointed to provide warnings to corrupt politicians, and other government employees, and to obstruct investigations. The head of the Task Force against Corruption was himself arrested in April 2012 for engaging in bribery, and for covering up corruption involving prominent government leaders (Karadaku, 2012).

What is likely most disturbing is that the most identifiable corrupt officials in Kosovo are three previous Prime Ministers and the former Minister of Transportation and Telecommunications. The former Prime Minister Hashim Thaci, the leader of the ruling PDK political party, and presently the nation's Foreign Minister, has been recognized as the leader of the Drenica organized crime group (Marty, 2010). Although Thaci cannot account for his questionable financial resources in any credible fashion, the international community has permitted him to remain in the political realm. Another former Prime Minister Ramush Haradinaj, the leader of the Alliance for the Future of Kosovo (AAK) party, the ruling party in western Kosovo, is recognized as the leader of the Haradinaj organized crime group functioning throughout the western Province of Peja. Haradinaj has astonishingly survived a number of International Criminal Tribunal for the former Yugoslavia (ICTY) war crimes trials. Former Minister of Transport and Telecommunications Fatmir Limaj, a top member of the PDK party, stepped down from office due to recurrent allegations that he accepted bribes in return for major government contracts. Former Prime Minister Agim Ceku, a member of the PDK party, has been reported to be a key coordinator of narcotics trading that has, and continues to occur within Kosovo's borders. In addition and extremely noteworthy, is that the above four former KLA members and *national heroes* are all suspects in serious incidents involving genocide and war crimes that targeted both ethnic Serbian and Albanian populations during and after the Yugoslavian conflict.

Recommendations for Kosovo to Move Forward

Corruption will remain endemic among the political elites of Kosovo until the international community ensures that corrupt officials are removed from their positions and guarantees that their illicit actions are properly addressed through the criminal justice system. In addition, beyond their involvement in organized crime activities, it is imperative that they be held accountable in a court of law, be it at the Hague, in Serbia, or in Kosovo, or whether by local, regional, or international prosecutors, for the war crime atrocities that they have been associated with. There is presently sufficient evidence to at the least advocate that they all be removed from their present positions, and be barred from active involvement in Kosovo government and politics. Unfortunately these criminals have moved from one critical government position to the next without much of any criticism or input from key international players. As such, Kosovo has sincerely earned the title of *Europe's mafia state*.

There is clearly a strong need to improve the distressing situation in Kosovo and permit the nation and her citizens to move forward. The most critical step is for the international community, most notably the United States and the European Union, which have significant influence within Kosovo, to direct the immediate removal of suspects of serious war crime allegations, and those with noted affiliations with organized crime groups, and bar those individuals from government employment. A *fresh start* will permit Kosovo to integrate more rapidly into the European Union and to earn the cooperation of her regional neighbors. This may sound severe, but until this occurs, Kosovo will deserve the title of *mafia state*, and will continue to be looked on as an illegitimate regional presence, ruled by *thugs* and supported financially by rampant organized crime activity.

In addition, effort should be made to revise Kosovo legislation, so as to permit the criminal justice system to evolve into a functional institution. Political influence into the appointment of police commanders and the assignment of Kosovo Police personnel should be eliminated, and more importantly police criminal investigations must remain free of political interference. Overall justice effectiveness could be instantly and dramatically improved by enacting legislation to switch to a common law system, which would permit independent police investigations and arrests. This would eliminate the present legal requirement for personal direction by prosecutors and judges in order to commence and continue criminal investigations. It is also crucial that the legislated mandate to *renew* a criminal investigation before a judge every 60 days be immediately removed. Since the law presently delineates the statue of limitations for each crime, this suffices to ensure cases are not excessively drawn out. Mandatory court renewal of criminal investigations merely delays the investigatory process, and allows corrupt and politically influential judges the opportunity to bring an end to major cases, particularly those involving government officials or members of their families or clans.

It is apparent that, other than a small number of top police chiefs, the Kosovo Police are not noted for being overly corrupt, and impressively has been recognized as one of the least corrupt law enforcement agencies in southeastern Europe. It is imperative that the upper stratum of the Kosovo Police hierarchy, which includes police directors (i.e., department chiefs) and regional commanders, be revetted to ensure that they have no connection with the present political parties, no war crime associations, and no allegations involving affiliations with organized crime or other criminal groups. The process should be conducted under the direct supervision of the international community to ensure legitimacy. The European Union and the EULEX mission failed to take this critical step after the declaration of independence of Kosovo.

From a criminal justice perspective, a workload analysis must be conducted to rectify the overwhelming backlog of criminal cases and eliminate direct political interference or corruption in court cases. Efforts must be made to recruit, properly screen, hire, and train a sufficient number of prosecutors and judges with similar vetting instructions that are outlined above and have been recommended for the Kosovo Police. In addition, all personnel working in the Kosovo Anti-Corruption Agency and the Task Force against Corruption should be immediately terminated and international actors should implement a revised vetting and training process to hire new staff in order to root out political control, influence, and interference.

The predominant international actors present within Kosovo must take or support the necessary measures to bring legitimacy to Kosovo. Unfortunately, many countries appear to be more concerned with their own national interests than with the welfare of the people living within Kosovo. Uncomfortable decisions have to be made and all recommendations to Kosovo government officials to improve the current state of affairs and to eliminate corruption and organized criminal activity must be made with a *stick* and *carrot* mindset. There is hope for Kosovo, but not when the international community continues to exhibit indifference to clear unacceptable misbehavior and corruption.

Ukraine

Contemporary Ukraine

Ukraine is the second largest country in Europe located on the eastern end of the continent, and is geographically significant due to its location on the crossroads between Asia and Europe. Ukraine has a long coastline on the

Black Sea and possesses the third longest European river, the Dnipro, which is relevant domestically for the production of hydroelectric power. Ukrainians, as their geographic neighbors, are ethnically Slavic. Ukraine first became an independent country in 1919, only to be overtaken by Russia in 1920. Ukraine once again became a sovereign state in 1990 after the fall of the Soviet Union. A new constitution was adopted in 1996, followed shortly thereafter by presidential and parliamentary elections. In 2004, the *Orange Revolution*, a large public demonstration against corruption, brought about political change, but this was short lived as the new political actors were forced out of office due to allegations of misconduct. Later elections were affected by counter claims of corruption and impropriety by competing political parties, which has brought further instability to the nation, and criticism from the United States and the European Union. Ukraine is divided into 25 oblasts (or states) including the capital Kiev. The former autonomous Republic of Crimea has recently been annexed by the Russian Federation through military invasion in March 2014. Due to military aggression and separatist movements in a number of eastern oblasts, and owing to the uncertain stability of recent agreements to bring an end to conflict in those areas, it is presently not clear if those oblasts will ultimately be autonomous, semiautonomous, or return to their previous status as a Ukrainian oblast under central government control.

The two predominant ethnic groups in Ukraine are Ukrainians and Russians, with ethnic Tartars (predominantly Muslims) in the southern most regions of the country, mainly in Crimea and the surrounding Ukrainian oblasts. Ukraine has established the contemporary goals of eventual NATO and European Union membership.

Instability and Conflict in Ukraine

In November 2013, protests were organized in the center of Kiev, the capital of Ukraine, to counter the government's recent orientation to deeper cooperation with the Russian Federation. The majority of protestors favored a stronger alliance with the European Union. These *Euromaiden* protests eventually evolved into widespread violent civil unrest that culminated with the pro-Russian president of Ukraine fleeing to Russia in February 2014. Russia responded with the deployment of Russian military forces into the Crimean territory, and the annexation of Crimea to the Russian Federation, following a vote of the Russian Parliament.

As a result, demonstrations arose in March 2014 in all large cities across Ukraine, with the eastern Ukrainian cities of Donetsk and Luhansk, located closest to the border with Russia, declaring their independence, and receiving support from Russian government officials. An armed separatist conflict commenced, as Ukrainian forces responded with the mass deployment of military and police assets to the region. A military conflict ensued even with a partial ceasefire agreement in place as of September 2014. Unfortunately armed conflict continues as Ukrainian military personnel are routinely attacked by Russian backed separatist groups in eastern Ukraine.

Crime and Corruption in Ukraine

Ukraine, as many other eastern European nations, has been plagued by organized crime, transnational criminality, and corruption since the collapse of the Soviet Union in 1990. In 2013, Ukraine ranked 144th out of 177 rated nations with a corruption score of 2.5 (out of 10), and continues to maintain her reputation as being one of the world's most corruption-prone countries (Transparency International, 2014). Approximately 37% of the population has reported paying a bribe to a government official within the past 12 months. A further analysis of anticorruption program effectiveness has revealed that desired results have not been achieved, and that high ranking government officials have been actively involved in these detrimental practices (Transparency International, 2013). The U.S. Department of State (DOS) (2011b) has reported that both the police (a national organization called the Ukrainian National Police or the *militsia*) and the judiciary rate at the top of the list of the most corrupt actors within Ukraine. Given the rampant corruption, the limited number of arrests and prosecutions involving criminal justice related misconduct and abuse is a reasonable and clear indication that little has been done by the government to implement effective anticorruption measures. In addition, the common practice of legislators in the *new* democracies in Eastern Europe to grant themselves with immunity, although holding political office has undoubtedly been done to protect themselves from corruption investigations (Harasymiw, 2003). It has not been uncommon for criminals to run for political office when they have been made aware of criminal investigations against them.

Shortly after the commencement of democratic principles in Ukraine in 1990, the country has been affected by chronic bribery as influential figures and organized crime organizations have managed to gain control in the privatization process and in business dealings. It has been estimated that between 33% and 50% of criminal capital has been regularly spent on bribing public officials over the first 10 years of Ukraine's modern existence (Kalman, 2001). The flaw is that Ukraine, even with extensive legislation in place to counter corruption, continues to act in reactive mode with little public trust in prosecutors and judges (Grodeland, 2010). As many other Eastern European nations, Ukraine has been hampered by political interference into corruption investigations and prosecutions, lending support to stated claims of the exorbitant amount of bribes paid to government and justice officials. The lack of enforcement has created an atmosphere of indifference with little confidence in rule of law practices within Ukraine (Markoyskaya et al., 2003).

In addition, the diminished confidence in the police also has created the perception that they are not effective in controlling crime (Ivkovic, 2008), which is counter to the reality, that shows that the crime rate in Ukraine is relatively low when compared to other industrialized nations. The excessive amount of corruption involving law enforcement officials has also hampered initiatives to implement criminal justice reform measures promoted by the international community, which could potentially have increased citizen satisfaction in and support for the police, if properly institutionalized (Robertson, 2005).

The limited amount of trust in the police and government institutions in Ukraine is endemic. Regardless of the support and recommendations made by international allies, it is clear that the law enforcement actors within Ukraine are not adequately trained, nor properly prepared, to deal with significant and recurring issues. Police reform has been negligible since Internal Ministry management positions (which oversee the law enforcement and justice sectors) are directly tied in to corrupt federal officials (Harasymiw, 2003). The United States has been instrumental in providing training to Ukrainian criminal justice personnel, but has quickly learned that the priority of the participants was not first-rate training, but rather the opportunity for travel and comfortable accommodation (Kenney, 2002). Medical experts in Ukraine have also criticized the competence of the police to deal with drug addicted citizens and noted the police indifference to the plight of HIV-afflicted prisoners, and others in need of medical attention (Mimiaga et al., 2010), which further raises questions about human rights abuses committed by police personnel. On the other hand, it should be highlighted that corruption and bribery appear to be pervasive in all aspects of Ukrainian society. The flawed health care system reportedly cannot function without bribery payments for treatment, and purchase of medication and hospital equipment (Markovska and Isaeva, 2007). And many employees are paid both official and unofficial (i.e., cash payments in envelopes) salary payments in order for business owners to avoid paying payroll taxes and decrease operating costs (Rodgers et al., 2008). One could conclude that even as more than 20 years have passed since the fall of the socialist government within Ukraine, many of the ideological practices, including those involving expected bribery and government abuses remain evident. There continues to be a need for not only effective police and government reform, but also cultural transformation in order for democratic principles and rule of law practices to take hold, and become institutionalized over the long term.

The European Union has noted that vast improvements in customs and border control through technological and training assistance have been attained as a result of their (i.e., ESDP) interaction with Ukrainian and Moldovan counterparts (European Union Institute for Security Studies, 2009). The European Union has reported enhanced Ukrainian capabilities, as it has related to limiting the transborder smuggling activities of criminal and terrorist organizations (Howorth, 2007). This is significant, as border and customs control are often likely targets of bribery attempts, corruption, and other forms of official misconduct. However, the claims of success by the European Union in civilian crisis management assistance have routinely been found to be overstated (Chivvis, 2010). In slight contrast to the European Union statements, the United States continues to report the significance of Ukraine as a critical transit country for narcotics trafficking, most notably the transfer of heroin from Afghanistan to western Europe. On the other hand, the United States has highlighted the recent increase of more than 2% in drug seizures by Ukrainian law enforcement agencies (United States Department of State, 2012). Yet Ukraine remains a major transit country for illegal immigrants from the Middle East, Southeast Asia, and Asia (Luptakova, 2009), and for Afghani heroin due to porous borders with four European Union countries and evidently involving the illicit cooperation of Ukrainian border and customs officials (Layne et al., 2001).

In summary, it is easy to conclude that, although corruption is at the forefront of public concerns within Ukraine, very little has been accomplished in the fight against this threat. Ukraine has implemented a number of comprehensive anticorruption strategies, and related legislative initiatives over the past two decades, yet the public and the international community still perceive Ukrainian government, justice, and law enforcement officials as being chronically prone to bribery and to self-serving political interference. This ineffective response has created an atmosphere of mistrust, and has caused a decline in foreign investment and national welfare. There is an obvious need to improve public trust in the police and it is believed that rule of law and law enforcement reform initiatives may commence a trend in this direction. The *Euromaiden Revolution* of 2014 was another clear example of the frustrations based on the latest wave of overwhelming mistrust in government and political practices, and a call for the transformation of the pervasive corruption, and fraudulent practices endemic in all aspects of society. It is imperative that the new national leaders and supportive international partners welcome this call for constructive change.

Recommendations for Ukraine to Move Forward

Ukrainian's newly elected leaders have opted to steer toward European integration and democratic reforms in line with accepted rule of law and human rights standards and expectations. In exchange for geopolitical support and financial aid, the current Ukrainian government has agreed to address the scourge caused by corruption and political interference into the procurement and justice arenas. Ukraine is apparently in need of organizational police and criminal justice reform, and has accepted the guidance of the OSCE and the United States DOS in these regards. Two potential options strongly being considered involve revising the organizational ideologies of the Ukrainian National Police and the Ukranian Traffic Police to embrace community policing and related crime control practices, and a concrete and comprehensive initiative to deter governmental corruption, fraud, political interference, and abusive conduct within the criminal justice sectors and across the business spectrum. Reform within Ukraine is ongoing and appears to be accepted at all levels of government and society, but only time will reveal whether these efforts will prove to be fruitful (particularly during a time of interethnic conflict).

Criminological Explanations for Public Corruption

Public Corruption and Abuse

Corruption is noticeably endemic in most Eastern European nations and across the Balkans, and this is apparent whether discussing government officials, private organizations and corporations, and front line public servants, including the police. Before specifically examining police criminality and other forms of societal deviance, it would be best to contemplate explanations for the widespread nature of this phenomenon in this region of the globe.

State Crime Theory

One theoretical perspective that may explain the overwhelming prevalence of corruption within and across many Eastern European government agencies is state crime theory. Although state crime can take a variety of forms, the one aspect that could be viewed as being most relevant would be organized state crime. Criminal behavior at the hands of government officials may be the result of three primary factors, specifically the pressure for goal attainment, coupled with the appeal of illegitimate means, and the absence of effective and legitimate social control mechanisms (Kauzlarich and Kramer, 1998). This in essence would merge three criminological theories into one that could best explain state level criminality, including certain forms of police deviance that plague the criminal justice sectors. As such, *strain theory, differential association theory*, and *conflict theory* have been combined to explain organized state crime, and as a result, participating individuals, whether in the police or in another government agency, who have engaged collectively in criminal activity, may use this ideology to justify their chronic criminal and abusive practices, and could feel immune from prosecution and punishment.

International Strain Theory

Another plausible explanation for the widespread acceptance of bribery and fraud between political actors and business representatives in many developing nations could be achieved by applying Merton's strain theory (Merton, 1968) to the broader global market. Merton proposed that struggling individuals engage in deviant practices and crime in order to remain competitive and attain the *American Dream* (i.e., financial stability). It is therefore conceivable that political leaders in nations with overwhelmed economies have recognized and acknowledged that, in order for the country to meet international expectations and to maintain at least a sense of financial balance, there is the need to *cut corners* and support fraudulent and corrupt practices to preserve the expected status quo. As such, the prevalence of corruption and fraud in many Eastern European nations could be explained through *international strain theory*.

Police Deviance and Corruption

A more specific form of public corruption involves the police, the front line actor within the criminal justice sector of government. Police deviance can take many forms, from serious crime to simple violations of agency rules. In simplest terms, police deviance can be defined as disregarding agency policy, rules and regulations, policies and/or criminal law. Using more distinct terminology, Albrecht (2012, 2013) delineated five basic types of police deviance:

1. Police corruption
2. Police criminality
3. Excessive use of force
4. Abuse of authority
5. Police misconduct

Police Corruption involves situations, when police officers lose integrity in their professional actions and accept benefits or rewards in exchange for violating their mandated responsibilities. Examples include bribe receiving, receiving reward for official misconduct, and official misconduct. Police criminality occurs when police officials engage in direct acts of crime, such as robbery or theft, whether on or off duty. The use of excessive force involves engaging in menacing (i.e., threatening with a weapon) actions, assault, battery, and perhaps murder, when it is not justified although acting in the capacity of a police professional. Abuse of authority involves violating the legal mandate of the police position. Such infractions could include illegal stops, searches, and arrests. Finally, police misconduct includes acts that violate the rules and regulations of the respective law enforcement agency.

Such agency infractions could include arriving to work late or an unprofessional appearance (which could be indicators of other serious personal issues that could negatively affect police performance).

Theories of Crime and Police Deviance

A number of criminal justice researchers have attempted to apply theories of crime to explain police deviance and corruption. One interesting viewpoint promoted by Kappeler et al. (1998) and Erikson (1962) is that deviance must be measured from two separate perspectives, the perception of the actors, and the other through the eyes of the observer. As such, although the public may view certain actions of the police as being inappropriate or deviant, the law enforcement officers involved, due to the subcultural atmosphere, may believe that their acts were appropriate or correct. Some examples could include professional courtesy at traffic stops, not reporting police misconduct involving others to supervisors or administrators, and even courtroom perjury. Unfortunately fidelity to other police officers at times exceeds their loyalty to their oath of office and their service to the public. The use of excessive force against criminal suspects and falsifying evidence or courtroom testimony are often justified by the *just desserts* conception, in which no true harm has been done since criminals deserve to be punished. Such acts have often been referred to as *noble cause* corruption (Crank and Caldero, 1999), since officers may have considered their efforts to ensure that criminals be properly punished, regardless of methods used, to be an acceptable practice of crime control.

An attempt was made to apply control balance theory (Tittle, 1995) to police deviance. Hickman et al. (2001, p. 511) theorized that "the amount of control to which one is subject relative to the amount of control one can exercise (the control ratio), affects both the probability of deviance as well as the specific form of deviance." Control balance theory opines that actual deviance is a product of complex interactions between three factors: motivation, constraint, and opportunity. Each person has a *psychic need* that draws them toward deviant action and a desire for autonomy. Their actions within a specific opportunity are therefore triggered by an imbalance within their *control ratio*. A person could then be motivated to act in a deviant fashion if they could escape a *control deficit* and extend a *control surplus*. As a result, the opportunity for some type of deviance is almost always present (Tittle, 1995). Within police work, the frequency of the opportunities and the isolated and unsupervised nature of the events, add to the potential that officers may act in a deviant fashion. The findings of this limited research revealed that police personnel with control deficits were more likely to report police misconduct to supervisors and agency administrators (Hickman et al., 2001), which is counter to what is commonly observed in many police organizations.

As such, officers with stronger attitudes toward ethics were more likely to engage in appropriate conduct, and less likely to engage in activity that would support the *blue wall of silence* phenomenon.

Unfortunately none of these theories can be applied generally to all five of the defined categories of police deviance. It would be prudent, therefore, to attempt to specifically and comprehensively analyze the theoretical explanations for two of the more serious versions of police deviance, that is, corruption and criminality as exhibited by many police agencies across Eastern Europe.

Criminological Explanations for Police Corruption

Police corruption involves situations in which police officers lose integrity in their professional actions and accept benefits or rewards in exchange for violating their mandated responsibilities. Examples include bribe receiving, receiving reward for official misconduct, and engaging in official misconduct. In applying theories of crime to police corruption, which involves the willful acceptance of bribes and other rewards, the officer has in essence committed to engaging in official misconduct. In most cases, the incentive to engage in this deviance would involve the reception of money or other valuable item(s). One possible theory of crime that could be applied to police corruption as defined is strain theory, as it has been clarified by Merton (1968). One can identify the potential for these police personnel to desire more material goods to keep up with the social pressures of the cost of living, and the yearning for expected material goods. A common recommendation made by a number of government commissions that have followed major American police scandals, has been an increase in salary, for law enforcement personnel to counter the potential for temptation to engage in unacceptable corruption or other profit oriented criminality (Mollen, 1994).

Some police officers may have had preemployment associations or contacts with criminal gangs or street level criminals. These relationships were not likely revealed during the prehire screening process, or were disregarded due to political influence into the hiring process. These officers may have continued their involvement with some of these criminal elements, and were further drawn into corrupt activities to further their commitment to their private associates. These officers have likely been influenced by differential association, but in this case their loyalty is stronger to outside contacts and friends, rather to their work cohort. As such, their socialization to the deviant elements in the community had been developed prior to their police employment. In these isolated cases, this form of corruption (and associated criminality) could be attributed to Sutherland's differential association theory (Gaylord and Galliher, 1988).

An additional theoretical explanation for police corruption could involve Becker's rational choice theory. Rational choice theory proposes that, criminals (as all individuals) weigh the costs, risks, potential rewards, and benefits when considering participation in criminal conduct. Economic factors also play a significant role. Proper planning to avoid detection and apprehension will be devised, and criminals will actually conduct a probability analysis before engaging in deviant acts (Becker, 1976). In the case of police officers, they may believe that, since they are the actors charged with the enforcement of the law, the potential for detection or arrest would be relatively low. As such, some corrupt police personnel believe that their position has elevated them to being *above the law*.

Criminological Explanations for Police Criminality

Police criminality encompasses criminal actions undertaken by law enforcement personnel, other than corruption and the excessive use of force. These incidents would involve theft, robbery, drug dealing, and other illegal endeavors. Within the state crime model, many police officials could easily express frustration when seeing corrupt government officials going unpunished, and other criminal offenders promptly returned to the street with little or no penalty. When more closely evaluated, there has often been a notable evolution to the level of deviance and criminality that ultimately develops (Albrecht, 2012).

However, from a theoretical perspective, the most likely explanation for these developments would rely on Becker's rational choice model (Becker, 1976). It would appear that criminal police officers had likely calculated the likelihood of detection and noting its improbability, progressed from low level criminality to serious crime. In the perspective of these criminal officers, Tittle's proposed *control ratio* (Tittle, 1965) would have weighed in on the side of engaging in deviance, rather than considering personal restraint. In addition, since police criminality and deviance is reported to be endemic in many Eastern European nations and Balkan states, one could propose that Sutherland's differential association theory (Gaylord and Galliher, 1988) plays a significant role in this illicit behavior. In may also be that many officers believed that they would not be identified as a member of *the team* at their respective police station or unit, unless they participated in criminal activities.

Summary and Conclusion

Kosovo, Ukraine and Eastern Europe

Although it would be easy to conclude that certain remnants of the *Soviet* ideology are to blame for the pervasive nature of the corruption and fraud present in Eastern Europe, it will be made clear that these illicit practices are present across the globe, even in those nations considered developed and economically stable. These major flaws in the societal fabric clearly involve the overwhelming cultural acceptance and the pervasive nature in which corruption permeates both private and public aspects of daily life. Until government leaders acknowledge that global legitimacy cannot be attained until public fraud and corruption are addressed and eradicated, and until the public recognizes that both public and private services can be obtained without the payment of a bribe or *proactive tip*, these unacceptable practices will unfortunately continue to be accepted as common events and a part of *daily life*.

Even with international supervision for more than a decade, corruption and fraud remain apparent within Kosovo. And there is still hope that the second *revolution* in Ukraine to counter government corruption and gross mismanagement will be effective. It would be wise for the nations across Eastern Europe and the Balkans to take notice in the successes observed in the nation of Georgia following the *Rose Revolution* in 2003. Widespread reform measures have been implemented, that have led to the eradication of most incidents of corruption and bribery across the public sector (The World Bank, 2012). The experiences and lessons learned should serve as an example and promote a sense of optimism for regional countries. *Where there is a will, there is clearly a way*, and government leaders in the nation of Georgia have grasped and supported this dramatic transformation in political and cultural ideologies.

The Challenges of Countering Public Corruption through Foreign Assistance

The criminological theories raised above could point to potentially significant challenges involving future political and rule of law reform endeavors across Eastern Europe. History has shown, whether talking about the *Orange Revolution* in Ukraine, or the international supervision of a fledgling republic such as Kosovo, that dramatic legislative amendments and extensive foreign aid will not impressively result in a corruption-free government or society. Widespread ideological and cultural alterations may have to be considered and comprehensively implemented, in order for there to be hope for effective and positive societal reform. These efforts would therefore require willing, supportive, and enabling government leadership. This may prove to be both exceptionally difficult and frustrating, when many of the government and public service administrators that seek foreign assistance are often the most culpable *leaders* in fraudulent and corrupt practices. The international community must therefore take steps to address these phenomena before pledging significant support. The *carrot and stick* approach, although not considered noble, may prove to be the wiser option.

References

Albrecht, J.F. (2012). *Applying Theoretical Explanations for Crime to Police Deviance within the New York City Police Department,* Paper presented at the American Society of Criminology annual conference in Chicago, Illinois.

Albrecht, J.F. (2013). *Effective Leadership Principles and Pre-Employment Screening Mechanisms to Deter Police Deviance and Corruption: Lessons learned from the NYPD and Contemporary Research,* Paper presented at the International Association of Chiefs of Police annual conference in Philadelphia, Pennsylvania.

Becker, G.S. (1976). *The Economic Approach to Human Behaviour,* Chicago, IL: University of Chicago Press.

Bislimi, M. (2011). *An Assessment of Road Traffic Safety in Kosova*, Pristina, Kosovo: American University of Kosovo.

Chivvis, C.S. (2010). *EU Civilian Crisis Management: The Record So Far.* Santa Monica, CA: Rand Corporation.

Crank, J.P. and Caldero, M.A. (1999). *Police Ethics: The Corruption of Noble Cause.* Cincinnati, OH: Anderson Publishing Company.

Erikson, K.T. (1962). Notes on the sociology of deviance, *Social Problems,* 9: 307–314.

European Union Institute for Security Studies. (2009). *European Security and Defence Policy: The First 10 Years (1999–2009),* Paris: EU-ISS.

Filiminova, A. (2010). *Kosovo: Europe's Mafia State and the Rule of Law,* Montreal, Canada: Centre for Research on Globalization.

Gaylord, M.S. and Galliher, J.F. (1988). *The Criminology of Edward Sutherland.* Piscataway, NJ: Transaction Publishers.

Grodeland, A.B. (2010). Elite Perceptions of anti-corruption efforts in Ukraine, *Global Crime,* 11 (2), 237–260.

Hagan, W.H. (1999). The Balkans' lethal nationalisms, *Foreign Affairs,* 78: 52–64.

Harasymiw, B. (2003). Policing, democratization and political leadership in post-communist Ukraine, *Canadian Journal of Political Science,* 36 (2): 319–340.

Hickman, M.J., Piquero, A.R., Lawton, B.A., and Greene, J.R. (2001). Applying tittle's control balance theory to police deviance, *Policing,* 24 (4): 497–519.

Howorth, J. (2007). *Security and Defence Policy in the European Union*, Houndmills, England: Palgrave Macmillan.

International Crisis Group. (2010). *The Rule of Law in Independent Kosovo: Executive Summary and Recommendations,* Washington, D.C.: International Crisis Group.

Ivkovic, S.K. (2008). A comparative study of public support for the police, *International Criminal Justice Review,* 18 (4): 406–434.

Kalman, A.G. (2001). Organized economic crime and corruption in Ukraine: The problem of countermeasures, *Trends in Organized Crime,* 6 (3/4): 68–77.

Kappeler, V.E., Sluder, R.D., and Alpert, G.P. (1998). *Forces of Deviance: Understanding the Dark Side of Policing,* 2nd Edition, Prospect Heights, IL: Waveland Press.

Karadaku, L. (2012). Head of anti-corruption task force arrested for corruption, *Southeast European Times,* April 4, Pristina, Kosovo.

Kauzlarich, D. and Kramer, R.C. (1998). *Crimes of the American Nuclear State: At Home and Abroad,* Boston, MA: Northeastern University Press.

Kenney, D.J. (2002). Training the police in Ukraine, *Police Quarterly,* 5 (4): 470–493.

Ki-moon, B. (2007). Letter dated 26 March 2007 from the United States Secretary General to the United Nations Security Council. United Nations Headquarters, New York.

Layne, M., Khruppa, M.S., and Muzyka, A.A. (2001). The growing importance of Ukraine as a transit country for heroin trafficking: U.S.—Ukraine Research Partnership, *Trends in Organized Crime*, 6 (3/4): 77–93.

Luptakova, M. (2009). Legal and illegal migration from Ukraine: An analysis of social and security issues, *International Journal of Criminal Justice Sciences*, 4 (2): 144–159.

Markovska, A. and Isaeva, A. (2007). Public sector corruption: Lessons to be learned from the Ukrainian experience, *Crime Prevention and Community Safety*, 9: 118–129.

Markoyskaya, A., Pridemore, W.A., and Nakajima, C. (2003). Laws without teeth: An overview of the problems associated with corruption in Ukraine, *Crime, Law & Social Change*, 39 (2): 193–213.

Marty, D. (2010). *Inhumane Treatment of People and Illicit Trafficking in Human Organs in Kosovo*, Report to the Parliamentary Assembly of the Council of Europe in Brussels on December 12, 2010.

Merton, R.K. (1968). *Social Theory and Social Structure*, New York: Free Press.

Mertus, A.J. (1999). *Kosovo: How Myths and Truths Started a War*, California: University of California Press.

Mimiaga, M.J., Safren, S.A., Dvoryak, S., Reisner, S.L., Needle, R. and Woody, G. (2010). "We fear the police, the police fear us:" Structural and individual barriers and facilitators to HIV medication adherence among injection drug users in Kiev, Ukraine, *AIDS Care*, 22 (11): 1305–1313.

Mollen, M. (1994). *Commission Report: Commission to Investigate Allegations of Police Corruption and the Anti-Corruption Procedures of the Police Department*, New York.

Robertson, A. (2005). Criminal justice policy transfer to post-soviet states: Two case studies of police reform in Russia and Ukraine, *European Journal on Criminal Policy & Research*, 11 (1): 1–28.

Rodgers, P., Williams, C.C., and Round, J. (2008). Workplace crime and the informal economy in Ukraine: Employee and employer perspectives, *International Journal of Social Economics*, 35 (9): 666–678.

Sklias, P. and Roukanas, S. (2007). Development in post-conflict Kosovo. *South-Eastern Europe Journal of Economics*, 2: 267–287.

Solana, J. (1999). NATO's success in Kosovo. *Foreign Affairs*, 78: 114–120.

Spector, B.I., Winbourne, S., and Beck, L.D. (2003). *Corruption in Kosovo: Observations and Implications for USAID*, Washington, D.C.: Management Systems International.

Strohmeyer, H. (2001). Collapse and reconstruction of a judicial system: The United Nations mission in Kosovo and East Timor, *The American Journal of International Law*, 95 (1): 46–63.

Tittle, C. (1995). *Control Balance: Toward a General Theory of Deviance*, Boulder, CO: Westview Press.

Transparency International. (2013). *Corruption Perceptions Index 2012*, Berlin, Germany: Transparency International.

Transparency International. (2014). *Corruption Perceptions Index 2013*, Berlin, Germany: Transparency International.

United Nations Development Programme. (2010). *Dogs Join Fight Against Weapons in Kosovo*, New York: United Nations.

United Nations Office on Drugs and Crime. (2008). *Crime and Its Impact on the Balkans and Affected Countries*, Vienna, Austria: United Nations.

United States Department of State. (2011a). *Money Laundering and Financial Crimes Country Database*, Washington, D.C.: US DOS Bureau for International Narcotics and Law Enforcement Affairs.

United States Department of State. (2011b). *Ukraine 2011 Crime and Safety Report*, Washington, D.C.: United States Department of State OSAC Bureau of Diplomatic Security.

United States Department of State. (2012). *2012 International Narcotics Control Strategy Report*, Washington, D.C.: US Bureau for International Narcotics and Law Enforcement Affairs.

Wilson, J.M. (2006). Law and order in an emerging democracy: Lessons from the reconstruction of Kosovo's police and justice systems, *Annals of the American Academy of Political and Social Science*, 2006, 152–177.

The World Bank. (2012). *Fighting Corruption in Public Services: Chronicling Georgia's Reforms*, Washington, D.C.: The World Bank.

Yannis, A. (2004). The UN as Government in Kosovo, *Global Governance*, 10 (1): 67–81.

Whistle-Blowers in Corruption Detection in Norway

5

PETTER GOTTSCHALK

Contents

Introduction

White-collar criminals are individuals who commit financial crime in a professional setting where they have legal access and hide misconduct in legitimate transactions. Corruption is a white-collar crime involving two parties. White-collar corruption in public procurement is characterized by a public official who is offered or asks for an unreasonable favor from outside vendors, often in return for a special treatment of the supplier (Ksenia, 2008 and Passas, 2007).

Corruption scandals involving public officials are regularly presented in the media in the United States and many other countries. For example, former middle manager of the technology department in the District of Columbia, Yusuf Acar, was sentenced to 27 months prison for corruption (Sidley, 2010). Another example is former major John Lee Cockerham who was sentenced to 17½ years in prison for corruption (Thompson and Schmitt, 2007).

It is an interesting question whether the detected corrupt public officials are only the tip of an iceberg. If they are, there is certainly a need to address the issue of detection sources. One detection source is whistle-blowers who are former or current organizational members disclosing misconduct and crime under the control of their employers (Stieger, 2012 and Vadera et al., 2009).

This article addresses the following research question: *What is the role of whistle-blowers in detection of white-collar corruption in public procurement?*

Based on a sample of convicted white-collar criminals in Norway, the objective of this article is to present research results of the role of whistle-blowers.

Procurement is highly susceptible to fraud, waste, and abuse. While public service motivation theory argues that some individuals work in the public sector based on values different from people in the private sector (Kjeldsen and Jacobsen, 2013; Perry et al., 2010), opportunity theory suggests that wherever there is an opportunity for financial gain, many will be tempted as long as the risk of detection is low (Benson and Simpson, 2014).

Public Procurement Corruption

To detect, investigate, prosecute, and otherwise combat, and prevent white-collar crime is a challenge in most countries all over the world. The Federal Bureau of Investigation (FBI, 2015) characterizes white-collar crime as the full range of frauds committed by business and government professionals. Fraud is a general type of crime that involves using deception for illegal monetary gain. White-collar crime includes violations of law committed by both individuals and organizations. White-collar offenders generally are recognized as those who are in high-status positions, including positions of trust. Public corruption is one form of white-collar crime that involves a breach of trust or an abuse of position by federal, state, or local government officials (Cordis, 2014). In general, white-collar offenses may be handled through the criminal justice system, the civil system, or through the regulatory means.

Public corruption is one form of white-collar crime that involves a breach of trust or an abuse of position by federal, state, or local government officials. In 2015, the National Institute of Justice (2015) supports research related to public corruption. FBI (2015) states that public corruption is their top priority among criminal investigations, and for good reason:

> Public corruption poses a fundamental threat to our national security and way of life. It impacts everything from how well our borders are secured and our neighborhoods protected...to verdicts handed down in courts...to the quality of our roads, schools, and other government services. And it takes a significant toll on our pocketbooks, wasting billions in tax dollars every year. The FBI is singularly situated to combat this corruption, with the skills and capabilities to run complex undercover operations and surveillance.

Cordis (2014) studied public corruption in the United States. She studied the relation between corruption and composition of state government spending. Her analysis reveals that corruption lowers the share of government spending devoted to higher education and increases the share of spending devoted to other and nonallocable budget items.

Elite public criminals can use the power and apparent legitimacy of their office to extort bribes or direct procurement to entities they control or from which they profit. They can shape the environment by organizing procurement processes and formulating regulatory requirements. Private elites can indirectly achieve the same profitable result by suborning public officials to modify the environment to benefit the private party, for example by going to a nonbid, sole-source market (Passas, 2007).

Some of the approaches applied in the private sector to combat corruption include corporate social responsibility programs (Eadie and Raffert, 2014), business process re-engineering (Bertolini et al., 2015), and e-procurement programs (Mahallik, 2014). These approaches are adaptable to the public sector.

Financial crime by white-collar criminals can be classified into four categories (Gottschalk, 2010) such as fraud, theft, manipulation, and corruption. Corruption can be defined as the giving, offering, promising, requesting, receiving, taking, agreeing to taking, or accepting an improper advantage in terms of money or other consideration related to position, office, or assignment (Boles, 2014). The improper advantage does not have to be connected to a specific action or to not doing this action. It is sufficient if the advantage can be linked to a person's position, office, or assignment. An individual or group is guilty of corruption if they accept money or money's worth for doing something that they are under a duty to do anyway or that they are under a duty not to do, or to exercise a legitimate discretion for improper reason (Ksenia, 2008). Corruption destroys or perverts the integrity or fidelity of a person in his discharge of duty, it induces to act dishonestly or unfaithfully, it makes venal, and it is to bribe. Both the bribed and the briber are criminals in most legislations, such as the United States and Western Europe. In some countries, only the receiver of a bribe is considered and treated as a criminal.

Transparency International (2014) defines corruption as the abuse of entrusted power for private gain. In the case of public corruption discussed below, private gain is interpreted widely to include gains accruing to the government official, his or her family members, close friends, political party, favorite charity, hometown, or a corporate, or other entity in which the official or the official's family or close friends have a financial or social interest. A public official is any officer or employee of government, including legislators and judges, and any person participating as juror, advisor, consultant, or otherwise in performing a governmental function (Boles, 2014).

Cordis and Milyo (2013) also defines corruption as the abuse of entrusted power for private gain, and public corruption as the misuse of public office for private gain, or more broadly as an abuse of public trust. They include, for example, postal employees charged with theft of mail. Their definition seems to include almost all kinds of financial crime and is thus not useful in our context. In their table of U.S. code titles for lead charge, the most relevant titles seem to be Paragraph 201 Bribery of Public

Officials and Witnesses, Paragraph 641 Public Money, Property or Records, and Paragraph 666 Theft/Bribery in Programs Receiving Federal Funds.

Corruption is a concealed abuse of a position of trust by an expectation that one will do what one is relied on to do (Boles, 2014). From an economic perspective, corruption generally is defined as the misuse of a position of authority for private or personal benefit, where misuse typically constitutes a breach of legal norms. Corruption is expected to occur where (1) there is a control over economic benefits and costs and, thus, the potential for economic rents—that is, profits; and (2) persons in positions of authority have discretion over the allocation of such benefits and costs. Corruption can reflect rational, self-interested behavior by persons using their discretion to direct allocations to themselves or to other social actors who offer rewards in return for favorable discretionary treatment (Misangyi et al., 2008).

In corruption, an external opportunity can supply benefits to solve a problem. Typically, a problem is solved by providing benefits to persons in positions of authority. According to Misangyi et al. (2008), the rational choice perspective on corruption assumes that corruption is a response to situations that present opportunities for gain and the discretionary power to appropriate that gain. Corruption involves behavior on the part of officials in the public or private sectors, in which they improperly and unlawfully enrich themselves and/or those who are close to them, or induce others to do so by misusing the position in which they are placed.

Corruption covers a wide range of illegal activities, such as kickbacks, embezzlement, and extortion. Kayrak (2008) includes money laundering as well in his definition of corruption, which is too wide for our research purpose.

The notion of corruption may be classified as sporadic or systemic corruption, bureaucratic or political corruption, grand or petty corruption, personal or organizational corruption, and active and passive corruption. For example, Lange (2008) defines organizational corruption as the pursuit of individual interests by one or more organizational actors through the intentional misdirection of organizational resources or perversion of organizational routines, which is commonly understood to be highly undesirable for any parties holding a stake in the organization's performance.

Pinto et al. (2008) focused on two fundamental dimensions of corruption in organizations, that is, whether the individual or the organization is the beneficiary of the corrupt activity, and whether the corrupt behavior is undertaken by an individual actor or by two or more actors. While an organization of corrupt individuals is a scaling-up of personally beneficial corrupt behaviors to the organization level, a corrupt organization consists of a group of employees carrying out corrupt behaviors on behalf of the organization. This is similar to a distinction between bribed and briber, where the bribed is an individual beneficiary of the corruption while the briber is an organizational beneficiary of the corruption.

Bowman and Gilligan (2008) suggest that corruption may be a greater issue for the Australian public than has been assumed in the past, given the relatively low level of reported systematic corruption in Australia. Moreover, while there may be widespread agreement that corruption in Australia is harmful and perhaps inevitable, people can find it difficult at times to differentiate between what is corrupt and what is not.

Public corruption is defined as corruption involving public officials. Section 201 of Title 18 of the United States Code governs the offenses of bribery and illegal gratuity. Relevant definitions are set forth in § 2011. To prove corruption, the government must generally establish that: (1) a thing of value was given, offered, or promised to be given (or, in the case of a recipient, demanded, sought, received, or accepted); (2) a present or future public official; (3) for an official act; and (4) with corrupt intent or intent to influence (or be influenced). Corruption requires proof of intent (Dwyer et al., 2014).

Detection by Whistle-Blowers

A city manager told us that corruption in procurement happens every day and that when he first started with the town, the FBI was already investigating the public works' director and a purchasing director. We asked him how the FBI knew to investigate, and he said it was someone inside the organization or maybe people just talking outside of work. That is the difficulty in the detection—you really have to depend on people within the organization to blow the whistle. Auditors could also be relevant, but they may only be called in after a complaint or report has been filed.

In the United States, it is possible to make money by blowing the whistle. A whistle-blower can get a share of the retrieved and recovered sum of money. In 2014, the securities and exchange commission (SEC) paid $30 million in a whistle-blower award. It was the largest award so far, and the reporter wrote: "Blowing the whistle is increasingly worth big bucks." The SEC did not identify the tipster, where he or she is from, or the case this award was tied to. Andrew Ceresney, director of the SEC's enforcement division, said in a statement that "this whistle-blower came to us with information about an ongoing fraud that would have been very difficult to detect" (Ensign, 2014). The Office of the Whistle-blower at SEC (www.sec.gov/whistleblowers) is authorized by congress to provide monetary awards to eligible individuals who come forward with high-quality original information.

Public whistle-blowers are not entitled to awards. Stieger (2012) argues that offering monetary rewards to public whistle-blowers represents a proposal for attacking public corruption at its source. He suggests offering a carrot: if a public official reports a bribe offer, leading to the conviction of the offeror, the state will pay the reporting official the full amount of the offered bribe. By tying the amount of the reward to the amount of the bribe, any financial incentive the official would have to take the bribe is removed.

According to Kaplan et al. (2011), employee tips are the most common form of initial fraud detection, suggesting that employees frequently are aware of fraud before others professionally charged to detect fraud, such as internal and external auditors. The willingness of employees, who learn about fraud, to report this information, varies with several factors. For example, if the executive, to whom misconduct should be reported, is not trusted, employees will tend not to report. Whistle-blowing decisions are dependent on information, trust, security, predictability, self-confidence, job security and organizational culture in general.

Johnson (2005) has the following definition of whistle-blowing:

> Whistle blowing is a distinct form of dissent consisting of four elements: (1) the person acting must be a member or former member of the organization at issue, (2) his or her information must be about nontrivial wrongdoing in that organization, (3) he or she must intend to expose the wrongdoing, and (4) he or she must act in a way that makes the information public.

Vadera et al. (2009) have the following definition of whistle-blowing:

> Whistle blowing is the disclosure by organizational members (former or current) of illegal, immoral, or illegitimate practices under the control of their employers, to persons or organizations that may be able to effect action.

Atwater (2006) defines whistle-blowing as an act by which an individual reveals wrongdoing within an organization to those in positions of authority or to the public, with hopes of rectifying the situation.

Vadera et al. (2009) identified the following characteristics of whistle-blowers and whistle-blowing:

- Federal whistle-blowers were motivated by concern for public interest, were high performers, reported high levels of job security, job achievement, job commitment, and job satisfaction, and worked in high-performing work groups and organizations.
- Anger at wrongful activities drove individuals to make internal reports to management. Retaliation by management shifted individuals' focus away from helping their organizations or victims and toward attaining retribution.
- Whistle-blowing was more likely when observers of wrongdoing held professional positions, had more positive reactions to their work, had longer service, were recently recognized for good performance, were male, were members of larger work groups, and were employed by organizations perceived by others to be responsive to complaints.

- Whistle-blowing was more frequent in the public sector than in the private.
- Whistle-blowing was strongly related to situational variables with seriousness of the offense and supportiveness of the organizational climate being the strongest determinants.
- Inclination to report a peer for theft was associated with role responsibility, the interests of group members, and procedural perceptions.

Zipparo (1999) identified the following two main factors, which deter public officials from reporting corruption:

- Concern about not having enough proof
- Absence of legal protection from negative consequences

One of the more successful whistle-blowers is Michael Lissack. He worked as a banker at the Smith Barney brokerage. In 1995, he blew the whistle on a fraudulent scheme, known in municipal financing as "yield burning." Dr. Lissack filed a whistle-blower lawsuit against more than a dozen of Wall Street firms under the False Claims Act. In April 2000, 17 investment banks agreed to pay approximately $140 million to settle charges that they defrauded the federal government by overpricing securities sold in connection with certain municipal bond transactions. The U.S. Government has recovered more than $250 million as the result of Dr. Lissack's whistle-blower action. His allegations have brought on more than a dozen of civil and criminal investigations by the SEC, internal revenue service (IRS), and the U.S. Department of Justice. Dr. Lissack has written editorials about whistle-blowing for the New York Times and the Los Angeles Times, and has been profiled in many international publications, including the Wall Street Journal, the Financial Times, Fortune, Business Week, the Economist, and USA Today (www.whistleblowerdirectory.com).

In 2001, Sherron Watkins, an employee in the American energy company Enron, notified her chief executive officer Kenneth Lay about a perceived accounting scandal. Watkins did so hoping Lay would act. He did not and was later arrested due to his involvement in the wrongdoings because she blew the whistle (Bendiktsson, 2010).

Negative consequences, after whistle-blowing, suffered by some whistle-blowers are labeled retaliation. Retaliation implies to take an undesirable action against a whistle-blower—who reported wrongdoing internally or externally, outside the organization. Retaliation can be defined as taking adverse action against an employee for opposing an unlawful employment practice or participating in any investigation, proceeding, or hearing related to such a practice (Bjørkelo and Matthiesen, 2011).

Thus, receivers of complaints and reports have two issues to consider when dealing with whistle-blowers as an information source. First, not all that is said and not all accusations from a whistle-blower are necessarily true. Therefore, information from a whistle-blower has to be carefully checked and verified. Second, a whistle-blower may be in danger of retaliation, making it a requirement for receivers to protect the whistle-blower. Report receivers have to make sure that a whistle-blower contributing to an investigation does not experience negative consequences.

The national whistleblowers center (NWC) in the United States lists a number of whistle-blowers (www.whistleblowers.org). A few of them blew the whistle because of public procurement corruption. An example is Bunnatine Greenhouse who stood alone in opposing the approval of a highly improper multi-billion dollar no-bid contract to Halliburton for the reconstruction of Iraq. In retaliation for her courage, she was removed from her position as the highest ranking civilian contracting official of the Army Corps of Engineers. On June 27, 2005, she testified to a congressional panel alleging specific instances of waste, fraud, and other abuses, and irregularities by Halliburton with regard to its operation in Iraq since the 2003 invasion. Vice president Dick Cheney had been the CEO of Halliburton. Criminal investigations into Halliburton were opened by the U.S. Justice Department, the Federal Bureau of Investigation, and the Pentagon's inspector general. These investigations found no wrongdoing within the contract award and execution process. On July 25, 2011, the U.S. District Court in Washington, DC approved awarding Greenhouse $970,000 in full restitution of lost wages, compensatory damages, and attorney fees.

The Whistleblower Directory (www.whistleblowerdirectory.com) is a comprehensive database showcasing individuals who reported financial crime. An example is Jim Alderson who worked as an accountant for Quorum Health Services in Montana and a Chief Financial Officer at the Whitefish hospital. In 1992, he blew the whistle on the hospital's fraudulent book-keeping practices, wherein reimbursements were routinely sought after filing fraudulent cost reports with Medicare. In retaliation for his whistle-blowing disclosure, Alderson was fired. He filed a whistle-blower lawsuit against his former employer, Quorum Health Services, and its former owner, Hospital Corp. of America. Five years after Alderson filed the lawsuit, the federal government joined the case. In October 2000, Quorum settled the case. Under the False Claims law, Alderson received $11.6 million and Quorum paid a fine of $77.5 million.

Research Methodology

Our conceptual framework is detection sources for convicted white-collar criminals. To identify a substantial sample of white-collar criminals and to collect relevant information about detection sources, there are several options available. However, in a small country like Norway with a population of only five million people, available sample size is limited. One available option would be to study court cases involving white-collar criminals. A challenge here would be to identify relevant laws and sentences that correspond with our definition of not only white-collar crime, but also required characteristics of white-collar criminals. Another available option is to study newspaper articles, where the journalists have already conducted some form of selection of upper class, white-collar individuals convicted in court of financial crime. Another advantage of this approach is that the cases are publicly known, which makes it more acceptable to identify cases by individual white-collar names. Therefore, the latter option was chosen for this research.

Based on this decision, our sample has the following characteristics applicable to newspaper reporting: famous individuals, famous companies, surprising stories, important events, substantial consequences, matters of principle, and significant public interest. This is in line with research by Schnatterly (2003) who searched the Wall Street Journal for several years in her study of white-collar crime published in the Strategic Management Journal. Media often pick up examples of companies and their leaders by negative media coverage because of white-collar wrongdoings (Briscoe and Murphy, 2012).

Verification of facts in newspaper accounts was carried out by obtaining court documents in terms of final verdicts. After registering newspaper accounts as an important indication of a white-collar offender, the contents in newspaper articles were compared to and corrected by court sentences, which typically range from five to 50 pages in Norwegian district courts, courts of appeal, and Supreme Court. Thus, we reduce the effects of counter measures by firms and individuals to cover up for their wrongdoings (Zavyalova et al., 2012).

We only included cases where someone involved in the case was sentenced in court to imprisonment. For this study, it was considered sufficient that the person was sentenced in one court, even if the person represented a recent case that still had appeals pending in higher courts. As the case developed, data were updated in our database. A sentence was defined as a prison sentence. Therefore, cases ending with fines only were not included in the sample.

Research Results

A total of 390 white-collar criminals were convicted in Norway from 2009 to 2015. Thirty-three of these cases (8 percent) were concerned with white-collar corruption in public procurement as listed in Table 5.1. There are seven cases where 33 offenders were involved. Table 5.1 lists what the corruption case was

Table 5.1 Convicted White-Collar Criminals in Public Procurement Corruption

Corruption Case	White-Collar Criminal	Position	Prison Years
Construction permission	Gouravan, Mohammad	City planning manager	1
Construction permission	Mahmood, Nasir	Property developer	0,6
Construction permission	Mahmood, Tariq	Property developer	0,6
Recycling waste	Gunnerød, Ralph Kevin	Sales manager	1
Public utility	Hansen, Morten	Director	0,25
Police help out of prison	Henriksen, Helge	Entrepreneur	1
Police help out of prison	Isaksen, Sverre	Police officer	2
Police help out of prison	Kollen, Ernst Ole	Police officer	1,25
School buildings	Eide, Per Øyvind	Entrepreneur	2,75
School buildings	Bastiansen, Ronny	Entrepreneur	2,17
School buildings	Knudssøn, Jarle I.	Entrepreneur	1,58
School buildings	Kjøllesdal, Jon Arild	Entrepreneur	1,58
School buildings	Nettli, Harald	Project leader	5
School buildings	Pawlak, Jaroslaw Jozef	Project leader	2
School buildings	Olafsen, Tor Åge	Consultant	2
School buildings	Hauger, Arild	Managing director	1
School buildings	Skjerven, Jens Erik	Craftsman	1,5
School buildings	Dyrnes, Roger Klinge	Entrepreneur	3
Municipality buildings	Ramstad, Per Arne	City maint. manager	5,5
Municipality buildings	Ramstad, Nils Aage	Construction builder	4
Municipality buildings	Ramstad, Anders	Construction builder	3,6
Municipality buildings	Fjeld, Fredrik	Construction builder	2
Municipality buildings	Hartmann, Terje	Construction builder	2
Municipality buildings	Ramstad, Martin Petter	Construction builder	1,5
Procurement of busses	Tunold, Odd Gunnar	Sales director	0,1
Procurement of busses	Dahl, Erik Terje	Managing director	0,7
Procurement of busses	Helminen, Hannu Mikael	Construction manager	0,7
Procurement of busses	Leite, Helge	Chief Executive Officer	3,5
Procurement of busses	Ellingsen, Nils Aksel	Technical Manager	5,5
Procurement of busses	Andersson, Erik Ernst	Procurement Manager	5
Procurement of busses	Hagerup, Dag	Sales Manager	5
Procurement of busses	Gaarder, Tor	Entrepreneur	4
Procurement of busses	Øverbø, Knut	Construction Site Chief	0,8

about, the name of convicted white-collar criminal, the offender's position when committing the crime, and the sentence in court in terms of number of years imprisonment.

Table 5.2 lists sources of detection for the seven corruption cases. The last three cases are based on whistle-blowing. In the school buildings' case, a person blew the whistle by contacting journalists in the daily Norwegian

Table 5.2   Source of Detection for White-Collar Public Procurement Corruption Cases

Corruption Case	Source of Detection
Construction permission	Competing property developer who discovered that corruption was involved
Recycling waste	Criminal friend in money laundering who was cheated
Public utility	Internal auditor in the organization who distrusted the director
Police help out of prison	Divorced wife who wanted to hurt her ex-husband
School buildings	Journalists Gjernes and Skaalmo who received tips from city employees
Municipality buildings	Whistle-blower to internal control in the organization
Procurement of busses	Employee on vacation in German reads local newspaper about MAN corruption

Table 5.3   Detection of White-Collar Crime

Rank	Crime Detection Source	Criminals	Fraction
1	Journalists investigating tips from readers	101	26%
2	Crime victims suffering financial loss	47	12%
3	Internal controls of transactions in organization	44	11%
4	Bankruptcy lawyers identifying misconduct	41	11%
5	Tax authorities carrying out controls	25	6%
6	Commercial banks controlling accounts	18	5%
7	Accounting auditors controlling clients	18	5%
8	Police investigations into financial crime	5	1%
9	Stock exchange controls of transactions	4	1%
10	Other detection sources	87	22%
	TOTAL	390	100%

business newspaper *Dagens Næringsliv*. In the municipality buildings' case, a whistle-blower informed people in the internal control function about misconduct. In the procurement of busses' case, an employee blew the whistle when he came home from vacation. Thus, three out of seven cases were detected based on whistle-blowing. Although the sample is small, whistle-blowing is the most important source of detection in the sample.

If we look at all the 390 white-collar criminals in Norway, we find the following list of detection sources in Table 5.3. In our database of 390 convicted white-collar criminals, we were able to identify crime detection sources based on media reports, court documents as well as personal inquiries. In Norway, there are no whistle-blower awards. Therefore, we applied no separate crime detection source for whistle-blowing. Instead, whistle-blowers can be assumed to have contributed to several of the other sources in the table.

Tipsters are often whistle-blowers who provide tips to investigative journalists in the media. Tipsters are typically also the source for internal controls and accounting auditors. Given that these three groups make out a total of 26 + 12 + 5 = 43 percent of detections, it can be assumed that most of the detections were caused by whistle-blowers, since the last category of other detection sources also can be assumed to involve whistle-blowers.

We phrased the research question: *What is the role of whistle-blowers in detection of white-collar corruption in public procurement?* We found that almost half of all the cases were detected based on whistle-blowing. Whistle-blowers informed investigative journalist, internal control function person, and own employer. Therefore, this research indicates that whistle-blowers are the most important source of detection of white-collar corruption in public procurement.

Discussion

As illustrated in the Norwegian sample as well as the U.S. cases mentioned below, the role of whistle-blowers is important in detecting white-collar criminals in general and also in public procurement corruption. If the situation for whistle-blowers was improved, we might expect that more white-collar criminals would be detected.

In recent times, corruption has become an issue of major political and economic significance when developing countries are trying to make their transition into becoming developed countries. In the past, bilateral donors, such as the United States, not only overlooked partisan self-enrichment on the part of developing country governments, but also supported many corrupt regimes in Africa and other parts of the world in return for bilateral relationships (Abdulai, 2009).

Janet A. Garrison and Herb F. Hyman were procurement professionals who blew the whistle. During the course of their employment with public entities in Florida, they uncovered unethical procurement practices. They then became whistle-blowers. In their jobs as government purchasers, both Garrison and Hyman believe that they are entrusted by the public to spend taxpayer dollars wisely and fairly. Each individual also notes that codes of ethics govern their membership in professional procurement associations, as well as their certifications: Thus, Garrison and Hyman felt it was their public and professional duty to report ethics breaches that clearly violated our nation's laws or specific procurement statutes. However, their efforts to "do the right thing" met with unanticipated outcomes, ranging from the mixed reactions of others to a complex maze of ongoing legal proceedings (Atwater, 2006).

Janet A. Garrison's whistle-blowing experience occurred when she worked as a purchasing analyst for the Florida Department of Education (DOE). Back in 2003, she was asked to help to develop a solicitation for privatizing about 174 jobs in DOE's Office of Student Financial Assistance (Atwater, 2006).

For Herb F. Hyman, procurement manager with the Town of Davie, FL, his whistle-blow experience was related to the purchasing practices of the town administrator, Christopher J. Kovanes. Hired by the town council as a contract employee, Kovanes was the town's top leader. Thus, Kovanes was Hyman's boss (Atwater, 2006).

It is often argued that detection of white-collar crime is low and that detectors are reluctant to blow the whistle. Social conflict theory might support this argument in that the elite does not really want to punish their own. According to social conflict theory, the justice system is biased and designed to protect the wealthy and powerful. The wealthy and powerful can take substantial assets out of their own companies at their own discretion whenever they like, although employed workers in the companies were the ones who created the values. Similarly, public officials can abuse their positions for personal gain. As Haines (2014: 21) puts it, "financial practices that threaten corporate interests, such as embezzlement, are clearly identified as criminal even as obscenely high salaries remain relatively untouched by regulatory controls."

Conflict theory is a perspective in criminology that emphasize the social, political, or material inequalities of a social group (Seron and Munger, 1996), that draw attention to power differentials, such as class conflict. Crime stems from conflict between different segments of society fueled by a system of domination based on inequality, alienation, and justice. Crime is harm that comes from differences in power (Lanier and Henry, 2009).

Conflict is a fundamental social process. Society is largely shaped by the competing interests of social groups who struggle for dominance in order to enact or maintain a social structure most beneficial to them (Petrocelli et al., 2003: 2)

> Conflict theory asserts that the relative power of a given social group dictates social order in that powerful groups not only to control the lawmakers, but also the law enforcement apparatus of the state. In essence, laws are made that serve the interests of the privileged, and the police are used to suppress and control any segment of society that poses a threat to the status quo.

According to conflict theory, economic inequalities and repression lead to deviant behavior. Laws, law-breaking, and law enforcement are factors that evolve from and contribute to social conflicts, and strengthen the dominant position of powerful individuals. Laws tend to penalize the behavior of certain classes, and not individuals, because it is the more powerful class that is in a position to pronounce certain actions as illegal. The ruling class is faced with the decision, which values to enforce when making laws. Criminal law plays the role of a social control mechanism. Certain types of conduct are prohibited, and certain kinds of sanctions are imposed for their infringement.

In addition to, conflict theory, public service motivation theory should inform future research into white-collar crime in the public sector and public procurement. Because the theory speaks to the motivations of individuals who choose to work in the public sector, it could explain why some public sector employees will become whistle-blowers despite the risks inherent in doing so, while other public sector employees will either ignore the corruption or attempt to profit from it themselves.

Conclusion

The role of whistle-blowers is important in detecting white-collar crime, as evidenced by our study sample as well as some cases. Whistle-blowing seems to be the most important source of detection, particularly with regard to public procurement. Despite the procedures and protocols established to protect the procurement process from corruption, bad actors have been found at all levels of government. While audits and other checks and balances are useful in exploring the claims of corrupt procurement practices or the fraudulent award of contracts, these are insufficient in the initial detection of corruption. To detect more crime, whistle-blowing has to be encouraged and revenge and retaliation need to be prevented. This is no easy feat, as whistle-blowers have few protections and generally suffer large reputational and financial losses. The ruling class in society has the power to define certain behavior as deviant, while the ruled class might be of a differing opinion about what is right and what is wrong. Criminal laws are established mainly for the protection and development of the institutions of capitalism. Through laws, the powerful class exercises its power and controls the resources.

The unique contribution of this research can be found in the empirical side of public procurement corruption. A managerial implication is that whistle-blowing should be further enhanced, while at the same time discouraging false accusations. A theoretical implication can be found in future research that may focus on the links between public service motivation theory and whistle-blowing for detection of public procurement corruption.

References

Abdulai, A.G. (2009). "Political will in combating corruption in developing and transition economies: A comparative study of Singapore, Hong Kong and Ghana," *Journal of Financial Crime*, Vol. 16, No. 4, pp. 387–417.

Atwater, K. (2006). "Whistle blowers enforce procurement ethics," *American City & County*, published October 23, http://americancityandcounty.com/mag/ whistle-blowers-enforce-procurement-ethics.

Bendiktsson, M.O. (2010). "The deviant organization and the bad apple CEO: Ideology and accountability in media coverage of corporate scandals," *Social Forces*, Vol. 88, No. 5, pp. 2189–2216.

Benson, M.L. and Simpson, S.S. (2014). *Understanding White-Collar Crime—An Opportunity Perspective*, New York: Routledge.

Bertolini, M., Bevilacqua, M., Ciarapica, E., and Postacchini, L. (2015). "Business process reengineering of drugs storage and distribution: A case study," *International Journal of Procurement Management*, Vol. 8, No. 1/2, pp. 44–65.

Bjørkelo, B. and Matthiesen, S.B. (2011). "Preventing and dealing with retaliation against whistleblowers," in: Lewis, D. and Vandekerckhove, W. (editors), *Whistleblowing and Democratic Values*, International Whistleblowing Research Network, London. https://whistleblowingnetwork.org/about/.

Boles, J. (2014). "The two faces of bribery: International corruption pathways meet conflicting legislative regimes," *Michigan Journal of International Law*, Vol. 35, No. 4, pp. 673–713.

Bowman, D. and Gilligan, G. (2008). "Public awareness of corruption in Australia," *Journal of Financial Crime*, Vol. 14, No. 4, pp. 438–452.

Briscoe, F. and Murphy, C. (2012). "Sleight of hand? Practice opacity, third-party responses, and the interorganizational diffusion of controversial practices," *Administrative Science Quarterly*, Vol. 57, No. 4, pp. 553–584.

Cordis, A.S. (2014). "Corruption and the composition of public spending in the United States," *Public Finance Review*, Vol. 42, No. 6, pp. 745–773.

Cordis, A.S. and Milyo, J. (2013). *Measuring Public Corruption in the United States: Evidence from Administrative Records of Federal Prosecutions*, Working Paper, University of Missouri, http://economics.missouri.edu/working-papers/2013/WP1322_milyo.pdf.

Dwyer, L., Golden, K., and Lehman, S. (2014). "Public corruption," *American Criminal Law Review*, Vol. 51, No. 4, pp. 1549–1600.

Eadie, R. and Rafferty, S. (2014). "Do corporate social responsibility clauses work? A contractor perspective," *International Journal of Procurement Management*, Vol. 7, No. 1, pp. 19–34.

Ensign, R.L. (2014). "SEC to pay $30 million whistleblower award, its largest yet," *The Wall Street Journal*, published September 22, http://www.wsj.com/articles/sec-to-pay-30-million-whistleblower-award-its-largest-yet-1411406612.

FBI. (2015). *It's Our Top Priority Among Criminal Investigations—And For Good Reason*, Federal Bureau of Investigation, http://www.fbi.gov/about-us/investigate/corruption, downloaded February 4, 2015.

Gottschalk, P. (2010). "Categories of financial crime," *Journal of Financial Crime*, Vol. 17, No. 4, pp. 441–458.

Haines, F. (2014). "Corporate fraud as misplaced confidence? Exploring ambiguity in the accuracy of accounts and the materiality of money," *Theoretical Criminology*, Vol. 18, No. 1, pp. 20–37.

Johnson, R.A. (2005). "Whistleblowing and the police," *Rutgers University Journal of Law and Urban Policy*, Vol. 1, No. 3, pp. 74–83.

Kaplan, S., Pope, K.R., and Samuels, J.A. (2011). "An examination of the effect of inquiry and auditor type on reporting intentions for fraud," *Auditing: A Journal of Practice & Theory*, Vol. 30, No. 4, pp. 29–49.

Kayrak, M. (2008). "Evolving challenges for supreme audit institutions in struggling with corruption," *Journal of Financial Crime*, Vol. 15, No. 1, pp. 60–70.

Kjeldsen, A.M. and Jacobsen, C.B. (2013). "Public service motivation and employment sector: Attraction or socialization?" *Journal of Public Administration Research and Theory*, Vol. 23, No. 4, pp. 899–926.

Ksenia, G. (2008). "Can corruption and economic crime be controlled in developing countries and if so, is it cost-effective?" *Journal of Financial Crime*, Vol. 15, No. 2, pp. 223–233.

Lange, D. (2008). "A multidimensional conceptualization of organizational corruption control," *Academy of Management Review*, Vol. 33, No. 3, pp. 710–729.

Lanier, M.M. and Henry, S. (2009). "Chapter 3: Conflict and radical theories, in: *Essential Criminology*, 3rd Edition, Westview, Member of the Perseus Books Group, New York.

Mahallik, D.K. (2014). "Measuring success of e-procurement: A case discussion of MCL using fuzzy approach," *International Journal of Procurement Management*, Vol. 7, No. 5, pp. 508–519.

Misangyi, V.F., Weaver, G.R., and Elms, H. (2008). "Ending corruption: The interplay among institutional logics, resources, and institutional entrepreneurs," *Academy of Management Review*, Vol. 33, No. 3, pp. 750–770.

National Institute of Justice (2015). *Research and Evaluation on White-Collar Crime and Public Corruption*, Office of Justice Programs, U.S. Department of Justice, https://www.ncjrs.gov/pdffiles1/nij/sl001155.pdf, downloaded February 4, 2015.

Passas, N. (2007). *Corruption in the Procurement Process/Outsourcing Government Functions: Issues, Case Studies, Implications*, Report to the Institute for Fraud Prevention, shortened version by W. Black, 33 pages, http://www.theifp.org/research-grants/procurement_final_edited.pdf.

Perry, J., Hondeghem, A., and Wise, L. (2010). "Revisiting the motivational bases of public service," *Public Administration Review*, September/October, pp. 681–690.

Petrocelli, M., Piquero, A.R., and Smith, M.R. (2003). "Conflict theory and racial profiling: An empirical analysis of police traffic stop data," *Journal of Criminal Justice*, Vol. 31, pp. 1–11.

Pinto, J., Leana, C.R., and Pil, F.K. (2008). "Corrupt organizations or organizations of corrupt individuals? Two types of organizational-level corruption," *Academy of Management Review*, Vol. 33, No. 3, pp. 685–709.

Schnatterly, K. (2003). "Increasing firm value through detection and prevention of white-collar crime," *Strategic Management Journal*, Vol. 24, pp. 587–614.

Seron, C. and Munger, F. (1996). "Law and inequality: Race, gender...and, of course, class," *Annual Review of Sociology*, Vol. 22, pp. 187–212.

Sidley (2010). *Report of Investigation Regarding Procurement Practices at the Office of the Chief Technology Officer of the District of Columbia*, Sidley Austin LLP, July 14, DRAFT, 60 pages, http://assets.bizjournals.com/cms_media/washington/pdf/Sidley%20Report.pdf.

Stieger, C.J. (2012). "Offering monetary rewards to public whistleblowers: A proposal for attacking corruption at its source," *Ohio State Journal of Criminal Law*, Vol. 9, No. 2, pp. 815–829.

Thompson, G. and Schmitt, E. (2007). "Graft in military contracts spread from base," *The New York Times*, published September 24, http://www.nytimes.com/2007/09/24/world/middleeast/24contractor.html?_r=1&.

Transparency International. (2014). *Curbing Corruption in Public Procurement—A Practical Guide*, www.transparency.org, 40 pages.

Vadera, A.K., Aguilera, R.V., and Caza, B.B. (2009). "Making sense of whistle-blowing's antecedents: Learning from research on identity and ethics programs," *Business Ethics Quarterly*, Vol. 19, No. 4, pp. 553–586.

Zavyalova, A., Pfarrer, M.D., Reger, R.K., and Shapiro, D.L. (2012). "Managing the message: The effects of firm actions and industry spillovers on media coverage following wrongdoing," *Academy of Management Journal*, Vol. 55, No. 5, pp. 1079–1101.

Zipparo, L. (1999). "Factors which deter public officials from reporting corruption," *Crime, Law & Social Change*, Vol. 30, pp. 273–287.

Corruption—The Nobel Way in Norway

6

HARALD N. RØSTVIK

Contents

Introduction

Norwegians like to think of themselves as kind, welcoming, and peace-loving, as illustrated by the handing out of the annual Nobel Peace Prize in the capital Oslo, every December. Many assume that corruption is something that happens elsewhere, in countries far away. Generally speaking, though, in a global context, Norway is not very corrupt, but Norway is the most corrupt among the Nordic countries and has never been as corrupt as after the shift of the millennium (TI, 2002). In 2002, Norway was the World's 12th least corrupt countries; in 2014, it was a little better, as the World's seventh least corrupt country, but still, the most corrupt country among the Nordic ones are Sweden, Denmark, Iceland, and Finland. Why is this so? How did this country originally filled with farmers and fishermen, with its tiny cities only, turn to corruption? Who gets involved in corruption in Norway, which sectors does it involve, and is public procurement one of them? These are some of the questions that will be highlighted in this chapter.

An Overview

First and foremost, let us have a look at the big picture to see Norway with a bird eye's view. This is a necessary exercise in order to understand the forces behind procurement corruption and how the corrupting of the Norwegian minds has evolved. In doing so, we find many contradictions and dichotomies splitting the mind-set of the people. The almost richest, almost most beautiful, and almost best country to live in the world, according to several international indexes, have many other sides that monitoring carried out from afar rarely uncover. A few are as follows:

- Norway is a considerable exporter of arms, ammunition, and used to be involved in napalm. The Norwegian state owns a range of companies supplying the world with these goods. This is of course in sharp contrast to the objective of the Nobel Peace Prize; to honour organizations or individuals that "shall have done the most or the best work for fraternity between nations, for the abolition or reduction of standing armies and for the holding and promotion of peace congresses" (Nobel, 1895). The Nobel committee consists of high-profiled Norwegian politicians. This inevitably links Norwegian politics to the prize.
- Norway has become a considerable contributor to the bombings being carried out by Western forces since 1990. No nation has participated so heavily, apart from the United States. The engagements in Afghanistan, Iraq, and Libya have created fury in many places and it has been questioned if Norwegians now have blood on the hands and if the engagements also had a hidden objective of securing access to the oil fields where state-owned Norwegian oil companies are engaged. The former Norwegian Prime Minister Jens Stoltenberg (Labor) assumed office as the 13th Secretary General of the North Atlantic Treaty Organization, NATO, in Brusselson October 1, 2014. Stoltenberg, when being Prime Minister in Norway, did get a reputation for having handled the atrocities after the mass murderer Anders Behring Breivik very well. Breivik had killed young labor party members at the Utøya camp, after placing a bomb in the high-rise Government Headquarters in Oslo on July 22, 2011. Stoltenberg was praised for his peace and no-revenge speeches. But in spite of this, it was Stoltenberg that was one of the key pro-bombing Libya politicians. When the bombs started falling over Libya in March 2011, Norway and Stoltenberg's engagement were considerable. Norwegian planes dropped 567 bombs over Libya. It was the heaviest Norwegian bombardment since the Second World War. According to a book by the Swedish writer, Daniel Suhonen, Stoltenberg's attitude shocked

Swedish social democrats when he expressed in meetings with them that the Libya bombing "was an excellent training for the Norwegian air force" (Suhonen, 2014).

- Norway is a colonial power. Its early explorers and later the hunt for fossil fuels, minerals, and fish have placed Norway in a position where it controls land area on so many continents—among these on the North and South poles—that the sun never sets on Norway. Queen Maud's land in Antarctica alone is seven times larger than the Norwegian mainland, including Svalbard (Røstvik, 2015).
- It was a Norwegian company, Aker Kværner, with strong ties to the Norwegian state that through its ownership of a U.S. company, maintained the Guantanamo base on Cuba from 1993 to 2006 when it lost the contract to a cheaper competitor (Røstvik, 2015).

We need to ask ourselves if the above dichotomies may make many think that it is possible to get away with almost anything. If so, it is tempting. The reward to entering the grey ethical zones, if it is possible to get away with it, can be tremendously rewarding in a monetary sense. Some will think; when the state can get away with it, why cannot I, an individual, be-rich myself, and get away with it? Some have tried it and some got caught. One interesting sector is procurement.

Procurement Fraud

In order to understand procurement fraud, a quick reminder of what corruption is, how it develops, and why so many get entangled in this is helpful. In Norway, like all of the European Union area, there are competitive challenges in most people's and businesses' daily life. A lot is centered around winning contracts and as one of the several measures introduced in Norway by EU regulations, public procurements are nowadays regulated by size. Procurements over $11,000 have to be subject to tender. The larger the possible contract, the more detailed the tender and procurement procedure, and the more costly for the buyer to control and compare tenders as well as developing and for the supplier submitting them. But there are many ways of getting around this system and designing tender documents so that the buyer has a fair chance of getting the preferred supplier. One way is to use the evaluation system to define which "weight" shall be put on different tender components? By formulating how the tenders shall be evaluated, a buyer can put "weight" on the specific qualities or advantages of the preferred supplier, for example, through demanding a list of relevant reference projects, past experience, or a specific competence. By putting numerical "weight" on the different components in the weighting system (20%, 30%, 40% etc.), the buyer can in many ways control the system. Another way of controlling who wins is to start with a small project below the $11,000 limit, by giving the start project to the preferred supplier without any tender competition at all. This happens every hour of the working day in Norway and thereafter, when the project is completed, more projects are added—each one below the legal limit size. This is however more difficult because each project has to be defined as different and not just a string-like prolongation of the past project. In situations where a public servant is in sole individual control of such tender competitions, or is strong, and excludes others into the process, procurement fraud can more easily develop. But in most cases, decisions are not taken by one person, but by a small group of people that can have a controlling effect on the process unless they leave it to the strong man in the group.

Regardless of how the public procurement process is designed and how it develops, in most cases, it boils down to the challenge that the chain is not stronger than the weakest component. All the Norwegian examples shown in this chapter have clearly emerged because there are personal gains to be had. It is tempting because there is only a small chance of being caught. Since many people do not have the inbuilt reflections as to where the ethical lines are supposed to be drawn, they get into trouble in the grey zones. It is all a matter of ethical standards and of the conditions for whistle-blowing when something suspicious is going on. The Norwegian cases in this chapter show that with the enormous international activity in oil, energy, and arms of a small country like Norway and with the state being a major owner in the most international companies, procurement fraud in such public or semi-public companies are still taking place and the scale is very unclear because there is the likelihood of many, not yet uncovered cases.

In such a climate, where the Norwegian state is trying to set high-ethical verbal standards in all of its companies, why do so many huge corruption scandals take place in many of those companies? Is there a particular Norwegian corruption culture? If so, how did it start, why could it keep on evolving? In the book *Corruption the Nobel Way* (Røstvik, 2015), this was the main subject. Through documenting a range of cases, some known from media and some not, many of the latter category based on personal experience, the author pondered around the question of why and how corruption and moral decadence have emerged and prevailed in such a "happy" country. The conclusion more than indicates that there has not been a culture for preventing corruption in Norway, until recently. On the contrary, in a smug atmosphere where being on good terms with the boss and others in the hierarchy above to gain the benefits like wage increases and other advantages, it has a money-focused oil economy that led to a culture of greed. It has become natural to demand higher and higher wages, more benefits, and other multiple advantages because of the money pouring into the world's richest country's oil fund, while spilling a lot to all sides on its way there.

The game has become one that circles around how best to get a piece of the pie, while it lasts. The result is a particularly Norwegian form of corruption, a noble form, not one where money in brown envelopes are changing hands—although there are also many cases of this too—but one where nepotism is practiced. People help each other; friends help friends by giving them jobs, projects, and other benefits by twisting the system—in spite of stricter and stricter procurement procedures. It is a noble form of corruption, not a dirty one, and it is hard to uncover it because it remains among friends and has not yet damaged the image of Norway as "clean," as expected by the home of the Nobel Peace Prize.

Where and Why Does Corruption Occur?

The definition of nobel or noble corruption is expanding on the traditional everyday use of the word corruption or fraud. Through simple dictionaries, helpful words that come up are indicating where it all starts; spoil, deprave, fake, falsify, forge, and seduce. This is the Norwegian way, according to the uncovered examples. This is where it all starts. It is the basic ethical reflexes that are not functioning. The traditional word "corruption" does not cover what is going on because it focuses too much on "hidden transactions." This is not sufficient because corrupt activities also change character. Bribes to get access to business secrets have increased dramatically in Norway, according to the former head of Økokrim, the Norwegian authority investigating economic and environmental crimes (Dugstad, 2013).

There are few in-depth studies documenting the extent of corruption in Norway, but a World Bank study among 130,000 companies in 135 countries showed that bribes in the building sector were particularly extensive. The building industry is particularly exposed because there is a lot of money involved and on many levels. Professor Tina Søreide, a Norwegian corruption expert at NHH, is clear on this (Søreide, 2016) as follows:

> "Small adjustments in the procurement of tender criteria can decide which company gets to build a motorway, hospital, or other large projects."

Case 1—Municipality

According to paragraph 276 of Norway's Criminal Law, corruption is illegal and punishable with prison up to three years. During the 10 years from 2003 to 2013, 24 Norwegians have been caught and sentenced to all-in-all 49 years of prison for receiving bribes of $23 million in municipality-related cases (NRK, 2013).

In the book essay entitled *Corruption risk in Norwegian Municipalities* (Eriksen, 2014), Tor Dølvik demonstrated how important municipalities are in the decentralized Norwegian welfare model.

> "In principle, it is the people, through their elected representatives in county councils and municipalities, that handle almost 1/5 of the GDP,"

and studies (Baldersheim and Rose, 2011) show that people have considerable confidence in the municipal institutions.

But how does this compare with other countries on the European continent? The first EU report on corruption in the Euro-zone (EU, 2014) pointed at considerable corruption challenges in the member countries. Although Norway is not an EU member, but adheres to most of the EU-Directives through the European economic area (EEA) affiliation, corruption in Norway exists on many levels and the EU report was hence relevant when it stated the following:

> "Corruption risks are found to be higher at regional and local levels where checks and balances and internal controls tend to be weaker than at central level." "In many Member States, wide discretionary powers of regional governments or local administrations (which also manage considerable resources) are not matched by a corresponding level of accountability and control mechanisms. Conflicts of interest raise particular problems at local level."

If this is the situation in municipalities, what about the situation a few steps up in public administration, at state level? After decades of oil activity in the North Sea outside Norway's West coast, and with Norwegian oil companies, and their employees having engaged themselves in a range of countries where corruption is far more widespread than in Norway, how has this impact played out and have attitudes to corruption changed? It can be argued that because of the huge oil activity, the enormous state assets generated thereof and part of it stored in the world's second largest sovereign fund first named the "Oil Fund" later renamed the "Pension Fund," Norway has become a target for all kinds of money-seeking individuals, companies, and nations wanting to get their hands on a part of the wealth.

In January 2016, Norwegian TV stations showed a female municipality employee being secretly filmed on her way to a meeting she was invited to by the local police in Drammen, a middle-sized city near Oslo. She must have understood what the meeting was all about. Before entering the police building, the police cameras and the telephone surveillance showed her calling a relative asking her to remove documents from her home. The police had expected this and were hiding near her home. When the relative, minutes later, had done the job and carried several plastic bags full of documents out of the female municipality employee's home, the police caught that person and the bags, and possibly said thanks for making the police search work so easy.

The female municipality employee, still in the meeting with police, was confronted with suspicion that she had received payments from build-ers to grant them doubtful building permissions. Although the case is now under investigation and the woman is not sentenced, she was imprisoned for four weeks from January 15, 2016 charged with gross corruption for having received bribes in almost 30 building cases. Five days later, a man was also taken into custody charged with collaboration. He disputed the allegations, while the woman admitted breaking the rules. But she clearly stated that she would leave it to the court to decide whether what she did was punishable or not (NRK, 2015).

Case 2—Development Aid and Oil

The enormous Norwegian oil and gas exporting industry has not diminished the corruption challenges around the huge honey jar created by high oil prices. Many new institutional constructions that tap the jar have emerged. Some are procurement-based constructions. The public buys services from them, or engage them to perform certain tasks, very often without any com-petition at all. Many have, at first glance, very idealistic goals, but it need to be discussed whether they are just mere instruments to promote export-oriented Norwegian oil, gas, and oil services companies. One such con-struction is Petrad. Based on Stavanger, the oil capital, Petrad was set up in 1989 and its offices are located in the Norwegian petroleum directorate (NPD) building. It has, until now, worked in more than 50 countries. On its website, it is stated as follows:

> "Petrad delivers courses and other programs for building competencies for the petroleum sector. Petrad programs are particularly suited for public admin-istrators, oil company professionals, civil society professionals, and others whose work concerns the petroleum sector and its implications for society" (Petrad, 2016).

Petrad's values and fundamental beliefs are summed up in six main points whereof the last (F) states: Corruption is unacceptable.

Petrad was found on the vision that oil and gas anywhere in the world should be exploited for the benefit of the societies where they are found. It was set up by the Norwegian state's agency for development aid, Norad. The head of NPD at the time was Gunnar Berge, a former key labor party politi-cian who was the Finance Minister from 1992 to 1996 in the Gro Harlem Brundtland government. He was also a member of the Norwegian Nobel

Peace Prize Committee for many years and its chairman from 2000 to 2002. He has been and still is one of the major promoters of further oil exploration in Norway. He speaks warmly about the oil age and how it will last another 50 to 100 years. One of the board members of Petrad was Per Øyvind Grimstad, a former head of Norad from 1988 to 1996. He has also had key positions in the labor party. This mix of development aid, oil, and strong political figures seems to have opened doors for Petrad and secured stable state funding over the annual state budgets. But this type of procurement has not been subject to competition. I have raised this question several times and never been responded to. I have also questioned whether such and organ should not instead be developing the renewable energy competence in developing countries instead of just teaching them how to extract more oil and deal with the income from oil in a proper manner. In the 1994–1995 development aid state budget, it was described what activities Petrad were involved in:

> "Marketing/door opener and contact-creating development aid, where the Norwegian petroleum industry is at the receiving end" (The National Budget, 1994–1995).

This statement clearly indicates that there are benefits to be expected for the Norwegian petroleum industry. Does this mean increased exports of services and goods? What else can it mean? It seems to be the monetary gain for Norwegian industry that is the bi-product of the Petrad activity. It is a mutual gain; the developing countries get access to crucial knowledge about administrating its oil activity and the funds it generates, and in return the Norwegian industry gets access to the networks established by Petrad and later to the potential projects in developing countries that could include Norwegian companies, often state-owned. This is not corruption in the classic sense of the word, but it is more than indicating a corrupting attitude. Norwegians offer fossil fuel-related development aid programs and in return, Norwegians get lucrative fossil fuels' projects. This is far from untied, independent development aid, and it seems far from the ethical standards that Norwegians claim to operate under when entering developing countries. This is not the Norwegian version of "Mother Theresa" at work and it does not have to be, but it is a way out on the other side of the scale. In September 2004, the largest nation in the world, China, showed its gratitude by giving the Managing Director of Petrad The Friendship Prize in the Great Hall of the People in Beijing. In an extensive interview, the recipient, Øystein Berg, stated the following:

> "For more than 20 years Petrad has, on behalf of the Norwegian State, assisted the Chinese in their hunt for oil." "We do this development work with the new oil nations on their terms. We do this without demanding any returns" (Petrad, 2004).

The interview continued. The journalist asked if this then was not just giving away valuable knowledge free of charge. Berg did not agree and expanded on this by stating as follows:

> "No, Norway and Norwegian companies get a competitive advantage through this new way of marketing" (Petrad, 2004).

In another interview, Petrad's project manager Ellinor Melbye reconfirmed the agenda of Petrad as follows:

> "In addition to doing development aid, we provide soft marketing of the Norwegian oil industry" (Fedde, 2004).

So "soft marketing" is what is going on, with development aid funds, by an organization that does not have to participate in procurement competitions for its "soft marketing" style projects. Meanwhile, at the yearly autumn Thanksgiving feast at that same year, 36 persons in China were executed according to the Chinese State Press. Petrad did not comment upon that event.

Petrad also co-operates with another oil/developing world program, Norway's Oil for Development Program (Oil for Development, 2016), whose aim is to reduce poverty by promoting responsible management of petroleum resources. The focus is good governance, anticorruption and environmental issues. But again the program can be viewed as a way of positioning the Norwegian oil industry. Although this is not a corrupt practice in the traditional interpretation of the word corruption, there can be corrupting elements in this way of ensuring projects for the Norwegian oil industry in the developing world, because it is a procurement-free activity hidden behind the do-good façade of development aid.

In a University of Oslo Master's dissertation, Kristin Dypedokk concluded that the program was strategically important for Norway, and the foreign political, development aid, and industrial policies were mixed:

> "I argue that OfD is a strategic part of Norwegian foreign politics, mixing foreign, development, and industrial policy to serve both altruistic and commercial objectives of the Norwegian state, but that the programme's economic motivation of contributing to internationalization of the Norwegian petroleum industry is not openly debated. The mix of policy agendas in itself is not a new phenomenon, but the way in which this is institutionalized through the OfD initiative represents something new in Norway's development landscape" (UiO, 2010).

To lead the program, the OfD employed the manager of Norsk Hydro's international oil division, Petter Nore. The program has up to now spent huge sums in corrupt countries like Angola and Mozambique, both crucial oil exploration countries for Norwegian Statoil and Norsk Hydro. The program included a range of other countries where Norwegian oil and oil services companies had huge interests or were seeking to become involved in oil exploration activities. Many of the companies were owned by the Norwegian state. It is hence the Norwegian state with its multiple roles, through the interests of the departments of development aid, oil, and natural gas as well as the state through the Ministry of Trade and Industry and Fisheries controlling ownership in many of the companies involved, that need to be questioned. The question is if it is at all possible to separate these roles, or if they are all part of a stew with many contradictory interests in relation to ethics, corruption, and crossing interests.

The dilemmas at hand were underlined when the financing body for the OfD, the development aid institution Norad, placed under the Ministry of Foreign Affairs employed Villa Kulid as its new head in 2010. She came straight from the Department of Oil and Energy, where she had been having key positions during 20 years. Why, is the natural question, this focus on oil in a development aid context? Is oil an energy source of the future that developing countries should base its future energy supply on? Would not renewable energies be more suitable and futuristic?

In 2016, after having carried out "soft marketing" of the Norwegian oil industry, Petrad's annual financial support from the Norwegian state was finally cut. The organization had by then received state funds for 25 years without having had to bother about procurement procedures, competitions, and the hazzle that is included in all that. But as the EU—not the Norwegian state, its courts and laws—finally clamped down on the 25-years practice, funding stopped immediately. Six of the seven well-paid oil-promoting employees had to leave. At the peak period, Petrad had 12 employees and generous budgets. During the 25 years, 90% of the funding had arrived from the Norwegian state. The monopoly-like oil-marketing organization had been allowed to carry on for 25 years without protests. Finally, the EU regulations kicked in and stopped the monopoly. From now on, the work Petrad undertakes must be subject to public procurement simply because the EU directive on public procurement does not allow the state to just fund an organization at this scale and repeatedly without competition (Riiber, 2016).

Case 3—Research

The research sector received huge sums of money from the state every year. Competition is fierce and sometimes unfair, biased, and has the character of corruption. Here is a typical case, a crude one that involves public procurement of research. It would most probably not happen today, but it shows all the symptoms of what has been wrong and was only corrected because individuals blew the whistle repeatedly for years.

In Norway, it is the department of oil and energy (DoE) that provides the state funding for solar research. The money is mainly distributed through the selection procedure organized by the public Norwegian research council (NRC). But due to lack of capacity, the DoE and the NRC decided to engage an external company to run the secretariat needed to deal with sorting the funding applications and the buying of research services or procurement, preparing meetings, advising on, recommending and rejecting projects and consultants to the committee making the final decision. The person chosen to lead the secretariat was the co-owner of the private company that was engaged. The vacancy had an approximate annual value of 200,000 Euros. It stayed with the same person for 25 years. During those 25 years, he was employed in three private companies. In the last one, he had a considerable ownership when the company recently was sold with a nice profit. How could the DoE and the NFR allow a secretariat function with continuously renewed contracts end up in the hands of the same individual for 25 years, and all the way up to 2010? It is a mystery that calls on restraint not to use too strong words. During this period, I personally and repeatedly raised the issue with bot DoE and NRC. I asked if this monopoly was legal? My criticism was never really taken seriously until during the last years before the apparently cosy relationship between the pleased public procurement officers and the engaged consultant was finally abolished. The fact that this kind of procurement of one person's services could go on for so long indicates that there was a culture for this at the DoE and NRC. There must have been, since the internal alarm bells that should have rung, never did ring.

What kind of a job did this person do, then, that was in such a demand at the DoE and NFR? Was he known for his integrity? Was he blowing the whistle when necessary or was he just muddling on? The answer to this lies in another example of how this particular secretariat, for solar energy research that he administrated, worked. The committee that procured solar research and also considered applications for solar research funding was depending on the preparatory work of the secretariat. Were the funds evenly spread to give many research institutes the chance to carry out research? It was not—not at all! As a result of repeated complaints, an external study uncovered that the committee members from 1985 to 2002 had made sure that 87% of the funds ended up in their own institutions (Bellona Informasjon, 1993). During this entire period, the same person had led the secretariat and only outsiders to blew the whistles. When finally pushed to the brink in the media, the committee appointed a small internal group to study the matter. Its conclusions were immediately stamped confidential, for good reasons. It uncovered a practice out of hand and not in line with laws and regulations. But it took 25 years to fix it (Røstvik, 2015).

The solar research case was in many ways uncovered by one man fighting the malpractice of the procurement system. Many others that agreed with him were afraid of the consequences of blowing the whistle and refrained from doing so (Bellona Informasjon, 1993). In the aftermath of this mishap, the Parliamentary Ombudsman for citizens was asked to look at the case. A part of his job objective is to look at the way bureaucrats handle individuals. His judgement was that everything was fine. There were no reasons to question the way the committee had dealt with external applicants, in spite of the committee ensuring that 87% of the funds for solar research ended up in the institutions of the committee members. The publicly paid Ombudsman was then asked to find out if there was some kind of amnesty imposed on public procurement committees like the solar research one or on NRC itself. The question went as follows: "Is it true that the Ombudsman has never looked at any case relating to NRC (The Norwegian Research Council)?" His reply was clear. He confirmed that he had never had a case related to the NRC.

This was disturbing, because it could either mean that everything was perfect—an assumption that many examples including the one above proved wring—or that fellow researchers, colleagues, and companies were too afraid of taking the cost of becoming stigmatized and put outside the "good company" if they complained about the priorities of the committee procuring and funding solar research work.

The fact that the committee system that allowed a small group of insiders to distribute practically all the money between them has, however, been changed so that this cannot happen anymore. But it documents that the old system had grave design faults that nobody has yet admitted publicly, although the changing of the procurement committee procedure speaks for itself. The worrying part is, however, that the necessary public debates on these issues do not emerge to the extent necessary to fix the system in a more fundamental way, because of the secrecy emerging as a result of the stamping of the internal report as confidential. The danger is hence that there are still design faults inbuilt in the system.

Carl August Fleischer, professor of law at University of Oslo, has repeatedly drawn the attention to nepotism and the reasons for lacking whistleblowing among academics in Norway. It is a challenge indicating that when silence prevails among academics, that normally are supposed to be open and frank, how bad is the situation in other sectors really? Fleischer's response is as follows (Fleischer, 2006):

> "...It is documented that being critical in an academic setting is problematic. It can even be seen as un-collegial." "Critics can be downgraded." "The lack of real freedom of expression in academic circles is a very serious problem." "Critics are overseen."

Discussion

In a Norwegian study (TI, 2002) was originally carried out for a research institute in Angola, AIP, as a contribution to the domestic preparations for a public procurement reform, the findings were later generalized, without any specific country in mind. The generalization indicated that the challenges of corruption are universal, but above all, corrupting attitudes in one country can rub off on another. More specifically, if Norway engages a lot with corrupt regimes, how does that have an impact on corruption levels in Norway? The summary of the report stated the following:

> "Corruption is rarely a one-sector phenomenon, occurring only in one institution of the state, or at one level of the bureaucratic hierarchy. Where it exists as a problem, it tends to pervade large parts of the state administration."

During the last decades of intense international oil activity, the one-to-one contact points between Norwegian citizens employed by Norwegian companies abroad and citizens in fairly corrupt countries have become extensive. It is not very ingenious to assume that temptation to receive bribes has been increasing in line with increasing activity in such nations. The result is readable from statistics, as it has been revealed that Norwegian companies have been involved in huge corruption scandals. The partly Norwegian state-owned Telenor (54% state ownership) owns 33% of Vimpelcom, the Russian telecom giant that has accepted to pay fines equivalent to U.S. $795 million for breach of the U.S. Foreign Corrupt Practices Act. This is the second largest fine in the U.S., after the Siemens one of U.S. $800 million other huge corruption scandals involve Norwegian state-owned companies like the fertilizer exporter Yara (36% state ownership) and oil and gas giant Statoil (67% state ownership). The latter with huge oil activities and money transfers in Angola, among those a $50 million research center transfers where no research center can be found. The transfer is not yet counted for and still being investigated.

The touchpoints between individuals in these companies and the individuals on the other side of the table in the more corrupt countries are many and since corruption is a phenomenon that involves people, where there are people involved, there is a chance that corruption will be taking place. Many of the contracts involved are procurement based.

In order to understand how such corrupt practices arise, a study of the human condition, human behavior, greed, and the like is a useful tool—as well as the technicalities involved in the weaknesses of the controlling mechanisms that were designed to stop corruption from taking place. The Dean of Insead University in Paris, Dipak C. Jain, has expressed that corruption is latent in human nature and has the best conditions for growth during economic boom times (Røstvik, 2015). If Jain is right, Norwegians—through the past decades of oil boom—have exposed themselves to corruption and mainly through transatlantic operating companies. The largest single owner of such companies is the Norwegian state, so corruption takes place by individuals working in the companies as state employees. These are companies placing huge procurement contracts. In addition to, the above-mentioned companies, in 2014 the Norwegian state ownership involves arms and ammunition exporters Nammo (50%) and Kongsberg Group (50%), coal producer Spitsbergen (100%), power supplier Statkraft (100%), the former oil company and now aluminium exporter Norsk Hydro (34%), oil services company Aker Kværner Holding (30%), and fish farming giant Cermaq (59%).

In other words, in 2014 the Norwegian state held ownerships worth 62 billion Euros in most of the Norwegian companies that have been involved in corruption scandals or allegations. What does this indicate as regards to the people employed by these companies? It is hard to tell, because human errors or greed is exposed in all parts of society and whether a company is state-owned or private does not necessarily indicate the level of potential corruption that can take place. However, it is puzzling how many of the state giants that get entangled in corruption in spite of their clear zero-corruption-target texts in their internal ethical guidelines?

In Norway, if you own more than 50% of the shares in a company, you have "full control" over decisions needing plenary majority. If you own over one-third of the shares, it ensures so-called "negative control"—one is able to block several types of major decisions. The above-listed companies are hence under the "full" or "negative" control of the Norwegian state and it is the state's responsibility when their employees get entangled in corruption. The scale of this problem at public company state level makes one wonder if this is just a signal of a major problem that is not yet altogether uncovered or if it is limited? Have everybody been caught? Of course not! If this is the state of things in state-owned Norwegian companies, what about the huge jungle of private enterprises and in the municipalities and country councils? The task of cleaning-up seems, in view of the actual uncovered cases, very hard and signals very strong that the "zero corruption target" is just a dream.

Many Norwegians have a naive view of the level of corruption actually taking place in the country. Based on the number of grave cases having been uncovered, the level of corruption is more widespread than the typical naive view of Norway as a zero corruption zone should indicate. If, so, corruption happens on many levels—also in procurement related to small and large contracts, the smaller the more widespread since it then is the nepotism effect that kicks in—and following from this, corruption is not at all something that only takes place in countries far away. Corruption is about human weakness on many levels. A study in 2013 confirmed the typical naive Norwegian perception of the level of corruption. Only 17% of Norwegian employees believed corruption was widespread in Norwegian companies, only 2% thought that it happened in their own field or company (Ernst & Young, 2013). This is of course contradictory to the TI annual reports showing Norway as the most corrupt Nordic country. Corruption has been allowed to develop over time and the authorities have not clamped down on it, but looked the other way. In 2002, only two cases were reported to the police. From 2005 to 2007, the number of reported cases almost doubled from 18 to 31. In 2009, the number of actual convictions were 40. It is people in the public sector that dominate the number of convicted. This led Eva Joly, the French/Norwegian corruption hunter, to express as follows:

"Norway has never been more corrupt than now" (Røstvik, 2015).

Most of the corruption happens in connection with the public buying goods and services. Some public employees use their position to gain economical benefits or to serve friends—so called nepotism. Professor of economics and an expert on corruption, Petter Gottschalk put it in the following way:

"When you sit on top in one of the main corporations in Norway, it is very easy to embezzle. The chance of being discovered is microscopic" (Christensen, 2014).

Who then get caught? It is men and women in prestigious companies and in public administration that get caught for corruption, mostly men. But there are many surprising corruption cases caused by women too.

After 40 years of international oil activity, Norway may have seen an increasing corrupt activity developing and a loyalty culture along with it. Such a culture aims at involving those who know. They are invited inside the inner circles, to make sure they shut up and do not tell outsiders about budget overruns, corruption, and accidents in the company that need to be played down. In some Norwegian studies, every third employee expressed that they had experienced that their leaders did things that must be, and was expected to be, hidden in the dark (Røstvik, 2015). Whistle-blowers are rare in such a culture. They often become outcasts if they react. They do not get access to the "good company." They may be termed "not trustworthy" and pushed into the cold. This might be some of the reasons why there are so few whistle-blowers in Norway. It is easier to close the eyes than to blow the whistle. A research project as early as 10 years ago revealed that the Norwegian loyalty culture that is described above really exists. Women are becoming more and more interested in participating in this men-dominated loyalty culture. They see it is a way for them to reach higher positions by proving loyalty and being daring. A study based on 15,000 questionnaires and 400 interviews confirmed this view (UiO, 2005).

Conclusions

What can be drawn out of the selected cases presented in this paper? Do they indicate something about the level of procurement-related corruption in Norway that is not readable straightaway from statistics? Yes and no. There is certainly a level of corruption in Norway far higher than in the neighbouring countries. This is mainly due to the international character of the Norwegian oil, gas, arms, and telecom businesses that are present in many countries with a high general level of corruption. It will hence be necessary to discuss whether the number of identified and prosecuted fraud and corruption cases give a correct picture of the situation or is it just the top of the iceberg that has become visible? The wide mix of types of cases, of professions involved, and of places involved certainly indicates that corruption is not only limited to one sector or industry, like for example, the arms-exporting industry. It is wider than that and when it is wide, it is harder to detect. The next assumption to be considered would hence be, if the general richness that has flooded over the Norwegian landscape due to the major industries' successes has created greed and envy? Everyone wants a part of the pie and since everyone does not have access to the table where the big chunks of the pie is split, it is natural to assume that those that split the pie takes the biggest chunks for themselves and leave dust to the others. This in itself is unfair and creates envy; among some, it also creates an urge at trying to get a bigger piece. If corruption is the way to get a bigger piece, then corruption might be one way of ensuring one owns' wealth. Such processes lead to the corrupting of the people involved. Few are probably caught. The cases we can write about are hence only those where facts are clear or where prosecution has taken place. The rest will remain speculation.

References

Baldersheim, H. and Rose, L. (2011). How does local democracy function? Ministry of Local Government and Modernisation. Hvordan fungerer lokaldemokratiet? Oslo, Norway: KS, Kommunal-og regional departementet.

Bellona Informasjon. (1993). Frank Hugo Storelv: Forskerne deler ut penger til seg selv. *Journal*. Oslo, Norway. 1/1993. pp. 3–5.

Christensen A.R. (2014). Risikoen for å bli oppdaget er mikroskopisk. *Aftenposten* Oslo, Norway. January 11, 2014. pp. 58–59.

Dugstad, L. (2013). Bestikker for informasjon. *Dagens Næringsliv*. Oslo, Norway. March 30, 2013. p. 5.

Eriksen, B. (2014). Editor. To fight a social evil. Å bekjempe et samfunnsonde. Transparency International Norge. Oslo, Norway: Gyldendal Publishing. pp. 92–107.

Ernst & Young. (2013). *EMEIA Fraud Survey 2013*, Navigating today's complex business risks, EYG AU1870.

EU. (2014). Report from the Commission to the Council and the European Parliament. EU Anti-Corruption Report. Brussel, Belgium: EU-Commission.

Fedde, A.M. (2004). Petrad vil gi Bolivia oljeopplæring. *Newspaper.* Stavanger, Norway. October 6, 2004. p. 14.

Fleischer, C.A. (2006). Corruption culture, camaraderie and breach of trust. Korrupsjonskultur, kameraderi og tillitssvikt i Norge. Oslo, Norway: Koloritt Publishing.

The National Budget (1994–1995). Item 70 of the development aid budget. Norwegian Ministry of Finance.

Nobel. (1895). The third and last will of Alfred Nobel November 27, 1895. Several sources. https://www.nobelprize.org/alfred_nobel/will/will-full.html (accessed July 8, 2016).

NRK. (2013). Twenty-four sentenced for municipality corruption. http://www.nrk.no/norge/24-domt-for-kommunal-korrupsjon-1.10848559 (accessed February 23, 2016).

NRK. (2015). Municipality employee in Drammen charged with gross corruption. http://www.nrk.no/buskerud/kommuneansatt-i-drammen-siktet-for-grov-korrupsjon-1.12754802 (accessed February 23, 2016).

Oil for Development (2016). https://www.norad.no/en/front/thematic-areas/oil-for-development/ (accessed September 19, 2016).

Petrad. (2004). http://www.petrad.no/news/2013/plaque-recognition-dr-øystein-berg (accessed September 20, 2016).

Petrad. (2016). Petroleum Knowledge for the World/Capacity development for managing petroleum resources. www.petrad.no (accessed March 8, 2016).

Riiber, K. (2016). *Newspaper.* Stavanger, Norway. February 23, 2016. pp. 8–9.

Røstvik, H.N. (2015). Corruption the Nobel way. Dirty fuels & The sunshine revolution, Oslo, Norway: Kolofon Publishing. pp. 19–22; 154–160; 249–257.

Søreide, T. (2016). Interview in Byggeindustrien. *Journal.* Oslo, Norway. Nr 2–2016. pp. 14–16.

Suhonen, D. (2014). The story of Juholt's fall and the new politics. "Berettelsen om Juholts fall och den nya politiken." Stockholm, Sweden: Leopard publishing.

TI. (2002). Transparency International, Corruption Perception Index 2002.

UiO. (2005). Læringslaben. Referred in Hegnar 29.1.2005. Do you know "things" about the boss? "Har du noe på sjefen." http://www.hegnar.no/Nyheter/Naeringsliv/2005/01/Har-du-noe-paa-sjefen (accessed April 16, 2016).

UiO. (2010). Kristin Dypedokk. Master Dissertation UiO, Centre for Development and the Environment; Serving Public or Private Interests? https://www.duo.uio.no/handle/10852/32608 (accessed May 15, 2016).

Tackling Corruption and Crime in Public Procurement in the 2012 London Olympics and Paralympics Games

The Role of Operation Podium, The Specialist Organized, and Economic Crime Unit of the Metropolitan Police

7

PERRY STANISLAS

Contents

Introduction

This chapter will interrogate the role of the Metropolitan Police's Specialist Organised and Economic Crime Unit (now SOC7), in tackling economic crime in the public procurement of construction projects for the 2012 London Olympic and Paralympic Games (hereafter called the Games). This chapter will first explore the history of organised crime and major construction projects, and second the role of the Specialists, Organised, and Economic Crime Unit (SOEU) and the work of its Operation Podium Team, in developing strategies to tackle procurement crime in the delivery of major construction projects for the Games. Third, the chapter details the preparation and evolution of the strategy and tactics used to reduce crime in this area of activity. Finally, the chapter will critically examine the effectiveness of the strategy and tactics of the police, and its partners, and the difficulties in tackling crime in the complex area of major construction projects. The chapter is informed by interviews that were carried out in 2014–2015 with police leaders and intelligence staff from Operation Podium Team who played an important role in the evolution and implementation of its strategy.

Problem

The domestic and international construction industry is a major driver of economic development and prosperity (Osei 2013). The British construction industry contributed £80 billon and 6% of the national output in 2012 (House of Commons 2013). The global building and construction industry is estimated to generate $7.2 trillion annually and expected to grow to $12 trillion by 2020 (Schilling 2013). Building and construction fraud is estimated to cost $1 trillion annually (Construction Manager 2013, Gardiner 2013). Concerns about corruption and public works have plagued important British construction projects, such as the London Millennium Dome, which damaged the careers of several senior ministers and resulted in arrests (Babbington 2000, Bird 2005). One specific crime involved a company called the Millennium Experience Lighting Company that was surreptitiously created by a director of the Millennium Dome Project. Using his position he was able to exclude other rival tenders from the bidding process and award the contract to his company (The Telegraph 2005). The Price Waterhouse Global Economic Survey (2014) found that 29% of all economic crime was related to procurement, and 27% bribery and corruption, with a significant number of these offenses being related to construction procurement matters. The Chartered Institute of Builders 2013 survey of members of Chartered Institute of Purchasing and Supply found that 40% of its members believed that the construction industry sector was the most vulnerable to corruption and fraud. One particular area of concern was contract or bid rigging (Goldstock 1990, Jones 2004).

Although little is known about the intricate workings of building and construction and related crime in most countries, many of the general characteristics of this industry seems to suggest that it is highly vulnerable to forms of criminal behavior (Albanese 2008, Vander Beken and Van Dael 2008, Kankaanranta and Muttilainen 2010). The building and construction sector has historically been associated with major organized crime groups in the developed world, transnational crime, and in the developing world (Harriot 2008, Dorn et al. 2010). One of the characteristics of large construction projects is the difficulty in formulating precise cost estimates, given their unique specifications and problems involved in the building process (Goldstock 1990: 17, Jones 2004: 87). The subjectivity intrinsic to costing projects can lead to overestimation of price and the conscious and unwitting facilitation of crime. Public construction involves extremely large sums of money (from millions to hundreds of millions in local currencies), and is characterized as a highly fragmented business sector with a large number of actors, such as contractors, subcontractors, technical specialists, inspectors, and gatekeepers of various kinds (Goldstock 1990: 13, Vander Beken and Van Dael 2008: 744–745).

Major building projects also involve a significant number of cash transactions at the construction site level in the purchasing of goods, materials, and services that can be the target of organized theft or false billing, and a variety of tax offenses (Harriot 2008: 133). Kankaanranta and Muttilainen's (2010) work highlights the high level of tax fraud that takes place within the construction industry in Finland, particularly that associated with false billing, which is a criminal offense in many countries (Goldstock 1990: 26). Kankaanranta and Muttilainen (2010) found 75% of respondents in their survey routinely were in possession of false receipts with a loss of approximately £25 million to the government in terms of taxation.

One of the most troubling forms of criminal activity that can occur in this industry is price-fixing or other activities designed to limit fair competition and or to achieve a monopoly over the various factors of production (Goldstock 1990, Dorn et al. 2010: 246–248). The result of these practices is inflating prices and profits to winners of contracts, who can often be those least qualified to carry out work, and has adverse consequences on society and key stakeholders. This can include distorting the building and construction costs, and those related industries that adversely affect property prices inter alia (Goldstock 1990: 37–38).

The building and construction industry in many parts of the world is not only vulnerable to organized criminal activities for financial profit, it also serves other important illicit purposes that make it particularly attractive to organized criminal groups or corrupt networks. The industry has historically been associated with money laundering (Goldstock 1990: 63–64, Savona 2010: 132), identity fraud in providing jobs for unqualified or illegal workers, as well as legitimate employment for criminals in order to mask their other illicit activities and associates. The term *ghost worker* is known in one form or another in many countries of the world. In the Caribbean it is often associated with fictitious jobs created by politicians to reward political loyalists or friends and a means to draw an extra salary (Reid and Scott 1994, Wayne 2010: 521). The unethical and potentially illegal treatment of many groups of labor involved in the building and construction industry around the world is a cause of concern in some quarters (Goldstock 1990). From what has been

Table 7.1   Construction Procurement Process

		Preprocurement
1. Commit to Invest	The point at which the client decides in principle to invest in a project, sets out the requirement in business terms and authorizes the project team to proceed with the conceptual design	Tender process and contract award
2. Commit to Construct	The point at which the client authorizes the project team to start the construction of the project	Contract and supply management
3. Available for Use	The point at which the project is available for substantial occupation/use, which may be in advance of completion	Occupation and defects rectification

Source: Fox, S. (2015). *A Guide to Construction Procurement Strategies*. Available from www.slideshare.net/sarahjvfox. Definitions are taken from Chapter 16, Key Performance Indicators and Benchmarking of the 2009 DTI Annual Statistics.

described the effective policing of building and construction crime involves a number of state policing and specialist law enforcement agencies, and other stakeholders that can include tax and immigration authorities and private sector security and auditing specialists (Ekblom 2002, Levi and Maguire 2004: 422–426, Jones 2004, Harriot 2008). It is also important to note that the construction industry is a location for a range of other crimes, which may not always require high levels of organization, and can include the buying and selling of stolen equipment and materials and other actions of lone individuals. It is suffice to say that the construction industry is often a site for a plethora of criminal activity (Harriot 2008: 132) and similar to procurement fraud the full-scale of financial loss caused in and around this area is nearly impossible to quantify.

Understanding the vulnerability of the public procurement process for construction work is assisted by Fox's (2014) simplification of the process, which is illustrated in Table 7.1. The commitment to investment phase is where the client is exploring the feasibility of the construction project. The types of vulnerabilities to corruption and fraud that exists at this level can include matters around compromising sensitive and confidential information or inflating project proposal costs inter alia (Jones 2004: 82–3, Harriot 2008: 135). A major area at this level, which is plagued with a number of potential risks, is the tendering and contract awarding process where many well-known frauds such as restricting advertising or bidders can occur (Goldstock 1990: 13, Vander Beken and Van Dael 2008: 744–745 Jones 2004: 33, Harriot 2008: 136). At this level there are different types of processes that can be used where bidders can compete for contracts. These can include open procedures where interested parties compete for bids. Restricted procedures where potential bidders are invited to apply and negotiated procedures where contracting authorities invite a small number of interested parties to negotiate the terms of the contract (Dorn et al. 2008). Negotiated procedures may not be advertised and utilized for emergency situations.

The commit to construct phase is vulnerable to a range of offenses, such as practices involving collusion between contractors and suppliers, and other actors operating at this level. An example of this is false billing (Kankaanranta and Muttilainen 2010). The final phase of activity, that is, making the structure available for client use, is associated with a number of practices such as shortcutting work, substitutions, and disposal of materials and billing offenses (Vander Beken and Van Dael 2008: 748). One of the features of construction activities is that many of the early phases of the work process are obscured by other subsequent phases of work that follow. For example, electrical wiring may be covered up by flooring or other forms of material that masks the quality of work previously carried out (Harriot 2008: 132).

Operation Podium and the Planning for the Olympic Games

The police involvement in the planning of the 2012 London Olympic and Paralympic Games (or Games) was twofold. The first was in the security preparations for athletes, attendees, venues, and policing of communities during the period of the Games (Fussey 2011, Stanislas 2014). The second dimension of police involvement was tackling economic crime during the preparations and duration of the Games, given the unprecedented amounts of money involved in staging and delivering the event. The total amount of public money spent on the Games was £9.9 billion with the overwhelming majority being spent on major construction projects (National Audit Office 2012).

Following the successful bid in 2005 a discussion document titled "Who Will Win Gold?" was produced for the Metropolitan Police's Economic Crime Command, which outlined the economic crime risks within what became known as the *Olympic Economy* and set out the opportunities to work in partnership with other stakeholders. The author, a Detective Sergeant with extensive experience of economic crime, was tasked to further explore the issues relating to the successful delivery of previous Games and major construction projects in the United Kingdom and Europe. He was also tasked to develop a holistic economic crime policing strategy. The strategy focussed on working in partnership to proactively prevent crime rather than simply reacting to crime allegations.

The MPS Serious Organised and Economic Crime Unit (SOECU) subsequently established Operation Podium, which initially focussed on the Olympic Development Authority (ODA), and the risk posed from the construction sector as a whole. Podium targeted the threat to the delivery of the

Olympic Games. The scoping exercise conducted by the SOECU highlighted the following crime types as being prominent within the construction sector:

- Corruption (Fraud)
- Plant/Haulage theft
- Metal theft

There were major concerns that the occurrence of crime during the Games could lead to significant financial harms, potentially lengthy time delays, and reputational damage (Stanislas 2014: 235). The MPS attempted to learn lessons from similar major projects. Some of the cases examined as part of this process was the construction of the Millennium Dome, Railtrack-Cross rail project, the Jubilee Line extension, and Welsh Slate Mining fraud inter alia (Walsh 2007, Serious Fraud Office 2009). The evolving strategy built on other SOECU policing initiatives based on intelligence-led proactive and partnership approaches to crime prevention (Bullock et al. 2010). The SOECU had previously launched Operation Sterling—a prevention strategy for various business sectors within London and other police/industry engagements. Operation Sterling targeted identity fraud, which is a crucial component of immigration and other forms of economic crime. Another major influence was Operation Maxim, which was a multiagency partnership that involved the Immigration Services and Crown Prosecution Services that focused on immigration offenses, including fraud and other economic crimes. The appointment of a Detective Superintendent as the new head of the SOECU further contributed to the body of expertise already accumulated by Operation Podium.

The career background of the new Detective Superintendent complemented the approach that had already been adopted by the Operation Podium team: "A lot of my work had been around proactive prevention and disruption and the enforcement side of things, that's very much my approach to combating organised crime." He continues:

> Drawing on all these experiences helped me design what I wanted to for the Olympics. I am very much a believer in prevention if we can prevent the crime in the first place, even if the potential victim don't know they are vulnerable to crime it just makes sense in terms of cost effectiveness and harm to potential victims that we do so.

A good example of this was the Detective Superintendent's role in the passing of the Specialist Print Equipment (Offenses) Act 2015, which was one of the objectives of the Genesius Project that consisted of the police and other stakeholders to regulate the purchasing and use of equipment that could be used for producing fraudulent documentation.[1] This project led to intelligence being developed in this area by its enforcement arm, Operation Maxim. Using their knowledge of a range of fraud and related crimes, and the various means to prevent them, the task of carrying out the initial work in preparation for the Games was given to the Detective Sergeant, who in 2005 started research on the types of economic crimes that could occur. The Detective Sergeant explains his thinking on the matter:

> I could see various opportunities for criminals to profiteer from the Games, especially within the construction phase. The more knowledge I obtained on procurement the more it became evident there were plenty of opportunities for people to make significant amounts of money illegally.

Operation Podium was established in 2006 in order to address economic crime in the context of the Games and the construction phase of hosting the event in particular. The opportunities for fraud and corruption within such a large infrastructure project was highlighted by the large amount of money allocated to the building of infrastructure for the Games to the ODA, which was an estimated £6.8 billion, and the largest part of the total expenditure for the event (National Audit Office 2012, Zayas 2012). The ODA was the client (on behalf of the public) who commissioned 70 construction projects for the Games, while a partnership of companies consisting of Chase Hill and Laing O'Rourke and Mace, which went by the acronym (CH2M), was responsible for delivering the construction projects (Zayas 2012, Department for Environment, Food and Rural Affairs 2013). These projects included the Olympic Village and a Media Centre.

The background to the SOECU's involvement in the Games has its roots in several successful antifraud operations that had taken place in the years prior to the event that contributed to the acquisition of a body of knowledge and skills by the specialist detectives and intelligence officers who worked on them. To supplement the police's knowledge of construction risks and issues, Podium engaged with a number of the United Kingdom's leading construction companies and subsequently formed the Construction Industry Fraud Forum (CIFF). An essential function of the CIFFs was improving understanding about the range of risks to crime and corrupt behavior that can occur in the procurement process. One respondent describes a prevailing attitude among many CIFF members. "A lot of people at the ODA and London Organising Committee for the Games (LOCOG) were of the view who would want to defraud the Olympic Games because everybody wanted it to be a success?" Changing this almost naiveté outlook was fundamental to the work of the Podium officers.

The CIFFs played a crucial role in educating stakeholders about various processes and actors involved in procurement and some of its challenges, which was particularly important for the police in developing their understanding of the workings of the sector (Cummings and Huse 1989: 168–169). Other aspects of the CIFs role included identifying and developing good practice in anticorruption work. They also undertook training and related activities. Creating an awareness of how major events provide opportunities for economic crime was fundamental to the work of CIFFs. This was achieved primarily by the police sharing their knowledge and experiences of procurement-related offenses drawn from some high-profile cases.

The CIFF consisted of construction companies, house builders, and professional bodies, such as the National Housing Building Council (NHBC) and the Chartered Institute of Builders (CIOB). These were major players in the construction industry, many of whom were specialist companies with expertise in building the types of infrastructure required for mega-events such as the Games. In 2007, the MPS was able to put together a business case for additional funding for its ideas for preventing economic crime for the Games, which was eventually agreed by the Home Office in the late 2009. Some of the funds applied for were used to continue to pay for dedicated police officers to carry out crime prevention work with the ODA. Given the amount of work involved in preparing for the Games, and the need to start work was immediate, it could not be left until a formal decision had been reached on the matter of funding from the Home Office.

The ODA's Building and Construction Anticorruption Strategy

The efforts of the Operation Podium team to introduce transparency into the building and construction processes for the Games was assisted by broader developments with the existence of the European procurement standards, which the ODA as a public body accepted from its outset as providing a framework of good practice. This was the first major British construction project to operate within European guidelines and one of the largest of its type in Europe (Ruddock 2011).[2] An example of this was the advertising of large contracts, such as the one for the Olympic Aquatic Centre, in European-wide publications, which resulted in the winner of the contract facing stiff competition from foreign-based companies (Dorn et al. 2008, Ruddock 2011). This was reinforced by the adoption of good practice in the form of a baseline budgeting strategy in the area of financial planning, and control for the construction process. Zayas (2012) details the budgeting strategy documented in what was referred to as the *Yellow Book* by key stakeholders in the design and delivery process for construction projects for the Games (DEFRA 2013).

The Yellow Book, which was agreed by ministers, was an important document in providing a detailed and transparent map of the work processes, construction activities, the costs and budget allocation, and the risks and contingencies involved. An important risk it identifies, and seeks to tightly control, is the potential fluctuations in project costs that provide opportunities for corrupt practices (Goldstock 1990: 59). These operating frameworks, values, and priorities served to promote transparency, and helped to contribute to a receptive environment within the ODA, and its leadership that was conducive to the work of Operation Podium personnel.

The reliance on a proactive preventative approach, which had become a standard feature of the Metropolitan Police's response to economic crime, was reinforced by the research undertaken on procurement crime and large-scale projects in preparation for the Games. Commenting on the length of time it took for suspicions of criminal activity to be reported in the context of the Millennium Dome project. The Detective Sergeant explains:

> The research I carried out showed that the average referral occurred about nine months after the Dome had been finished, and the auditors had gone in and reported, some concerns about potential offences.

The traditional approach of waiting until a suspected fraud was reported to the police was thought to be inadequate. The Detective Superintendent explains the weakness of this approach (Levy 1987: 141):

> People often see fraud as involving long investigations which takes years and also results in relatively light sentences received. So you spend four years carrying out an investigation and the offenders receive a two year sentence.

Fraud, which is one of the core constituent offenses in discussions around procurement crime, is carried out by individuals whose actions involve the planning, commissioning, and covering-up of offenses (Gottschalk chapter on convenience theory). This makes the investigation of these types of crimes as being largely reactive, contingent on when they come to light, and based on assessments of their legal merits and likelihood of successful prosecution. With these considerations in mind it should not be surprising that the number of successful convictions for fraud is relatively small (Levy 1987).

One dimension of Podium's proactive approach to tackling economic crime was the creation of specialist industry forums involving key stakeholders.[3] The establishment of the Construction Industry Forums (CIFs) was an important stage in the evolution of a shared approach to problem-solving in the area of preventing construction fraud (Goldstock 1990: 110). CIF consisted of tier one companies who were major players in the construction industry. This group included 96 firms such as Balfour Beatty, and McAlpine inter alia, who were represented by staff with responsibilities for procurement-related activities, such as heads of internal audit (Jones 2004, Zayas 2012). A key motivator for the involvement of companies in the CIFs included reputational concerns and the desire to be seen beyond reproach, similar to the reasons for complying with good practice in health and safety, and other regulatory priority areas (Tombs and Whyte 2007). The association of firms with the Olympic Games also added considerable value to their brands and reputations (Maguire 2005), which is summed up in the following remarks:

> It did not take much to sell the idea of being part of the Games.

The police was instrumental in establishing tier two CIFs that represented construction companies responsible for smaller and very specific aspects of larger projects. These subcontractors numbered approximately 900 in total (Goldstock 1990: 17, Zayas 2012: 2). Prior to Operation Podium, some of its staff had been involved in the establishment of regional ODAs and the ODA's Procurement and Contract Management Teams. These bodies provided hands on advice and support by highlighting areas of vulnerability and appropriate courses of action. Both CIFs were led by the ODA and cochaired by the Detective Sergeant from Operation Podium.

Creating an awareness of how major events provide opportunities for economic crime was fundamental to the work of CIFs (United Nations Convention Against Corruption 2013). This was achieved primarily by the police sharing their knowledge and experiences of procurement-related offenses drawn from high-profile cases. The CIFs played a crucial role in educating stakeholders about various processes and actors involved in procurement and some of the challenges involved, which was also important for the police in developing their understanding of the workings of the sector. Other aspects of the CIFs role included identifying and developing good practice in public procurement. They also undertook training and related activities. Although CIFs were Olympic specific, their establishment inadvertently gave support to discussions already taking place about corruption and crime in the building and construction industry (Construction Management 2013). For example, the CIOB newsletter cites various sources of research and data, highlighting serious concerns about perceived criminal behavior taking place within the industry. This includes reports from number of authoritative sources, such as the Chartered Institute of Loss Adjusters 2011 indicating as much as 10% of payments made in the construction industry were fraudulent in nature (Construction Management 2013).

The ODA was the central player in the commissioning of projects and able to influence the wider environment around anticorruption matters, which it did in several ways. The first and a relatively innovative course of action was the embedding of a Detective Inspector and Detective Sergeant from Operation Podium into the ODA's workforce. The Detective Superintendent explains the following the role played by these individuals:

They were there reviewing risk registrations and giving advice and guidance on that. They were working closely with procurements and making sure things were done properly. Just having police officers on-site had a significant impact in terms of communicating how serious these issues were being taken.

These individuals reported to senior heads of departments and their secondments were funded by the Home Office. Their role was to act as advisors and provide support to managers in identifying risks and areas of vulnerability in the procurement process and how to mitigate them. Some of the specific actions introduced by the detectives, in terms of good practice was reviewing and updating the ODA's Fraud Risk Assessment, writing the initial fraud and corruption risk registers, encompassing IT, travel, finance, transport, and procurement, and human resources. The introduction of a risk register which listed companies with histories of suspect practice is a standard procedure, and was supported by other actions that included forensically examining sample contracts (Goldstock 1990: 19, Jones 2004: 90). These good practices were reinforced by the designation of one of the detectives as the Podium Single Point of Contact (SPOC) for the MPS and others within the ODA. Finally, the adoption of a partnership approach assisted in fostering joint ownership of procurement fraud, further supporting efforts in introducing an antifraud culture. This also assisted in informing management decisions, resource allocation, and improved the process of identifying risk and confidence in the change process (Goldstock 1990: 110).

Perhaps one of the most significant interventions was the provision of training, for in the first instance 48 ODA and CLM officials/CIFF members, which was crucial in increasing awareness about procurement fraud. The training also included 120 procurement professionals from the ODA. Special packages were designed and delivered for staff from the Finance and Information and Technology Departments. The Detective Sergeant describes an important element of the training provided to Finance Team staff to identify basic fraud:

We gave them an invoice and asked them to find three things wrong with the invoice and as soon as they have done that to turn over the piece of paper. I would go around the class once they have completed the exercise and go through the issues they found in the invoice.

He continues:

There were numerous issues with the invoice. But once you direct people to look for those three basic things they become blind to other problems, which was an additional learning point.

This example illustrates an essential element of the work of the embedded detectives in using their experience and knowledge to increase awareness of the types of crimes and bad practices that can take place as part of the procurement process. The role of the Detective Sergeant was particularly crucial as the police liaison and SPOC for economic crime. His graduate educational and academic background in economics and accounting was useful in this context and general role (Stanislas 2014: 3). His primary responsibility was for mitigating economic crime risks and help to establish processes for reporting and responding to allegations of crime or related matters. Another dimension of the Detective Sergeant's role was to support, advise, and prepare an appropriate policing response to economic crime matters through the life of the Games. The Detective Sergeant reported to the Detective Superintendent from the SOECU on a weekly basis and bimonthly to the Commander of Organised Crime of the Metropolitan Police Service (MPS).

Although the MPS was the lead organisation on all crime prevention and security matters for the Games, it was part of the Olympic Economic Crime Forum. This body involved other regional police organizations hosting events as part of the competition (Stanislas 2014), where issues around risks or particular developments were discussed and shared. The Olympics Intelligence Centre played a crucial role in the collection, analysis, and dissemination of important information to relevant parties (Interview with Intelligence Analyst). An important set of national police priorities in regards to the Games, was reducing the risk to crime, and protecting the international reputation and *brand* of the country, given the unprecedented nature of mega events such as the Games and their global media exposure and implications (Stanislas 2014: 235). The importance of adverse publicity on a country's reputation and its political and economic consequences cannot be underestimated. This can be seen by the near hysterical response from Kenyan government, when CNN dubbed it *a hot bed of terrorism* and the international controversy that ensued (Justice 2015, Stanislas 2016). The commercial ramification of sporting mega events for investment is considerable (Maguire 2005).

Within this broader strategic context and institutional police framework, the work of the Operation Podium and its officers evolved. The Detective Sergeant, who played a critical leadership role from the earliest stages of the discussion and planning of the Games, elaborates on his primary responsibilities:

> My role in simple terms was to create an anti-fraud culture (from zero) to highlight the risk of economic crime, and build their understanding of fraud, as they (ODA) had very little initially and to prepare and plan for the police response as the project grew.

One of the primary steps required in bringing about this antifraud awareness is the use of influencing strategies directed at selected senior managers (Cummings and Huse 1989: 113–114, Neyroud and Wain 2014). Evidence of this thinking is illustrated by the Detective Sergeant: "I spoke to the head of security, the head of construction, the head of procurement, head of IT and transport and I gave them the arguments why it would be good to give some input and momentum to get some energy around this anticorruption concept, and this was taken on board." Like many staff specialist functions with limited amounts of power, the Detective Sergeant's primary source of authority was his ability to influence those more powerful in the organisational hierarchy (Cummings and Huse 1989: 23).

Evidence of the influence of the embedded officers on the ODA's evolving outlook on anticorruption matters is highlighted in the creation of a Head of Fraud Prevention post. The new post reported to the Head of Internal Fraud:

> The first thing that we did was to persuade the ODA to appoint a Head of Fraud, although they re-named it Head of Fraud Prevention, because they did not like the negative connotations of Head of Fraud, and we wanted someone in there who had a focus for fraud issues.

The appointment of a Head of Fraud Prevention was a result of advice and lobbying by the Metropolitan Police Service (MPS), with the support of key leaders within the ODA, such as the Head and Deputy Head of Procurement. There was a difference between how the post was conceived by the MPS and the ODA beyond the name. The original job specification as envisaged by the Detective Inspector who designed the post, perceived the role as being dynamic with freedom to exercise autonomy in the aggressive identification of risk and areas of vulnerability. Despite the police's disappointment in the differing perceptions about the new post and its workings, the decision to create a new post was viewed as a success. The police summed up this experience in characteristic pragmatic terms (Bittner 1972):

> Although it was not exactly what we wanted it was good to have somebody there raising issues at the Board level and had that access.

The new appointment came from a banking background, similar to the Head of Internal Audit and other auditing staff, with little experience of the construction industry. He was assisted in his induction into the role by the Detective Inspector, whose responsibility it was to *chaperone* the post holder, until they became familiar with the job and its requirements. The work of the Head of Fraud Prevention involved assisting and facilitating the relationship between the imbedded officers with heads of ODA departments, in terms of support and access, and contributing to the establishment of the Olympic Park Construction Fraud Forum that he chaired and involved all major tier one companies. He also assisted in arranging training for ODA and LOCOG staff. In terms of investigatory dimension of the Head of Fraud Prevention's role, this consisted of dealing with cases of suspected fraud, many of which were not shared with the imbedded police officers, and the establishment of an ODA Star Group to address urgent issues that arose.

It is important to note on one occasion the decisions to award a contract was taken against the advice of the police, or issues of concern raised by them ignored, which underscores their purely advisory roles, and the differences in values and priorities between law enforcement agencies and commercial enterprises (Levy 1987). An important addition to the anticorruption architecture of the ODA was the Cross Verification Teams that were responsible for checking the accuracy of invoices (Kankaanranta and Muttilainen 2010). Although difficult to comment on its detailed workings, the existence of mechanisms such as the Cross Verification Teams must have contributed to increasing awareness about fraud within the ODA, especially those whose activities it inspected. This is also reflected in the introduction of an online system for declaring and monitoring gratuities and gifts received by ODA staff. Anything not declared by officials opened them to disciplinary and other forms of action. The importance of this practice is elaborated:

> If there were any issues they could go back and find out whether staff had declared anything or not. That's part of a prevention strategy and makes things more difficult. It's like keeping out burglars and whether you have an alarm in your home, whether you have shutters on your shop or business premises.

In one instance the Podium Team inadvertently were able to prevent a fraud involving the sum of £28 million, when an e-mail was sent accidentally to the wrong people. On closer examination it was identified that the original cost of the bid referred to in the e-mail had been changed, based on an insider's information. This resulted in a member of the ODA being dismissed. The Detective Superintendent elaborates on the incident:

> We got hold of phishing letter that went out to one of the payment departments purporting to be from one of the tier one construction companies, informing them that they had changed their bank details. Unfortunately, because there were no checks and balances they nearly got away with it, the bank account was changed and £2.4 million was transferred to an account in the first instance. We received a phone call a day or so before Operation Podium started, informing us of this. I only had a skeleton staff who picked up the case, and we got back £2.3 million and 15 people got arrested and most of the principal characters were imprisoned.

After the incident, police were instructed to investigate the matter:

> I sent my prevention team in to review their systems and processes and identified another fraud in progress, involving another £6 million. This was

shared with the industry and published in articles in industry magazines which helped educate people in preventing fraud both for the Olympics and generally.

The success in preventing these incidents of fraud was hailed as a major victory for Operation Podium team, and justified its rationale, and judgment in making preventing fraud in the building, and construction process its priority. The amount of money saved by their intervention dwarfed the costs of the embedded detectives and the entire Operation Podium Team, and underscores the rationale behind private sector security and other forms of police provision in proving their value in hard currency (Button and Wakefield 2014). Another lesson drawn from these experiences was how businesses are organized and the implications for preventing fraud, in terms of their internal structures, and areas of responsibilities. Traditionally those responsible for internal audit are primarily tasked with matters related to detecting fraud (Jones 2004: 81). The Detective Sergeant questions this conventional wisdom based on the ODA experience. He explains:

> There is a KPMG report somewhere that found 19 per cent of all fraud is detected by internal audit. Are they the best people to do this work?

He continues:

> No. There should be someone ahead of them looking at those risks, but as a business they are about generating money.

According to his view the emphasis of companies is to generate profit, not saving money, or fraud prevention, this results in the relegation of the internal audit activities to that of back office staff function. This results in offenses being detected (if at all), after they have been committed as opposed to proactively prevent them from occurring in the first instance.

A lot of initiatives introduced by the ODA to tackle corruption and bad practice were already widely known within the construction industry, such as whistle-blowing policies that encourage employees or anyone with information of wrong-doing, to share it with those in authority (Jones 2004). A whistle-blowing policy and line had already been established by the ODA, which was the responsibility of health and safety personnel to administer and investigate complaints. This was viewed as inappropriate by the police, given the lack of expertise of health and safety officials in matters around procurement fraud and related concerns, and their ability to identify the potentially critical issues that could be contained in reports made to them (Levy 1987: 141). Changes were made to the reporting system so that all whistle-blowing reports went to the Head of Fraud Prevention. Another change of a much more mundane nature, but potentially important was the location of posters advertising the existence of the whistle-blowing procedures, originally placed in common areas such as works canteens. This made it difficult for individuals to read the information without potentially drawing attention to themselves. This was resolved by a relatively simple course of action. The Detective Sergeant explains:

> We found it more helpful to put that information on the back of toilet doors so when people are "powdering their noses," so to speak, they can read the information in private.

The key lessons learnt about how to reduce the opportunity for fraud in public procurement demonstrated that it required changes at the most senior levels of the company to more mundane interventions at the shop floor level (UNODC 2013).

Problems with Tackling Fraud

One of the prerequisites of building the various construction projects for the Game was purchasing land from landowners, which raises another important set of challenges for the ODA, in anticipating and mitigating the scope for fraud, and other forms of abuse. The embedded police officers and Operation Podium Team worked closely with other police organizations, such as the British Transport Police, who were responsible for many of the areas that were affected by the compulsory purchase of land. The need to purchase land created numerous opportunities for fraud and other suspect practices, many of which were very difficult to tackle. One of the most obvious was ascertaining the financial loss that would be affected by the ODA's efforts to purchase land. The Detective Sergeant explains:

> Once you have government and MP saying that they were committed to ensuring that those people who would potentially be affected by the compulsory purchase order would not financially lose out, it creates the obvious problem of people inflating their potential loss which is difficult to check in any robust way given the serious time constraints involved.

The problem created by compulsory land purchase as described demonstrates the numerous opportunities for fraud on major construction projects, whether they be one-off actions or reoccurring in nature, and the near impossibility to eliminate them all (Goldstock 1990). Under these circumstances, law enforcement agencies must have clear priorities in the areas and types of offense they target (Goldstock 1990, Levy and Maguire 2004). According to the police respondents, the majority of suspected fraudulent activities in the context of the Games took place on the actual construction sites, and lower ranks of companies, many of which were hard to detect. An example of this was the difficulty of ensuring that the work paid for was actually carried out in ways initially agreed (Goldstock 1990, Fox 2004). This can be seen in the case of the removal of soil for the building of various structures, such as in making venues wheel chair accessible. This entailed making the ground flat which required the use of a handheld calibration device that calculates the amount of soil to be removed. The difficulties in limiting the fraudulent abuse of this device are explained by the Detective Sergeant:

> If I balance that device on my boot, instead of the ground, that will add two extra inches which means people can be paid for work which they have not done. There are all these little tricks of the trade which experienced contractors and builders are aware of.

The above highlights how difficult it is to eliminate fraudulent practices at the micro level of construction work. It also throws light on the plethora of ways in which these activities can take place across most occupation and task areas. Another practice that purported took place at the site level is explained:

> There was an allegation, and a typical one during the Olympics, that if you wanted to work on a building site you had to pay a foreman £2 a day per piece of equipment; a kind of surcharge and you would hear that allegation up and down the country.

In this instance, concern was raised with the ODA officials, along with the identity of the individual in question, who in turn approached the company involved, who investigated the matter. Although the company claimed to have found no evidence to support this allegation, it paid back money to many individuals on the construction site due to what it described as an *oversight*, and the individual in question was transferred to another site. This information was passed on to police and other authorities in the new area, where the individual in question was moved to by Operation Podium, underscoring that this was someone of potential further interest in intelligence terms.

In some instances, as already alluded to, difficulties in tackling bad practice was constrained by intrinsic conflicts of interest, forcing senior officials to withhold information from their police colleagues (Levy 1987). A typical type of example of this is where a high performing manager, who was making significant amounts of money, or saving their employers money, is suspected of unethical and unlawful behavior. In this type of instance, senior management are often very reluctant to take disciplinary action. Despite many types of abuses that can occur, and without a doubt went undetected during the Games, due to the wide range of discretion open to individuals in the construction project delivery chain, the evidence suggests that the strategy adopted by the ODA to tackle procurement fraud was successful. No fraud reports have been made by auditors four years after the completion of the event. Moreover, the ability to prevent major frauds in progress by embedded Podium Officers, due to the increased awareness of staff in the first instance, highlights the success of a crucial component of the tactics deployed that clearly worked.

Conclusion

The unique nature of mega events such as the Olympic and Paralympic Games in terms of its sheer size, the amounts of money involved, and the political and reputational consequences led to government responding to the challenges entailed in a very robust manner. First, in protecting the large numbers of people attending the event, and second in preventing a range of unseen economic crimes primarily in the area of procurement fraud that enjoyed the majority of public expenditure followed by ticketing fraud. White-collar crime historically often constitute offenses, which has serious consequences for society, that is underplayed given the traditional structure of the police and government crime agenda. The Metropolitan Police's SOECU to its credit, recognized very early into the preparations for the Games, the potential for major crime that saw the creation of Operation Podium, which represents a very unique initiative in world policing and the history of the Olympic Games. The primary incentive of the government for supporting the work of Operation Podium was in promoting Britain commercially as a proven and exceptionally competent and trustworthy place for foreign investment. This follows from the Beijing Games and the cloud of suspicion surrounding China around corruption that saw the Chinese authorities taking unprecedented efforts in the development of what was termed *sunshine projects* to maximize transparency (United Nations Convention Against Corruption 2013: 15). Similar concerns have rocked the international football association FIFA.

One of the important outcomes of the strategy adopted by the Operation Podium Team, in partnership with the ODA, was evidence of success in preventing forms of corruption and fraud in some instances, and the effectiveness of some innovative practices. An example of this was embedding detectives working with procurement staff, the employment of fraud prevention personnel, and the establishment of the cross verification teams to check invoices inter alia. Many of the limitations in attempting to prevent corrupt and criminal practices were also highlighted, which is underscored by the sheer difficulty in reducing crime, given the large number of vulnerable areas and ways that discretion can be used in the construction process of major projects. Never mind, the opportunities for fraud and other crimes in the processes that precede the actual planning phase of building project, such as compulsory land purchasing. Eliminating opportunities for crime is even more challenging at the construction site level (Goldstock 1990: 63).

Equally of importance are the self-interests of businesses and major contractors, in not wanting to reveal wrong doing of staff, or those under their control for any number of reasons. Despite the successes and limitations of the strategy developed to reduce and eliminate procurement fraud for the Games, perhaps one of the most important things that have come from it is the development and sharing of good practice in many areas covered by this chapter. The MPS has shared its experience in planning the Games with numerous organizations domestically and internationally, similar to Police Scotland in the context of its role within the Commonwealth Games,[4] to assist others.

Operation Podium and other key MPS leaders involved in the Games played an invaluable role in preparing Police Scotland to lead and coordinate the Commonwealth Games. Many aspects of the ODA's work have been cited as best practice in combating corruption in planning for major international events by the United Nations Office on Drugs and Crime (2013). However, missing from this report is any detailed discussion about the crucial role of the police and Operation Podium. Other aspects of technical practice that came from the Games, such as its construction budgeting strategy, and procurement system has also been promoted by various agencies as best practice, which underscores the enduring legacy of the Olympics to the area of building and construction work and law enforcement.

Notes

1. www.projectgenesus.org.
2. See www.freshfields.com. Retrieved January 18, 2016.
3. See   http://content.met.police.uk/Article/Operation-Podium/1400005479316/ 1400005470676.
4. Interview with Deputy Chief Constable Police Scotland 2014.

References

Albanese, S. (2008). Risk Assessment in Organized Crime: Developing a Market and Product-Based Model to Determine Threat Levels, *Journal of Contemporary Criminal Justice*, Vol. 24: 263–273.

Babbington, A. (2000). Four Arrested in Millennium Dome Fraud Probe, www. independent.co.uk, October 12. Retrieved March 5, 2014.

Bird, S. (2005). Prison for Dome Chief Over £4 Million, www.thetimes.co.uk, September 14. Retrieved January 30, 2014.

Bittner, E. (1972). *The Functions of the Police in Modern Society: A Review of Background Factors, Current Practices, and Possible Role Models.* Washington, D.C.: National Institute of Mental Health.

Bullock, K., Clarke, R. and Tilley, N. (eds.) (2010). Situational Prevention of Organised Crime. Collumpton, UK: Willan.

Button, M. and Wakefield, A. (2014). New Perspectives on Police Education and Training: Lessons from the Private Security Sector, in Stanislas, P. (ed.) *International Perspective on Police Education and Training*, London, UK: Routledge.

Cummings, T. and Huse, E. (1989). *Organisation Development and Change*, 4th Edition, New York: West Publishing.

Dorn, N., Levi, M. and White, S. (2008). Do European Procurement Rules Generate or Prevent Crime, *Journal of Financial Crime*, Vol. 15(3): 243–260.

Ekblom, P. (2002). Organised Crime and the Conjunction of Criminal Opportunity Framework, in Piquero, A. and Tibbetts, S. (eds.), Rational Choice and Criminal Behaviour, London, UK: Routledge.

Fox, S. (2014). Guide to Construction Procurement Strategies, www.slideshare.net/sarahjvfox. Retrieved November 30, 2015.

Fussey, P. (2011). Surveillance and the Olympics, in A. Richards, P. Fussey, and P. Silke (eds.), *Terrorism and the Olympics: Major Event Security and Lessons for the Future*, London, UK: Routledge.

Gardiner, J. (2013). Construction Fraud Costs $1Trillon Globally, www.building.co.uk, October 25. Accessed July 10, 2010.

Goldstock, R. (1990). Corruption and Racketeering in the New York City Construction Industry. New York: New University Press.

Harriot, A. (2008). Organised Crime in Jamaica. Jamaica: Canoe Press.

Jones, P. (2004). Fraud and Corruption in Public Services, A guide to Risk and Prevention. Aldershot, UK: Gower Publishing.

Justice, A. (2015). Kenya Demands Apology from CNN over Terror Comments Ahead of Visit of President Obama, www.Ibitimes.co. July 24. Retrieved July 27, 2015.

Kankaanranta, T. and Muttilainen, V. (2010). Economic Crimes in the Construction Industry: The Case of Finland, *Journal of Financial Crime,* Vol. 17(4): 417–429.

Levi, M. and Maguire, M. (2004). Reducing and Preventing Organised Crime: An Evidence-Based Critique, *Crime, Law and Social Change*, Vol. 41: 397–469.

Levy, M. (1987). Regulating Fraud: White Collar Crime and the Criminal Process, Tavistock Publications Ltd, Cambridge University Press, Cambridge.

Maguire, J. (2005). Power and Global Sport: Zones of Prestige, Emulation and Resistance. London, UK: Routledge.

Neyroud, P. and Wain, N. (2014). New Perspectives on Police Education and Training, Lessons from the Private Sector, in P. Stanislas (ed.) *International Perspective on Police Education and Training*, London, UK: Routledge.

Osei, V. (2013). The Construction Industry and its Linkages to Ghanaian Economic Policies to Improve the Sectors Performance, *International Journal of Development and Economic Sustainability*, Vol. 1(1): 56–72.

Reid, G. and Scott, G. (1994). Public Human Resource Management in Latin America and the Caribbean, in Chaudhry, S., Reid, G. and Waleed, M. (eds.) *Civil Service Reform in Latin America and the Caribbean*, The World Bank, Washington, D.C.

Ruddock, G. (2011). London 2012 Olympics: The Olympic Stadium Made in Britain, www.telegraph.co.uk, July 16. Retrieved January 19, 2016.

Savona, E.U. (2010). Infiltration of the Public Construction Industry by Italian Organised Crime, in Bullock, K., Clarke, R. and Tilley, N. (eds.), *Situational Prevention of Organised Crime*, Cullompton, UK: Willan.

Schilling, D. (2013). Global Construction Industry Expected to Increase by $4.8 Trillion by 2020, www.industrytap.com, March 8. Accessed July 10, 2013.

Stanislas, P. (2014). Police Leadership and the Management of Mega-Events: Policing the London 2012 Olympics and Paralympic Games, in D. Das and D. Plecas (eds.) *International Perspectives on Policing Major Events*. New York: CRC Press.

Stanislas, P. (2016). The Challenge of Postcolonial Political and Social Leadership: Building Inclusive Citizenship, Safety and Security in East Africa, in L. Ruttere and K. Mkutu (eds.), *East African Policing*, Suffolk, VA: James Currey.

The Telegraph (2005). Designer Jailed for £4 Million Millennium Dome Fraud, www.telegraph.co.uk, September 13. Retrieved July 24, 2014.

Tombs, S. and Whyte, D. (2007). *Safety Crimes*, Cullompton, UK: Willan.

Vander Beken, T. and Van Dael, S. (2008). Legitimate Business and Crime Vulnerabilities, *International Journal of Social Economies*, Vol. 35(10): 739–750.

Walsh, F. (2007). MacAlpine Hit By Accounting Black hole at Welsh Mining Slate Quarry, www.theguardian.com, February 27. Retrieved January 13, 2014.

Wayne, R. (2010). Lapses and Infelicities: An Insider's Perspective of Politics in the Caribbean. St Lucia: Star Publishing Co Ltd Lucia.

Reports

Construction Manager (2013). Construction Fraud Cost Clients and Contractors Billions, www.construction-manager.co.uk, October 25. Retrieved July 10, 2013.

Department of Environment Food and Rural Affairs (2013). London 2012 Olympic and Paralympic Games: The Legacy: Sustainable Procurement for Construction Projects, A Guide.

House of Commons Library (2013). The Construction Industry: Statistics and Policy.

National Audit Office (2012). The London 2012 Olympic Games and Paralympic Games: post Games Review. www.nao.org.uk. Retrieved September 5, 2013.

Price Waterhouse Cooper (2014). Global Economic Crime Survey. www.pwh.com. Retrieved February 12, 2015.

Serious Fraud Office Annual Report (2009). www.gov.uk. Retrieved February 21, 2015.

United Nations Convention Against Corruption (2013). A Strategy for Safeguarding against Corruption in Major Public Events, United Nations Office on Drugs and Crime.

Zayas, D. (2012). Delivering London 2012: Managing the Construction of Olympic Park, www.p2sl.berkerly.edu. Retrieved December 15, 2015.

Other Nations

Tackling Corruption in the sub-Saharan African Extraction Industries

8

KENNEDY MKUTU AGADE
PERRY STANISLAS

Contents

Introduction

This chapter explores the strategic importance of the extractive industries in sub-Saharan Africa, the major issues involved in regulating it, and some of the outcomes and consequences. It focusses on the issue of corruption in the extraction industries and its social, economic, and other impacts, particularly with regard to the criminal justice system, and the security sector. It interrogates the theories and explanations for this corruption and the various ramifications. This chapter is an exploration of the attempts to regulate the extractive industries, and the successes and problems associated with this enterprise. Finally, the chapter will provide a case study of extractive industries in East Africa, and how many of the aforementioned issues manifest in this region of the African continent.

The Extractive Industry in sub-Saharan Africa

The killing of Patrice Lumumba, the newly elected prime minister of the Congo and its first independent leader in 1961, with the complicity and involvement of the United States and its Central Intelligence Agency, took place against the backdrop of fear about the control of precious natural resources (Nzongola-Ntalaja 2011). This occurred against a history of Belgian colonial rule, one of the most brutal and genocidal regimes witnessed on the African continent, that resulted in the killing of 10 million Congolese over a period of around 20 years in the ruthless, inhuman exploitation of people to access the valuable resources found in this naturally blessed part of Africa (Ankomah 1999).

The richness of the natural resources of African countries has shaped so much of its unfortunate past, as it has in the contemporary age, whether it has been the uranium that provided the source material for the first atomic bomb, or the coltan used to produce the microchips that drive postmodern technology such as mobile phones (Essick 2011, Nzongola-Ntalaja 2011). The extractive industries are critical to the economies of sub-Saharan Africa and its relationship to the outside world and their economies. From a strategic perspective, African countries provide natural resources critical to the industries of global economies. West Africa provides 12% of the oil and gas supplies to the West, with Nigeria providing one third of the petroleum consumed by the United States, and Angola supplying China with one third of its energy needs (Burgis and Chitoyo 2012).

The Niger Delta produces 90% of Nigeria's commercial crude, and accounts for roughly 70% of government revenue. The total dollar amounts are staggering. According to the Organization of the Petroleum Exporting Countries (OPEC), Nigeria made $77 billion from oil exports in 2014— and that was a low year. The U.S. Department of Energy says Nigeria's oil export earnings hit $99 billion in 2011. (The figures were $94 billion and $84 billion for 2012 and 2013, respectively.) Much of the wealth however, which is supposed to flow back to the states from the federal government, is simply siphoned off. A recent federal government audit showed that the state-owned Nigerian National Petroleum Corporation (NNPC) failed to pay $16 billion in revenue that it owed to the state treasury in 2014 alone. (NNPC officials disputed that figure, claiming it was closer to $1 billion). The revelation came after the then-Central Bank Governor Lamido Sanusi, accused the NNPC of failing to pay $20 billion to the federal government between January 2012 and July 2013. (Sanusi was immediately suspended after making the accusation and eventually forced out of his job.) Although benefits have passed them by, communities have borne the costs of environmental degradation. The discovery of oil in 1956 forever changed the face of the Niger Delta. Located in the southernmost part of Nigeria, it is the largest mangrove swamp in Africa and the third largest in the world. Its dense forest and complex labyrinth of creeks and waterways breathes life into over 339 plant species and more than 100 species of birds and fish. Tall palm trees with thick branches stretch upward before bending to touch the water below. The natural wonder stretches for miles and miles, but today it's only a fragment of what it once was.[*]

For most of the 2000s, an insurgency fueled by bitter resentment claimed thousands of lives and, at its height, cut Nigeria's oil production in half. Now, after a brief respite, it is beginning to reemerge. In August 2016, a militant group calling itself the Niger Delta Avengers has already claimed three separate attacks on oil installations, and promised to cut the country's oil output to zero. The Ijaw Youth Council, an influential grassroots organization that has its origins in the armed struggle of the 2000s and advocates for local control of natural resources, said in June 2016 that the security situation is "rapidly deteriorating and getting out of control."[†]

Much of Africa's natural resources have yet to be exploited, or have only recently begun to be extracted for industrial use. For example, Guinea has one of the largest underdeveloped iron ore deposits in the world; the Democratic Republic of the Congo (DRC) has the largest supply of cobalt (Burgis and Chitoyo 2012, Essick 2001), and Burkino Faso is the fourth largest gold producer in the world (Blair 2014). Africa is the home of the 20 most natural resource-rich nations in the world (Kateta 2015). The Metals Economic Group data for 2013 shows that Africa enjoyed the second highest level of investment for mining exploration after Latin America, while in the period 2003–2007 it received the highest amount of investment for these purposes. This demonstrates that the demand for mine-based products remains largely constant, but is difficult to sustain without new sources of material (Standing 2007).

Corruption and Procurement Fraud in African Extraction Industries

Le Billon (2005) notes that funds in the extractive areas often risk being captured by politicians, and are subject to corruption. An estimated U.S. $1.4 trillion has disappeared from the sub-Saharan African economy due to corruption from 1980–2009, which represents more money than direct aid and investment into the region's economy (Patrick 2014). A conservative estimate puts the loss due to corruption at billions of U.S. dollars annually (Patrick 2014). A significant amount of that money is assumed to come from the extractive industries, given the large amount of monies involved that

---

[*] Chika Oduah (2016). Trouble Is Brewing in Nigeria's Oil Country. http://foreignpolicy.com/2016/06/14/trouble-is-brewing-in-nigerias-oil-country, accessed June 15, 2016.

[†] Chika Oduah (2016). Trouble Is Brewing in Nigeria's Oil Country. http://foreignpolicy.com/2016/06/14/trouble-is-brewing-in-nigerias-oil-country, accessed June 15, 2016.

can relatively easily be diverted into private hands (Standing 2007, OECD Bribery Report 2014: 15). The issue of corruption has been posited as being critical in the poverty and underdevelopment of numerous African countries that include Nigeria (detailed in depth in Chapter 9), Angola, and the DRC inter alia, and has been a source of bitter acrimony and tensions. In South Africa, allegations of corruption have plagued the tenure of President Jacob Zuma (www.allafrican.com 2016), and have also become a major concern in Ethiopia (Kebede 2016).

According to the Organization for Economic Cooperation and Development in 2014, nearly 20% of foreign bribery cases involved the extractive industries, and this finding was particularly prevalent in developing countries (OECD Foreign Bribery Report 2014). The alleged financial benefits of corruption related to the extractive industries can be seen in the case of Angola, Africa's second largest oil exporter, where in 2003 approximately 50 Angolans in public office were estimated to possess a personal wealth worth $50 million, with 10 members of the government elite being worth $100 million, and the President believed to be among the wealthiest in the country (Standing 2007: 5).

The "resource curse" (Standing 2007: 4, Mkutu and Wandera 2016: 4) refers to the variety of problems, which accompany resource wealth, in particular to the distorting and detrimental impact on the national economy, whereby resource wealth, which is subject to fluctuations structurally contributes to underdevelopment. In oil producing Trinidad and Tobago, the neglect of agricultural production and self-sufficiency in the provision of food has led to greater dependency and poverty (Pino 2012, Jatto and Stanislas 2016). Another illustration of this is the destruction of the textile industry in Northern Nigeria due to the nations dependency on oil and subsequent currency inflation linked to it (Burgis and Chitoyo 2012: 3). With regard to this corruption, however, several writers have commented on how resource wealth may lead to the breakdown in democratic structures (Ross 2001; Fearon and Laitin 2003; Humphreys 2005; Snyder and Bhavnani 2005), a phenomenon to be discussed in more detail in the following section.

Corruption may be a factor in the exclusion of local people and their representatives from decision-making, when contracts between governments and the investors in extractive resources take place behind closed doors. Societal conflicts of various types may follow, focusing on rewards and opportunities from the industry. Ross (2008) comments that corruption and crime together with local grievance contribute to the increased risk of insurgency and separatism in oil rich countries.

A deep sense of grievance about unfairness and inequalities can be seen by the response of poor and unemployed black youth in South Africa, who cite the granting of very lucrative contracts by governmental elites to families and friends (www.allafrica.com 2016). Similar sentiments are highlighted by Mkutu and Wandera (2016: 19) in the response of local people in Turkana, Kenya, to what is perceived as exclusion from the economic opportunities brought about by extractive companies in their communities, as well as fears about threats to their pastoral livelihoods and land access and environmental degradation. The most extreme form these tensions can take is military coups and power struggles within state institutions. This is illustrated in the overthrow of Lumumba in the Congo, and Thomas Sankara in gold rich Burkina Faso (Blair 2014), and in Niger (Burgis and Chityo 2012: 4). Conflict about the impacts of petroleum production and its spoils were the driving force in the state killing of activist Ken Saro Wiwa and eight of his colleagues in the Delta region of Nigeria (Stanislas 2014: 229). One of the points of contention that led to the death of these activists was the environmental damage caused by petroleum production affecting the livelihood and agriculture of local people. Similar concerns have been highlighted by Mkutu and Wandera (2016: 17–18) and the Council on Foreign Relations (2014), in terms of the impact of the extractive industries on local livestock, and fishing and access to water and pastoral lands. The serious damage these industries can have on the environment can include soil contamination, land erosion, air and water pollution inter alia (Standing 2007: 11–12, see White 2011).

Greed theories on resource and conflict deserve a brief mention, Collier and Hoeffler (2004) conclude that resources can provide motivation and opportunity for insurgencies, which may happen through the looting or control of access to those resources. *Greed* motivations may combine with other factors such as grievances and weak governance to increase the likelihood of conflict (Mkutu and Wandera, 2016).

Understanding Corruption and Procurement Matters in the Extraction Industries

Although corruption is usually associated with politicians, tribal elites, civil servants, and administrators who run state bureaucracies, how it is conceived and explained, and the various forms it can take require further interrogation. The most conventional view of corruption is the abuse of public office for private gain, and usually takes the form of members of government or officials receiving *kickbacks* for giving companies or other interests, unfair advantages in obtaining contracts or in negotiating particular details or terms of such agreements (Standing 2007, Burgis and Chitoyo 2012, Mkutu and Wandera 2016). Corruption can also take the form of *skimming*, where sums of money are taken from agreed payment or in the forms of bonuses or *royalty payments*, for negotiating contracts in the extractive industries. The extremely large sum of money generated in this sector has spurned a whole range of ways in which payments by companies or foreign governments, find their way into private hands. Often this money is paid directly or takes the form of gifts, or some other benefit to family members or agents (OECD Foreign Bribery Report 2014: 28).

Corruption can also include politicians or civil servants colluding with private sector contractors to inflate costs, either to take money directly, or to offset tax liabilities (Blair 2014: 5). These forms of activity have often been called *grand corruption* (Standing 2007: 4, Council on Foreign Relations 2014, Patrick 2014), and is closely associated with countries, which lack basic infrastructure and transparency that enables the public or civil society to monitor the revenues gained from the nation's resources (Burgis and Chitoyo 2012: 6, Standing 2007: 3). By the same token, these features of government and society are also associated with totalitarian regimes and state corruption. According to Standing (2007), corruption in these instances is both a cause and symptom of deeper institutional and societal problems. A popular theory of state corruption advanced by Mahdavy (1970, cited in Standing 2007) has at its heart the notion of the rentier state that seeks to explain how the exploitation of natural resources contributes to the erosion of democracy and government accountability. The theory posits that the political and governmental elite are able to solicit undisclosed rents in resource-rich countries, which displaces the need for direct tax revenue that contributes to institutionalizing the different interests between those who rule and the ruled.

Political systems in sub-Saharan African countries are invariably based on competition among elites who seek to access the rents they are able to levy from the natural resources of the country, as opposed to engaging in rent producing activity, via good economic management and taxation (Mahdavy cited in Standing 2007: 4). Public spending in these political systems is not used for the public good, such as the building of new roads and adequate infrastructure, but in preserving the status quo. An essential element of maintaining power is weakening the key institutions of the state, such as the police, and criminal justice system, the media, academia and civil society, by a combination of patronage, corruption, and intimidation (Stanislas 2016b). It is not uncommon that the military and the police are co-opted into the systemic corruption of the state in the persecution of dissenters and rivals to the status quo (Standing 2007: 4, Council on Foreign Relations 2014: 4, Stanislas 2016). Taxation authorities are often weak in many developing countries, which makes it much easier for corrupt practices to occur (Burgis and Chitoyo 2012: 5). Standing (2007) explains the outcome of these dynamics:

> In this rentier state model the wealth derived from natural resources may result in a form of centralised government that is secretive, aggressive, paranoid, and uninterested in public welfare.

This explains why so many natural resource-rich African countries are among some of the poorest and underdeveloped in the world and highlighted by the: higher poverty rates, malnutrition, mortality rates, low amounts of money spent on health care, and low levels of adult literacy inter alia (Standing 2007: 4). The corrupt activities of government are only one dimension of the corruption dynamic. The other dimension is the role of corporations in bringing about the conditions to facilitate corruption of officials and government elites. Companies have been exposed paying bribes and other forms of inducement in order to obtain advantage in procurement matters, which is highlighted in the Haliburton controversy in Nigeria (Daniel 2014, Standing 2007: 6).

Many companies are averse to participating in corrupt activities, which are against their values and image. Moreover, the cost of illicit practices is often expensive in political, legitimacy, and financial terms by bringing respectable companies into close association with very unsavory characters, such as rebel military leaders, which can have negative effects on potential investors (Standing 2007: 6). However, the competition between rival companies to access natural resources, provides the elites in developing countries strong bargaining positions, being able to play companies off each other, in order to achieve favorable outcomes. At the same time competition between companies may lead to them using bribery to gain advantage (OECD Foreign Bribery Report 2014). It is misleading, as Standing (2007) points out, to view foreign companies simply as victims of circumstances that they have little control over, which in many instances is a convenient depiction. The concept of state capture, which is elucidated by Standing (2007), demonstrates the ways powerful corporations are able to shape, if not dictate in many instances, the terms by which it operates in many countries, particularly in the developing world, given the superior power of the former.

Very often the tactics used to gain governmental compliance can involve foreign corporations threatening to withdraw from a country if they do not obtain terms advantageous to them. This can be seen in the area of environmental crime and the way companies can evade the law or have policies put in place that suit their profit maximizing against the national and public interests (White 2011: 93–95). Often it is cheaper from the companies' point of view to pay bribes than complying with regulations, such in the area of environmental protection (Burgis and Chitoyo 2012: 5). According to the state capture thesis, the state is simply a tool of foreign corporations in the pursuit of their objectives (Standing 2007: 4). The police, military and courts, according to this view, are often used to regulate, persecute, and in the final instance, even kill dissenters. In many respects it is often difficult to separate the interests of foreign companies and local elites (Obi 2010), which contributes to obfuscation and lack of conceptual clarity when speaking about theories and models of corruption such as notions of *grand corruption* or state capture (Standing 2007: 8–9).

Therefore simple explanations or one-dimensional theories are inadequate to explain corruption in the extractive industries. For example, in 2004, a U.S. Senate special investigation into the conduct of many U.S. based oil companies abroad (including Exxon, Chevron, Texaco and Mobile), found that these companies paid millions of dollars in bribes to obtain oil drilling rights, to reduce tax liabilities, and to avoid environmental regulations. Among the charges made against some U.S. based oil companies, was money laundering in assisting many powerful members of the government elite, to get very large sums of money out of the country (Standing 2007: 8, Burgis and Chitoyo 2012: 5).

Although the profile around matters concerning corruption has increased over the past couple of decades due to the actions of NGOs, and influential transnational organizations such as the United Nations, the media, and other representatives of civil society (Blair 2014, Kateta 2015, Standing 2007: 14), less progress has been made in the area of legal prosecutions, which has undermined much of the campaigning work to increase awareness on the issue of corruption. Public confidence in anti-corruption rests on successful convictions that are few and far between, both in developed and developing countries. Transparency International monitored OECD conventions passed on the issue of corruption, and in 2005 discovered that only three of the 24 signatory countries had more than one conviction for a corruption related matter, and 13 countries had no successful prosecutions at all. What is particularly interesting is that many western countries with interests in the extractive industries such as Australia, Canada, and Britain had some of the weakest records of prosecutions (Standing 2007: 14).

Part of the reason for lack of prosecutions is the nature of many white-collar crimes (covered in this collection), in that in the immediate instance the offence may seem as though it is victimless, and if uncovered only comes to light usually well after the offense has occurred (See Stanislas Chapter 7); further in accordance with convenience theory, these crimes takes place in such conditions that make it very difficult to detect. Bribes often involve complex sets of activities, including the use of offshore transactions and multiple intermediaries and structures (OECD 2014: 15). Moreover, this is exacerbated in an environment where public accountability in terms of media exposure or independent investigation is literally nonexistent.

There are several barriers to legal prosecutions other than those already mentioned. Many companies enter agreements such as profit sharing arrangements that create a disincentive for governments to prosecute, or to frustrate legal challenges from other parties (Standing 2007: 15). Equally, the extractive industries often occupy an important strategic geopolitical role of resources such as oil to the economies of western countries. An example of this was the lack of action on behalf of the British government in response to complaints by United Nations experts about the practices of British mining firms in the DRC. By the same token, French investigators looking into the practices of company, Elf Africaine experienced considerable obstacles placed in their way by the French government that led to the investigation taking years. In addition, investigators experienced death threats resulting in them being forced to have police protection (Stanislas 2016a).

The OECD introduced its Anti-Bribery Convention in May 1997, which came into force in 1999. The signatory countries included many of the world's leading economies, and the most developed countries in Latin America, with South Africa being the only African country to be a participant in this process. The Convention was amended in 2009 and its membership currently stands at 41 countries. It recommended the introduction of a range of actions and sanctions, to tackle the attempts to bribe foreign officials. Article 3 of the Anti-Bribery Convention outlines the sanctions recommended for bribery:

1. The bribery of a foreign public official shall be punishable by effective, proportionate, and dissuasive criminal penalties. The range of penalties shall be comparable to that applicable to the bribery of the Party's own public officials and shall, in the case of natural persons, include deprivation of liberty sufficient to enable effective mutual legal assistance and extradition.

2. In the event that, under the legal system of a Party, criminal responsibility is not applicable to legal persons, that Party shall ensure that legal persons shall be subject to effective, proportionate and dissuasive non-criminal sanctions, including monetary sanctions, for bribery of foreign public officials.

3. Each Party shall take such measures as may be necessary to provide that the bribe and the proceeds of the bribery of a foreign public official, or property the value of which corresponds to that of such proceeds, are subject to seizure and confiscation or that monetary sanctions of comparable effect are applicable.

4. Each Party shall consider the imposition of additional civil or administrative sanctions upon a person subject to sanctions for the bribery of a foreign public official.

The OECD Anti-Bribery Report (2014) provides an interesting analysis of the occurrence of bribery based on reports from 1999–2013. The research informing the analysis was based on 427 cases drawn from 17 countries who were signatories to the Anti-Bribery Convention. It found that two-thirds of foreign bribery cases were found in four economic sectors, with the extractive industries having the most (19%) construction (15%), transportation and storage (15%), and information and communication (10%). An interesting for bribery, which have been adopted since the introduction of the OECD Anti-Bribery Convention came into being, between 2003 and 2011, the number of instances where sanctions have been enforcement has declined. One of the key factors for this outcome is the length of time to complete bribery investigations. The average time to complete bribery investigations increased to average of 7.3 years and in a few occasion have taken as long as 15 years. The evidence shows that corruption investigations are taking longer to conclude. The report highlights a number of factors in this, including length of appeal procedures, growing complexity of investigations and uncovering offenses that can involve transnational inquiries in trying to trace financial transactions.

The majority of reports of bribery were brought to light through self disclosure, often as an outcome of a range of organizational activities such as mergers and takeovers, and the work of accountants and auditors who found financial irregularities resulting in companies or senior staff disclosing this information, not uncommonly in a desire to mitigate any problems they may experience (OECD Anti-Bribery Report 2014: 15). Among the numerous recommendation made by the OECD to tackle bribery, is that signatories take steps to increase awareness, and greater use of criminal sanctions. Out of 427 cases of suspected bribery, the OECD found 80 (19%) led to imprisonment, and 38 (9%) suspended sentences. There were 261 (61%) instances of individuals and companies being forced to pay criminal/civil fines, 82 (19%) confiscations, and 12 (3%) instances of where offenders being forced to pay compensation.

Anti-Corruption Discourse, Practice, and Assumptions

Tackling corruption, especially in the extractive industries, has become increasingly important, and has drawn the support of major countries such as the United States and Britain who are playing an influential role in keeping the topic on the international agenda (Standing 2007: 21, Patrick 2014, Withnall 2016). One anti-corruption initiative that has drawn some support has been the notion of increasing transparency, thus decreasing the discretion of power elites, and government officials by publishing information on financial transactions, accounts, and internal reports. This is believed to assist the public, NGOs, and representatives of civil society to hold government and companies to account (Standing 2007, Patrick 2014). This emphasis on increasing transparency among reformers, although not without value is rooted on some questionable assumptions, which skate over many concerns. First, much of the information that the government may publish regarding its financial transactions is not easily understood by a lay audience and can involve some very complex information (Standing 2007, Patrick 2014). At bare minimum there is a serious training and educational need to assist wider society to engage with this process, as desired by various agencies and stakeholders. Second, many partners including government have potentially a vested interest in not making crucial information widely available, particularly if it has importance for its competitive advantage over rivals.

Third, another set of criticisms is that the focus of anti-corruption reform is too narrow and should place more emphasis on effective investigations and political and legal accountability (Burgis and Chitoyo 2012: 4, Standing 2007). Standing has stressed that effectively tackling corruption in the extractive industries is a technically challenging and complex enterprise, and requires a drastic improvement in the levels of policing capabilities to effectively regulate it. For example, in many instances such as in oil production, crucial decisions, which are open to potential corruption, are made years before any profit is generated, and outside any formal structure of arrangements that reformers seek to regulate (Standing 2007: 17). There are a plethora of areas of discretion in the various processes (both formal and informal) used by companies and governments that can conceal corrupt practices. An example of this is case of the Chad-Cameroon oil project that has been cited by the World Bank as a model of good practice, where transparency and anti-corruption practice is concerned. However, as Standing (2007) highlights, the decision concerning bonus agreements was signed outside the formal framework agreement.

The scope of the challenge facing anti-corruption reformers, in limiting the discretion of important decision-makers, and identifying and addressing the numerous gaps in the system or systems involved, can encompass trying to restrict potentially deviant behavior of multinational companies, and their interface with governments, officials and banks often located in third countries. Another area of concern is the revolving door practices where former politicians or administrators from natural resource-rich developing countries end up on the board of directors of foreign private companies, and exploit their insider knowledge and contacts to get around formal systems of accountability inter alia (Standing 2007).

Perhaps Standing's most important contribution to the discussion about corruption and the extractive industries in Africa, and no doubt elsewhere, is challenging the empirically untested, and taken for granted assumptions that have shaped much of the thinking of anti-corruption reformers. In fact some countries, such as Angola and several Asian countries, have experienced significant economic growth, which coexisted with clear evidence of corrupt practices (Standing 2007). Moreover, clarity is required to establish what are the key values and priorities that anti-corruption reformers are trying to maximize? Is their aim to achieve greater economic efficiency and growth, protect the environment or to establish democratic control, and authority over unaccountable governmental systems? Alternatively the lack of accountability of multinational companies at the expense of the citizens' power can also constitute a major plank in the narrative and agendas of reformers (White 2011).

The Extractive Industries Transparency Initiative (EITI) is the most popular development, which has taken place as response to demands for greater accountability and anti-corruption practice. EITI requires governments and companies to reveal contract details, and produce annual reports to demonstrate how signatory members have implemented good practice (Patrick 2004, Council on Foreign Relations 2014: 4). Views about this development are mixed. Some members question the effectiveness of the initiative (2014: 4), whereas other stakeholders view the EITI as being very positive. In particular it is seen as a model of good practice with regard to its governing board that consists of all key stakeholders such as NGOs and civil society interest (Council on Foreign Relations 2014: 4). There are many problems with the EITI and similar reforms, as already mentioned, but in particular even in developed societies there is a lack of expertise on extractive industries among civil society groups, and in many developing countries groups are unable to participate in such initiatives, due to victimization by governments such as in Liberia and Azerbaijan (Council on Foreign Relations 2014: 6). This creates an ethical dilemma of whether to allow repressive regimes to participate in these types of initiatives or not.

Despite the problems with initiatives such as EITI, it has had some effect in West Africa. Nigeria has introduced the Nigeria Extractive Industries Initiative, whereby government and oil companies have begun to publish information, in response to the barrage of criticism and allegations of widespread corruption with members of the elite living what some have described as *rock star life styles* amidst widespread poverty (Council on Foreign Relations 2014: 5, see Chapter 9, Stanislas and Iyah 2016). Ghana is the only West African country to be a signatory of EITI, and has also been proactive in ensuring that Tullow Oil company publishes its production agreement and related information (Council on Foreign Relations 2014). Several countries such as Britain, South Korea, and the Europe passed legislation to ensure that payments to foreign governments for oil and gas are published (Patrick 2014).

The Cases of Turkana and Mtwara

Mtwara is Tanzania's southernmost region, and the site of natural gas discovery in 2013. The region is marginalized and underdeveloped, and illiteracy is high. Turkana county in Kenya, where oil was discovered in

2012 is similarly underdeveloped, in the semi-arid northwest of the country, where nomadic pastoralism is the main economic activity. Through colonial and postcolonial regimes these seemingly unproductive areas were not afforded state penetration, in terms of development and provision of state services, nor administrative and security structures (Mkutu 2015). Now that the areas have resource wealth, the stakes for control of the area with its benefits are now high, but governance is likely to be a challenge. Both areas have witnessed riots by the local communities voicing their frustrations about the negative impacts and lack of benefits to themselves.

One concern in both Mtwara and Turkana is the lack of transparency surrounding the production sharing agreements between the investor and the national governments, which were concluded in Dar es Salaam and Nairobi with little knowledge of the local communities, and have since been the subject of heated debates. The production sharing agreement for Mtwara, between Tanzanian Petroleum Development Corporation (TPDC) and the Norwegian multinational Statoil, along with Exxon Mobile, raised important questions about transparency in 2014. A leaked document suggested that a contract that would benefit Tanzanians significantly through an eventual 80% share was discarded, and a final share of 50% was agreed on, the reasons for which are unclear.* Zitto Kabwe, a member of parliament and Chairman of the Public Accounts Committee commented on the issue in a blog and critiqued the fact that the contents of the agreement were not made publically available. This also illustrates the growing public awareness and dissatisfaction on the way in which the government handles such contracts and demand for information.

In Turkana the production-sharing contract for (10BB/13T) blocks were signed prior to 2010, when Kenya's new constitution called for a more participatory approach. The local government structure at the time, Turkana county council, was excluded from the discussions, and the new structure, the county government is now attempting to catch up and respond to the issues raised by the industry. Lack of participation has continued to be a common complaint by local communities, leading to many protests and road blocks. One demonstration halted operations for three weeks, whereas another besieged an oil site for four days and laid claim to all supplies entering by truck. These activities have been somewhat effective in forcing companies to improve communication with local people, and to employ more locals in unskilled jobs.

Another issue, in which participation has been hindered, is that of environmental impact of the industry. Statutory environmental impact assessments (EIAs) in Turkana have been deemed inadequate by a civil society organization, which is concerned that consultants may be biased by their

---

* The Citizen (2014) $1 billion loss: who's fooling Tanzanians? corrected July 14.

funding that comes through the investor. Reports are also supposed to be publically available, but these are in practice very large and difficult to access, download, and comprehend. No popular versions have been provided and this makes it almost impossible for the communities to participate and to question them, which is a legal right (Mkutu and Wandera, 2016).

In Turkana, non-public negotiations between a subcontractor to the oil company and a civil society organization took place to create conservancies in the county. These large portions of land are demarcated and overseen by the National Rangelands Trust in other parts of the country for the purposes of conservation, including security management using teams of rangers, and attempts to benefit the community through ecotourism and land use management; the trust also protects the interests of landowners who choose to turn their land into conservancies. However, the plans were made without adequately involving the county government and sufficient sectors of the community. Moreover, the impact on traditionally negotiated land access and management was not well understood. Finally there were significant concerns about the *buying* of state security to protect investors' interests, and the prospect of semiprivate armed teams of rangers in the areas that are already conflict prone. A stakeholders forum eventually highlighted the dangers to the county government and the plans were halted. It was also revealed that one investor interested in creating a conservancy paid elders 30,000 Kshs each, which ensured that they spoke in favour of the investor. The various interested parties and potentials for control of the benefits of oil wealth are evident in this example.

Land grabbing and allocation for investment is an enormous problem in East Africa. In Turkana, the majority of land is community land, being owned collectively by pastoralists and held in trust by the county (Land Act, 2012). To facilitate the security of this tenure the Community Land Bill (2014) is set to provide for communities to register their collectively owned land in order to secure their interests. The complex steps involved however, may be out of reach for the unschooled communities, and may easily be dominated by elites. (Further, the registering of defined portions of land could threaten existing looser arrangements based on patterns of pastoral mobility.) The Land Act does allow for forcible acquisition "in accordance with the law, for a public purpose, and upon prompt payment of just compensation to the person or persons, in full," terms that are rather vague, and may be easily interpreted to suit interests of elites, politicians, and investors. Compensation is not covered in any detail in either the Act or the Bill, raising the question as to who should be compensated when land is collectively owned.

In Tanzania most land is owned by the state, and the land targeted for investment is under *customary right of occupancy* that constitutes what the Village Land Act, 1999 calls as *village land* 4 (1). Again, for the purpose of *public interest*, land can be transferred for investment purposes on the decision of the Minister or Commissioner for Lands. Although provision is made in the Village Land Act (section 4) for affected villagers to represent their case to the village council, another section (7) of the same Act allows these provisions to be overridden, subject to the other Acts (Land Act and Local Government Act). It is easy to see how villagers' power is limited by ignorance of complex law, high illiteracy, and lack of resources for legal representation (Reisman et al. 2013).

In addition to, the land given for extraction, there is grabbing of land for speculation in surrounding areas. Such is the case for the areas marked out for the LAPSSET corridor (Lamu Port, South Sudan, Ethiopia Transport corridor), an oil pipeline with road and rail links that was planned to traverse Northern Kenya. Although plans have now been slimmed down and Kenya may now create its own internal corridor, much of the land has already been acquired in advance by elites. The Kenyan President is quoted to have encouraged communities along the proposed LAPSSET route to form cooperative organs, where they can jointly engage with the crude pipeline, although it is not clear how this should happen.

In May 2013, a conflict broke out in Turkana between an investor and the community. The county council had allocated an estimated six-square kilometer of land[*] to an investor to build a 600-bed hotel and an airstrip, foreseeing the future development of Turkana. The investor claimed to have paid 4.5 million Kenya shillings (U.S. $50,000) to the county council.[†] However, the area was part of an important grazing ground for pastoralists. The community burned and destroyed the investors' property worth six million Kshs ($80,000), including huge tents and fencing poles, saying that they had not been consulted before the leasing of the land, and that bribery may have been involved.[‡] Since the incident, the investor has continued to develop the area and has built an airstrip, which has been leased to the oil company.[§]

The strategic nature of the extractive industry requires security arrangements and contracts to be made in areas that may have previously lacked formal structures. These may also be vulnerable to corruption. In Turkana, the National Police Reserve (NPR), a locally recruited volunteer force armed by the state to supplement the role of the police, provide the only state-linked security presence for most of Turkana (Mkutu and Wandera, 2016). Local people have also acquired their own illicit arms, and use these in conflicts

---

[*] Sources interviewed noted 500 hectares or acres; with confusion among the various sources over which unit was being used. Six square kilometer is in fact 600 hectares or 1482 acres so the former unit is most likely. This, however, illustrates the general confusion surrounding these issues, which can heighten tensions.

[†] Interview several people and organizations including Oxfam, Provincial administration, civil society, May 25, 2013.

[‡] Interview, former director APAD, Lodwar, May 26, 2013.

[§] Observation, February 2015.

with other ethnic groups in international and internal border areas, over land access and in cattle raids. In practice, a mixture of local warriors and NPRs therefore protect Kenya's frontiers. To give them an income, NPRs also use their state arms in a variety of private security roles in urban areas and on roads, the illegality of which is overlooked by their police supervisors. NPRs are also known to misuse their arms in banditry and protection rackets (Mkutu and Wandera, 2013).

Since 2012, oil companies and their subcontractors have an agreement with the national government for the provision of armed guards and escorts, and NPRs are among those deployed in short-term contracts to guard oil exploration and drilling sites. Although they are paid for this, there were reports of cuts being given to security bosses (Mkutu and Wandera, 2013). The paid deployment of NPRs was also viewed by one respondent as a means of buying the community members so that they support the oil industry, and are silent about potential or real problems (Mkutu and Wandera, 2013).

The provision of state forces to guard oil, if not well overseen, could lead to the command and control of state-armed NPRs by nonstate entities, such as managers or private security companies. This kind of arrangement is not unheard of in private and community wildlife conservancies in Northern Kenya, which are allowed to recruit, equip, and train NPRs usually with very little police oversight (Mkutu and Wandera, 2013). Similarly, in Marsabit, G4S, a British security firm has been contracted to provide security to the Lake Turkana Wind Project. G4S in turn has been given freedom to hire NPRs,with their arms. It is not clear how this contract has been agreed or to what extent the police will cede responsibility for oversight of the NPRs to the private company.*

Finally in terms of security governance, oil companies are currently moving toward recruitment of private security guards, rather than NPRs for reasons that were not made clear. The Niger Delta is now awash with British and American private military companies (PMCs) engaged in security services for their clients in the oil and gas industry.[†] They have been accused of human rights abuse.[‡]

NPRs are also sometimes recruited by politicians for their personal protection, because they are located in constituencies, and because the work is paid. Fears were raised about how this might play into existing political tensions in the context of lucrative resource wealth (Mkutu and Wandera, 2013) of which 25% of royalties are supposed to reach the county level.

---

* E-mail correspondence with a researcher on LTWP, Marsabit, May 2016.

† Iyare, T (2009). Nigeria: Private Military Companies in the Niger Delta. http://www.pambazuka.org/global-south/nigeria-private-military-companies-niger-delta, accessed August 7, 2016.

‡ The Economist (2015). Private security in Nigeria-Rent-a-cop. *The Economist*. October 17.

Banditry could also get worse and take the form of oil bunkering (tapping) as in Nigeria, and local elites could also be involved in this.

Jobs, procurement, and corporate social responsibility (CSR) projects can be subject to corruption and partisanship, and the buying of elite favors. Subcontractors to the oil company in south Turkana were themselves involved in subcontracting, using companies that belonged to the employees themselves. A lack of documentation made it difficult to resolve issues when there were problems with payments to local community members for goods and services.[*]

As part of its CSR commitment, the oil company in Turkana paid 222 million KES (U.S. $2.5 million) for vehicles from Toyota Kenya that would be under a three year lease. These were then distributed to 36 companies that would provide transport services for the company and later own the cars.[†] Unfortunately, the process attracted problems, as a former company employee noted,

> When the list of the people given the cars came, we could not believe that the list was different from what had been agreed. Some families had three members in the list. These vehicles were entrusted to few individuals and the community did not feel that they benefited from the so called "community vehicles." The benefits of these vehicles went directly to well-connected individuals pockets.[‡]

Interestingly the oil company having access to the private airstrip also offered free flights to politicians in the county, which was criticized for creating conflicts of interest and silencing dissent.

In Mtwara (and neighboring Lindi) in south Tanzania, locals also lost out from benefits to their region when, instead of creating a local gas-processing plant, plans were made for a $1.2 billion pipeline from Mtwara to a plant in Dar-es-Salaam. In 2013, violent riots against the Chinese contractors building the pipeline ensued as a result, but the construction has continued.[§] The protests resulted in bloodshed, and large losses of property due to vandalism, amounting to around a million U.S. dollars. In such disputes, the government has often protected the interests of the companies as opposed to communities (Reisman et al. 2013). Similarly in North Mara, Tanzania, a region with one of the largest reserves of gold is home to some of the poorest

---

[*] Interview, former Tullow employee, August 8, Nairobi, 2016.
[†] Igadwah, L. (2014) Tullow woos Turkana locals car lease contract. November 12.
[‡] Interview, former Tullow employee, August 8, Nairobi, 2016.
[§] BBC (2013) Tanzania Mtwara gas riots: "Pregnant woman killed" BBC 24 May, http://www.bbc.com/news/world-africa-22652809, accessed August 8, 2016; Mgamba, R. (2013) Paper presented at "Africa Wide Convening on Governance of Oil and the Extractive sector: Experiences and lessons for Kenya." January 30–February 2, 2013, Naivasha, Kenya. Organized by ILEG and OSIEA.

residents. The region faces recurrent conflict between the investor and community, characterized by violent confrontations between armed locals and security guards. The investor's attempt to provide corporate social responsibility through provision of water, electricity, schools, and health has not transformed the situation (Reisman et al. 2013).

In Kenya, most laws relevant to the extractive industry are still in the process of being updated to reflect changing needs. This means that a legal framework and ensuing policies are lacking, leaving loopholes, contradictions and confusion. Lack of capacity in local and national government in dealing with matters pertaining to the extractive industry, along with illiteracy of communities, further contributes to the potential for corruption and pillage. The Petroleum Bill 2015 contains provisions for community rights to information/education and compensation for displacement/lost source of revenue and environmental damage. A revenue-sharing formula of 20% to the county and 5% to locals is also contained within the Bill, but would require a watertight policy to ensure that the benefits reach local people as intended, and to govern equitable distribution. The Bill has been faulted by some falling short of constitutional requirements to benefit locals adequately, and for failing to specify what should happen if resources are found on community (shared) land as is most of Turkana.* A constitutional requirement for affirmative action to offer jobs and opportunities to marginalized people is not reflected in the Bill.

On a larger-scale, there are concerns that benefits from resources may not reach east Africans due to international trade agreements that work in favor of developed nations, given the weak regulatory structures of developing countries, making it vulnerable to exploitation and corruption, both from the angle of tendering and revenue distribution.† A 2014 article by the Africa Progress Panel states that "every year, the continent loses an estimated 5.7% of its GDP [gross domestic product] to illicit financial flows. "The extractive sector is particularly affected. A report by Global Financial Integrity study for 10 years provides the amounts of domestic tax and tariff revenues that African countries in Africa lost due to lack of capacity and transparency to manage revenue from international trade. It shows that "Kenya lost $435 million, Mozambique lost $187 million, Tanzania lost $248 million, and Uganda lost $243 million on average per year in potential tax and tariff." (23) (Harris 2014). It also argues that "the value of Tanzania's mining exports grew to $1.5 billion in 2010, but annual government revenue from its sale was only about $100 million, or about seven percent" (Fletcher 2014). Without a clear legal framework and policy and watch dog, there are potential huge losses even as new resources are found.

---

* Okoth, (2012), http://www.standardmedia.co.ke/?articleID=2000072976&story_title=Kenya-Chaos-looms-over-oil-revenue-in-Kenya, accessed August 8, 2016.
† Devarajan (2011), http://www.theguardian.com/global-development/poverty-matters/2011/jun/29/africa-extracting-benefits-from-natural-resources, accessed August 8, 2016.

References

Ankomah, B. (1999). The Butcher of the Congo, New African, www.Hartford-hwp. com, October. Retrieved June 6, 2016.

Blair, A. (2014). Corruption Is Like Bad Breath, Oxfam, www.polticsofpoverty.oxfamamerica.org, December 9. Retrieved April 25, 2016.

Burgis, T. and Chitoyo, K. (2012). Manufacturing Instability? Extractive Industry, the State and the Resource Curse in West Africa, Chatham House, London.

Collier, P. and Hoeffler, A. (2004). *Greed and Grievance in Civil War,* Oxford Economic Papers, 56 (4): 563–595.

Daniel, S. (2014). Haliburton $185 Bribery Scandal EFCC Yet to Locate Refund, www.vanguard.ngr.com, February 14. Retrieved June 6, 2016.

Essick, K. (2001). Guns. Money and Cellphones, www.globalissues.org, June. Retrieved May 14, 2016.

Fearon, J. and Laitin, D. (2003). Ethnicity, Insurgency, and Civil War, *American Political Science Review,* 97 (1): 75–90.

Fletcher, M. (2014). More Transparency and Accountability Are Needed, if Tanzania Is to Truly Benefit from its New-Found Gas, Global Financial Integrity, July 18, 2014, http://www.gfintegrity.org/tanzania-needs-careful-gas-revenues/, accessed December 2, 2016.

Harris, E. (2014). "Africa citizens need a more transparent commodities trade" Remarks by Head of Communications, Africa Progress Panel to World Trade Organization public forum, October 2, 2014, http://www.africaprogresspanel. org/africas-citizens-need-a-more-transparent-commodities-trade/. Retrieved August 9, 2016.

Humphreys, M. (2005). Natural Resources, Conflict, and Conflict Resolution, *Journal of Conflict Resolution,* 49 (4): 508–537.

Jatto. A. and Stanislas, P. (2016). Contemporary Territorial, Economic and Political Security in Edo State, Nigeria, *International Executive Police Symposium Working Paper.*

Kateta, M. (2015). Extractive Industries in Africa, Extracted Profits, www.equaltimes.

Kebede, C. (2016). Ethiopia: Open Dialogue with the Public to Solve Corruption, allafrica.com. Retrieved April 23, 2016.

Le Billon, P. (2005). *Fuelling War: Natural Resources and Armed Conflict.* New York: Routledge, for International Institute for Strategic Studies.

Mkutu, K. (2015). Changes and challenges of the Kenya Police Reserve: the case of Turkana County, *African Studies Review,* 58 (1): 199–222.

Mkutu, K. and Wandera, G. (2013). Policing the periphery: opportunities and challenges for Kenya Police Reserves, March 2013. Working Paper No. 15, Small Arms Survey, Geneva, Switzerland.

Mkutu, K. and Wandera, G. (2016). Conflict, Security and the Extractive Industries in Turkana, Kenya, Emerging Issues 2012–2015.

Nzongola-Ntalaja, G. (2011). Patrice Lumumba: The Most Important Assassination of the 20th Century, www.theguardian.co.uk, January 17. Retrieved May 20, 2016.

Obi, C. (2010). Oil as the "curse" of conflict in Africa: peering through the smoke and mirrors, in *Conflict and Security in Africa,* Abrahamsen, R. (ed.), Oxford, UK: James Currey.

Patrick, S. (2014). Extracting Justice: Battling Corruption in Resource-Rich Africa. www.blogs.cfro.org, August 13. Retrieved April 19, 2016.

Pino, N. (2012). Trinidad Case Study, in Ellison, G. and Pino, N. (eds.) *Globalization, Police Reform and Development*, London, UK: Palgrave Macmillan.

Reisman, L., Mkutu, K., Lyimo, S., and Moshi, M. (2013). Tackling the Drift, Assessment of Crime and Violence, Open Society Initiative for East Africa.

Ross, M. (2001). Does oil hinder democracy? *World Politics*, 53: 325–361.

Ross, M. (2008). Blood barrels: why oil wealth fuels conflict, Foreign Affairs, May/June, http://foreignaffairs.com/articles/63396/michel-l-ross/bloodbarrels. Retrieved October 6, 2014.

Ross, M. (2012). *The Oil Curse: How Petroleum Wealth Shapes the Development of Nations*. Princeton, NJ: Princeton University Press.

Snyder, R. and Bhavnani, R. (2005). Diamonds, Blood and Taxes: A Revenue-Centered Framework for Explaining Political Order, *Journal of Conflict Resolution*, 49 (4): 563–597.

Standing, A. (2007). Corruption and the Extractive Industries in Africa, Institute of Security Studies, October.

Stanislas, P. (2014). *International Perspective on Police Education and Training*. London, UK: Routledge.

Stanislas, P. (2016a). The Challenge of Postcolonial Political and Social Leadership: Building Inclusive Citizenship, Safety and Security in East Africa, in Mkutu, K. (ed.) *Policing in East Africa, Suffolk*, VA: James Currey (forthcoming).

Stanislas, P. (2016b). Tackling Corruption and Crime in Public Procurement Fraud in the 2012 London Olympic and Paralympic Games: The Role of the Metropolitan Police's Serious and Organised Crime Command, in Gottschalk, P. and Stanislas.

Stanislas, P. and Iyah, I. (2016). Changing Religious Influences, Young People, Crime and Extremism in Nigeria in Sadique, K. and Stanislas, P. (eds.), *Religion, Faith and Crime*, London, UK: Palgrave Macmillan.

White, R. (2011). *Transnational Environmental Crime*. London, UK: Routledge.

Withnall, A. (2016). David Cameron's Corruption Comments: Nigerian President Won't Demand Apology-just a Return of Nigerian Assets, http://www. independent.co.uk. Retrieved May 11, 2016.

Reports

Council on Foreign Relations (2014). Workshop Summary Report: Governing Extractive Industries On A Global Scale: Challenges and Opportunities.

Organisation for Economic Cooperation and Development Foreign Bribery Report (2014). An Analysis of the Crime of Bribery of Foreign Public Officials.

Organisation for Economic Cooperation and Development. Foreign Convention on Combatting Bribery of Foreign Public Officials in International Business Transactions.

Recommendation of the Council for Further Combating Bribery of Foreign Public Officials in International Business Transactions (2009).

SNL Metals Economic Group (2013). Worldwide Exploration Trends.

Governance and Public Corruption in Nigeria

9

OYESOJI AREMU

Contents

Introduction

Governance and public corruption are attracting a lot of attention around the world, especially in developing countries such as Nigeria that is currently midwifing another civilian administration where the mantra is change. This issue has transformed from a predominately national phenomenon to a global issue. Global reaction against corruption has swept the international political landscape. No region and hardly any nation have been immune from this process. Indeed, any attempt to understand the tragedy of development and the challenges to development in Nigeria should come to grip withy the nature of governance, and public corruption, and stupendous wastage of scarce resources by public office holders. However, it is agreed that bad governance and corruption are inimical to public office holders, it undermines democracy, degrades moral fabrics of the society and development.

The subject of corruption and governance is a phenomenal trend that is on a constant public discourse in Nigeria. Far more than any socio-economic challenges that Nigeria as a country is bedeviled with, the twin concept of governance and corruption is like a Siamese twin that is constantly insepa-rable in the body polity of the country. While it could be asserted that in almost 55 years of Nigerian independence, the country has gained fortune in terms agrarian produce in the 1960s and later crude oil produce as from 1970. To date these economic resources have not transformed into expected developments due to poor governance and corruption. Generally, corruption is a function of national life in Nigeria. This permeates public and private sectors including the political class and criminal justice agencies. Myint (2000) in tandem with this submission notes that corruption occurs in all nations, both developed and developing countries, and in private and public sectors. A cue from Myint's submission is that corruption is general and permeates all facets of life. The general consensus of scholars, stakeholders, and transparency organizations is that while corruption is a "norm" in all countries, it is its degree that varies.

This chapter, therefore, examines science of public governance and intricacies of corruption in Nigeria. This chapter argues for the need of a continuous appraisal of the twin phenomenon with a view to giving governance a holistic human face. This chapter concludes on the premise that public governance should not be in tandem with best practices; corruption should be zero-tolerated and heavily sanctioned where this is violated.

Governance Defined

Governance as a concept has always being perceived generally from political point of view. While this is obvious in that, governance is a subset of politicization, it may not necessarily be as a result of political processes. This argument, notwithstanding, governance in the context of this chapter, is seen in the context of politics in that the subject of corruption is tied to its conceptualization. That advanced, the term governance has also become an important topic to scholars in political science. As expected, it is highly contentious like other terms. The concept of governance is notoriously slippery, frequently used by social scientists and practitioners without a concise definition. Nevertheless, governance implies the efficient management of state institutions in the area of public accountability, transparency in government procedures, rule of law, and public sector management. According to Ukaegbu (2010), governance means initiating, directing, and managing public resources, organizing people, directing subordinates to put in their best to achieve good result in given assignments. It is about ensuring that things are done accordingly, accountability is maintained through the instruments of governance. In the realm of public affairs, governance is seen as the range of policies that public officials make and means they employ to manage the affairs of society. Ojameruaye (2011) defines governance as the process by which governments are elected, monitored, and replaced; the capacity of the government to effectively formulate and implement sound policies; and respect of citizens and the state for the institutions that govern economic and social interactions among them. Governance is also seen as the process of steering state and society toward the realization of collective goals. Governance is an act controlling the affairs of the nation by making decisions and executing them on behalf of the citizens. It is the activity of governing a country or controlling a company or the way in which a country is governed or a company or institution is controlled.

Governance according to Awuudu (2012) is concerned with the structures and procedures for decision-making, accountability, control, and code of conduct. It is expressed through legislation, policies, and by-laws; and informal norms define governance as the control of an activity by some means such that a range of desired outcomes is attained. Thus, governance in a political sense is a more complex activity. Thus, governance has a lot to do with the allocation of values in the society, which to a large extent is political in nature. Although governance is related to politics, it is conceptually different. However, as a human phenomenon, governance is exercised within a given socio-cultural context and belongs to a broader department of politics. Ekei (2003) sees governance as the means through which public institutions manage public affairs to ensure effective use of resources to achieve the good life expected of citizens in a given state. Accordingly, Denis (2006) governance has a strong normative overtone, it is the practice of good government, and it remains essentially a fragile process that depends on the restraint of the ruler and the tolerance of the ruled. All these elements or attributes are the instruments of effective governance in the sense that they provide the necessary anchor and legal/moral justifications to the government. Governance in the context of this chapter is defined as the process of allocating resources, through the instrumentalities of the state, for the attainment of public good. This includes institutional and structural arrangements, decision-making processes, policy formulation, and implementation capacity, development of personnel, information flows, and the nature and style of leadership within a political system.

Nigerian nation that got weaned from the British colonial imperialism in 1960 has since being governed serially by the military personnel and the political class. While the military juntas have had the major part of the governance (20 years), the political class seems to be steady as from 1999 with Chief Olusegun Obasanjo's dispensation. In succession, Nigeria has been governed by Musa Yardua and Jonathan Goodluck whose administration brought an end to 16 years of people's democratic party (PDP) rule in Nigeria on May 29, 2015 with the government of President Muhamadu Buhari who had earlier governed Nigeria as a military ruler between 1983 and 1985. While Nigeria has witnessed self-governance between 1960 to date, the quality of the governance leaves more to be desired. Although the submission of Ogundiya (2010a) could suffice that while politics is the authoritative allocation of values or who gets what, when, and how, governance is the process and mechanism of allocating the values without jeopardizing the principle of equity, justice, and fairness; this notwithstanding governance, as a mechanism has not been fully felt by the citizenry. This, more often, in Nigeria due to perversion of governance through orchestrated corruption mostly at two of the three tiers of government (executive and legislative). At this point, this chapter discusses the concept of corruption having being linked surreptitiously to governance.

Anatomy of Corruption and its Etiology

Corruption and corrupt behavior have been variously defined by scholars. One defining thrust in all definitions of corruption and corrupt behavior is that it is seen as unethical and unapproved behavior expected of an individual holding a public office in trust for the citizens. Aremu, Pakes, and Johnston (2009) define corruption as the absence of integrity or honesty, and use of a position of trust for dishonest gain. The trio further apt it that corruption is an act done with an intent to gain an advantage that is inconsistent with one's official duty. It is well known that corruption is as old as human existence. In the Holy Bible of Christian persuasion, children of Prophet Samuel were alleged to have extorted people of Israel by perverting the cause of criminal justice and took bribe (1 Samuel 8:3). This led to the "revolt" that culminated in the kingship in Israel (1 Samuel 5-7). In relation to this, also in criminal justice, John—the Baptist in the Holy Bible—warned and admonished soldiers to be contented with their wages (Luke 3:14b). Akin to the public opprobrium of corrupt practices is the sanction in place in ancient Greece. According to Aremu et al. (2009), Plato on account of widespread of corrupt practices in his time recommended that any citizen who accepted gifts in exchange for public service should be buried without honor. This also affirms the depth of corruption in the ancient Greece. Aremu et al. (2009) then submits that: "It was from these rots of the ancient organisations, institutions and structures that the modern society emerged" (p. 60).

Nigerian nation has had its own full share of corruption majorly in public governance. This, more often, has always been in public domain and discourse. In reference to Adigun Agbaje's submission in Ogunsanwo (2015), corruption is regarded as one of the most dominant themes in Nigeria. Agbaje further enthused that since independence from Britain in 1960, Nigeria has grappled with the challenge of taming corruption. The analysis of Agbaje's submission in Ogunsanwo (2015) can be explained that while corruption has come to a monster in Nigeria, the perceived process of taming itself is fraught with corrupt practices most especially from the criminal justice. This assertion is premised on the fact that less than significant number of public officials found to be corrupt are punished and in some cases, they are asked to return insignificant portion of the loots to the state. Here, justice system has been found to be "more tolerant" of corruption and its perpetrators using the phrase, "plea bargaining." In Nigeria, there are specialized agencies economic and financial crimes commission (EFCC) and independent corrupt practices commission (ICPC) that are juristically established to determine what constitutes corruption by referring same to the court of competent jurisdiction. EFCC was established in 2003. Its jurisdictional framework could investigate all forms of financial crimes such as advance fee fraud (419 frauds) and money laundering. ICPC on the other hand was established in 2000. Its core mandate is to receive and investigate reports of corruption and in appropriate cases prosecute the offender(s). Often, these anticorruption agencies rely on the Nigeria Police and Department of State Service (State Security Service) for the arrest and prosecution of the offenders. The contention here is that war against corrupt practices and behavior is a multidimensional one that involves anticorrupt agencies, the police, DSS, and the judicial system.

Explaining what constitutes corruption is not as easy as defining it. Operationally, explaining it would give a definitive position on what corruption is. Be that as it may seem, corruption is simply an abuse of public trust perpetrated by an individual or a cohort either by proxy or real with the sole aim of advancing a selfish interest or gain. It is thus, a violation of established norms and values. According to World Bank (2000), corruption is a fraudulent act, dishonest, illegal behavior particularly of those in authority positions. In the same vein, Transparency International (2010) defines corruption as a general term for the misuse of a public position of trust for private gain. While Lipset and Lenz (2000) describe corruption as an effort to secure wealth or power through illegal means, private gain at public expense, or a misuse of public power for private benefit.

Taking a general cue from these definitions, the summation here is that certain behaviors could constitute corruption and these are not only in criminal act, they are also subjected to the interpretation of the judicial system. Behaviors like bribery, embezzlement of public fund, acceptance of gratification, misuse of office and trust, stealing, connivance to defraud, defraud, impropriety in office, inducement, tax evasion, laundering, and lodging of fund without a due process, and any form of behavior that is not in the interest of public trust could be explained as corruption. These plethora of behavior have said to constitute that corruption itself is not exhaustive. It is thus clear that any behavior that negates public trust is classified as corruption.

Governance and Public Corruption: The Synergy, Trend, and Magnitude

Public corruption is abused for private gain when an official accepts, solicits, or extorts a bribe. It is also abused when private agents actively offer bribes to circumvent public offices and processes for competitive advantages or profit. Agbu (2003) observes that public office can be abused for personal benefit even if no bribery occurs, through patronage and nepotism, the theft of state assets, or the diversion of state resources. According to Ocheje (2000), corruption in public office has existed in Nigeria since the establishment of modern structures of public administration in the country by the British colonial administrators. Nevertheless, its escalation has coincided with the expansion of administrative structures and the full development of the public sector (Ademolekun, 2002). Consequently, the administrative structures' development has been accompanied with lack of transparency and accountability arising from an over-bloated public service that is bedeviled with excessive bureaucracy and corruption.

The public service in Nigeria has been characterized by lack of culture of accountability and weak institutional structure; excessive centralization of administrative power; lack of access to citizens, and gross inefficiency (Ademolekun, 2002). Thus, the national wealth always disappear into private bank accounts of leaders, both military, politicians, civil servants, and their collaborators in the private sector. According to a report in Nigeria's newspaper (Guardian newspaper in June 11, 2014), corruption has taught the Nigerian a dangerous and wrong lesson that it does not pay to be honest, hard-working, and law-abiding. Through corrupt means, many political office holders acquire wealth and properties in and outside Nigeria; and many display their wealth that is beyond the means, but the society does not blink. This has made politics a big business in Nigeria, because anything spent to secure a political office is regarded as an investment, which matures immediately when one gets into office. This display of wealth by public officials which they are often unable to explain the source is a reflection of the social decay in terms of corruption in the society. however, many of these officials before being elected or appointed into offices had little or modest income, but become owners of many properties around the world (*This Day Sunday Online*, 2014). These kinds of behaviors have the tendency to scare way foreign and local investors, with tremendous negative effects on the economy (*The Daily Trust*, 2013). These features have and have fostered the practice of bare-faced theft and stealing of public funds and properties, waste and mismanagement of national resources and public assets. The resultant effects of which has been the phenomenon of inflated contracts, abandoned projects, lack of public infrastructures, poverty of the citizens, and general poor standard of living (Ocheje, 2000).

Given this development therefore, corruption connotes any behavior that deviates from an established norm with regard to public trust. It also means theft of public trust whether the person concerned is elected, selected, nominated, or appointed into office. Corrupt public servants bestrode the nation, masquerading as captains of business and power brokers with tainted and stolen wealth, and demanded the rest of us to kowtow before them (Ribadu, 2006). The Nigeria's economic and political landscape is pervaded by corruption and abuse of office. The National Planning Commission has noted that systemic corruption and low levels of transparency and account-ability have been major sources of development failure. Illegal activities such as money laundering have torn the fabric of Nigerian society (National Planning Commission, 2005). Unconventional and fraudulent trade, misap-propriation or diversion of funds, kickbacks, under and over in-voicing, brib-ery, false declarations, abuse of office, and collection of illegal tolls, among other malfeasant practices, are the forms that corruption take in Nigeria (Adeseyoju, 2006). In the international system, Nigeria is rated as one of the most corrupt nations of the world, a ranking that has denied the coun-try its pride of place in the international economic system (Transparency International, 2010).

Nigeria is the largest democracy in Africa. The country that was weaned from colonial subjugation of Britain on October 1, 1960 has about 170 million people and has most of its 55 years of independence being ruled by the military class. The country has come to witness a democratic stability as from 1999 till date with four civilian administrations of Olusegun Obasanjo, Sheu Musa Yaradua, Goodluck Jonathan, and Muhammadu Buhari. While the first three were of the PDP, the latter that took up the reins of government is of All Progressive Congress (APC), an amalgamation of four political par-ties (Action Congress of Nigeria, the Congress for Progressive Change, the All Nigeria Peoples Party, a faction of All Progressive Grand Alliance, and a splinter group of PDP).

Corruption is a huge challenge in the public sector in Nigeria. It is at the core of the crisis of governance and legitimacy, the establishment of a stable democratic order, rule of law, development, and the welfare of citizens. Of all forms of corruption, public office corruption has remained a major obstacle to national progress in Nigeria. Corruption is indeed the major explanation for the seemingly insolvable problem of poverty, diseases, hunger, and gen-eral acute development tragedy in Nigeria. No doubt, Nigeria's status as the sixth largest producer and exporter of oil with enormous revenue generation capacity from oil and nonoil exports, woefully contrasts with its decaying infrastructural and institutional development. It has also "seriously impeded the growth and effective utilization of resources in Nigeria (Egbue, 2007)". In terms of its cultural connotation, the prevalent value system of public acceptance of corruption as a way of life fueled the development of corrup-tion in terms of its behavioral traits, as well as the erosion of the separation between legal and illegal daily activities through social pressures without consideration for barrier hence, creating a conducive atmosphere for gener-alizing and trivializing corrupt practices in the Nigerian society.

The effects of years of dictatorial and corrupt governance by successive military administration and now civilian governments are glaringly mani-fest in the poor state of development in all the sectors of the nation's life, especially the level of poverty, and gross income inequality, and general low quality of life of its people. Understanding the existence, development, and impact of bad governance and corruption in the Nigerian state requires the conceptualization of its causes and effects to concretize the basis for a more effective criminalization policy and anticorruption techniques or mechanisms in combating it in Nigeria. The "Nigerian Factor" is the acronym for the practice of bribery and corruption based on the general perception that every public official has a "price" at which he or she may be "bought." It also translates into the general belief that public office/public service is for personal enrichment and accumulation of wealth, as part of every Nigerians' share of the "national cake" for himself/herself and for his/her family, and tribe/ethnic group. The whole result is the paling into extinction of the middle class, while the gap between the rich and the poor widened significantly with the value of the Naira drastically reduced, thus making the situation so unbearable for the common man.

From its mild manifestation in the 1960s, corruption grew rapidly at an alarming rate during the Second Republic. For instance, Aiyede (2006) aptly describes Shagari administration (1979–1983) as the government of the contractors by the contractors and for the contractors. The General Buhari regime took a more militant and practical approach to fight corruption and immorality in his "War Against Indiscipline," a measure considered too high handed that prompted the overthrow of the regime, which ushered in the General Babangida era that relaxed the "War" in favor of social and economic re-engineering policy that later led to the extinction of the middle class as a result of the structural adjustment program (SAP). At the end of the Second Republic, the probe panel set up by the General Buhari military administration found many government officials and state governors guilty of diversion, mismanagement, and misappropriation of public funds. Several millions of naira was siphoned out of the country, several millions squandered, and several others unaccounted for. However, the Federal Government White papers of the report of Justices Sampson Uwaifo and Mohammed Bello Review Panels (1986) are eloquent testimonies of public corruption in Nigeria. Compounded during the several years of military misrule, corruption became institutionalized and assaulted every facet of the country's political and socio-economic life (Aiyede 2006). The duo of Babangida/Abacha's rule, no doubt, galvanized the international position of Nigeria in 2000 as the most corrupt nation in the world, for example, the disappearance of the $5 billion Gulf Oil windfall in 1991. The one-year regime of General Abdul-Salami saw Nigeria's external reserve liquidated in the name of transition to democracy (Abdullahi, 2010).

Surveys of nations by Transparency International, a Berlin-based non-profit organization, rank Nigeria among the most corrupt countries in the world. In 1999, Nigeria was ranked the second most corrupt country in the world. In 2000, it was ranked the most corrupt country in the world. In 2001, 2002, and 2003, Nigeria was ranked the second most corrupt country out of the surveyed countries. From 2005 to 2007, Nigeria ranked the eight, twenty-second, and thirty-second most-corrupt country among the surveyed countries. By 2008, Nigeria's rating had significantly improved her rating, since the 2007 index Nigeria ranked 121 out of 180 countries. The Nigerian system, the product of more than 50 years of mismanagement, ethnic strife, military misrule, and political instability, provided a conducive setting for corruption to flourish. Control mechanisms were ineffective, and prospects of detection and prosecution were weak. The government's control and near domination of the economic sphere provided limitless opportunities for Nigerians who operate without any sense of accountability to seek rents with impunity (Gambo, 2006).

Corruption flourished in Nigeria mainly because no government credibly and honestly committed itself to fighting it. Neither civilian nor military regimes could stop corruption because each administration, in differing ways and to varying degrees, exemplified the pervading culture of public service: an amoral obsession with using public office for private gain. After several decades of military rule, Nigeria's democratic institutions had become weak and ineffective. A major challenge that faced the Obasanjo administration was how best to ensure genuine restoration of democracy and good governance in Nigeria and eradication of corruption. Weak and battered institutions, poor culture of accountability and transparency, abuse of human rights, and the neglect of the majority of the population created an environment in which reforms had been difficult. Faced with the tragic consequences of underdevelopment, which was propelled and sustained by dictatorial regimes and inept civilian governments, the country was challenged to induce qualitative transformation of the Nigerian economy and society.

According to Ogundiya (2010b), events in Nigeria since 1999 have shown that the tidal waves of reversal have been contending with Nigeria's democratic project. Consequently, democracy remains grossly unstable and the future seems to be very bleak because of rampant bureaucratic and political corruption. Corruption has reached a high crescendo such that an average Nigerian now possibly associates democracy with it. The consequences of political corruption are potently manifest: cyclical crisis of legitimacy, fragile party structure, institutional decay, chronic economic problem and unemployment, and above all general democratic volatility. Corruption in this country is generally characterized by looting of funds and wealth kept secretly: capital flight; misappropriation and mismanagement of public funds; money laundering (acquiring money through fraudulent ways); drug and child trafficking; illegal arms deal; and gratification, which involves monetary, material, or physical favors as a condition or reward for performing official duty, official abuse in which an official suppresses and violates an oath of office and nepotism that is granting underserved favors to one's relations.

The above features were legacies of decades of corruption and misman-agement, especially during the military administrations. In the context of an oil producing economy (with rents from oil as easy source of government revenue), a culture of rent-seeking developed. Government readily became an instrument for instant acquisition of wealth and therefore distorted the incentive to work and to create wealth in the private sector. With govern-ment as the major source of patronage and rent-seeking, the fight for public office became a matter of life and death. All these created an incentive frame-work that did not reward private enterprise, transparency, and accountabil-ity. According to former Governor of the Central Bank of Nigeria, Charles Soludo, bad governance evident as a result of inappropriate development frameworks, poor and frequently changing policies and programs, lack of clear development vision, and commitment to the Nigerian project (as well as a citizenry that acquiesced to the patronage culture) were the major causes of Nigeria's failed past (Soludo, 2007).

Some Examples in Perspectives

Corruption as expressed by scholars is universal. This has also been affirmed by Transparency International that corruption permeates almost all the countries, although with varying degrees. In China where population is around 1.357 billion with $11.212 trillion gross domestic product (GDP), there are incidences of corruption among public officials. Alluding to this, Ogunsanwo (2015) claimed that in 2014, some 15,450 officials were convicted for corruption. This phenomenon is not limited to the world populous coun-try. Other first world countries like France, Russia, United Kingdom, and the United States of America are also not immune to the problem of corruption. Other than these five permanent members of the United Nations Security Council, corruption thrives in other countries who boast of sound economy and security intelligence. Countries like Australia, Germany, Italy, Spain, and Singapore are also not free from the albatross of corruption. Similarly in Africa, countries like South Africa, Tanzania, Botswana, Egypt, and Ghana have had their own share of corruption in governance. It is also contended by Gray and Villa (2011) that the United States of America in spite of her strong legislative stance and severe penalties on corruption is not immune to the menace.

Generally, corruption remains a global threat, given the statistical fact that no country is immune from it. The global perception index as released by Transparency International (2014) shows that no country has a "perfect" score on the index. From the least ranked country (Denmark) to the most ranked country (Cambodia), corruption is perceived to be in governance of more than 150 surveyed countries.

The above perspectives of corruption in other countries in spite of their seeming zero tolerance for corruption show that the problem is inherent in humanity and not an exclusive happening in a particular country. Corruption is therefore a humanity problem. Thus, it requires some behavioral interventions of which emotional intelligence (EI) could be significantly efficacious, given some inferences from studies on EI.

Enhancing Governance and Curbing Corruption through a Psychological Process

While there have not been any known or empirically driven psychological solutions to the menace of bad governance and corruption worldwide, the interplay of some psychological models could be efficacious in this regard. American Sociologist, Edwin Sutherland in Brytting, Minogue and Morino (2015) in his classic white-collar crime expounded in Differential Association Theory that criminal behavior otherwise conceptualized as corruption in this chapter, is, somewhat, learnt. The contention of Edwin Sutherland is that criminal behavior (corrupt behavior inclusive) is sustained if the gain outweighs the consequence. This contention is also in tandem with the Choice Theory of Cesare Beccaria and Jeremy Bentham in which they argue that people weigh the benefits and consequences of their actions before deciding on a course of behavior (Aremu, 2014). Similarly, the Deterrence Theory holds that this choice can be controlled or deterred by the threat of punishment (Figure 9.1).

Not too far from the above opinion, Donald Cressey also in Brytting et al. (2015) proposed a model called the "Fraud Triangle." In the model, Donald

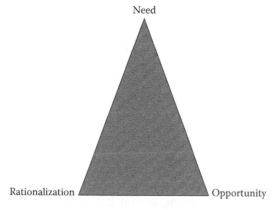

Figure 9.1 The fraud/corruption triangle model.

Cressey averred that corrupt behavior is a function of three elements: need, opportunity, and rationalization. These are contending elements that an individual could be engrossed in. According to Cressey, perceived need could range from affluence to power depending on the individual. This, in essence, means that what an individual feels as the most of his/her needs could precipitate a corrupt behavior if opportunity (environment) presents itself. People, especially those in government, have diverse opportunities. These opportunities could be physical, human or psychological. The human part of the environment is what psychologists refer to as 'significant others'. The human part of the environment is what psychologists refer to as "significant others." Sociologists call it "relevant others." When the opportunity confronts an individual, the decision to engage in corrupt behavior, however, depends on how rational the individual is. Rationalization itself is a function of the individual's cognitive or affective behavior.

Justifying the essence of psychological models and theories as related to criminal justice, Aremu (2014) advised that professionals and correctional psychologists could utilize the knowledge in ensuring social order in the society. Aremu advances further that in the present dispensation, the essence of knowledge is to meet the social needs.

The contention that cannot be suppressed is the fact that corruption is a behavioral problem that has behavioral underpinning. Other determinants of corrupt behavior could be inability to judge behavioral outcomes and social conformity.

Inability to judge outcomes are rooted in human insatiable desire to appease pleasure speaking part of personality refers to as *id* in Psychology. This could compel an individual toward corruption if found in a reinforcing environment. Social conformity, on the other hand, is a desire to be part of the social bandwagon where corruption thrives and unchecked. In doing so, the individual may slip into corruption. Moore, Tetlock, Tanku, and Bazerman (2006) refer to this as "the slippery slope" phenomenon. According to Moore et al. (2006), corruption will occur gradually in a number of successive steps, each of which moves an individual deeper into the untoward behavior. Similarly, Ashforth and Anand (2003) describe the slippery slope as incrementalism that is a gradual process that escalates corruption. Likewise, the individual, gradually get immersed into corrupt behavior and this becomes endemic. The affirmation of this was provided by Darley (2005) when he contends that once an individual get involved in corruption, the distance between the initial corrupt act and subsequent ones get thinned. The submission of Darley explains increased continuity in corrupt practices among government functionaries.

The work of Aremu et al. (2009) on corruption in the police in Nigeria could therefore be a good reference to start with. Aremu and his foreign colleagues note and conclude that it is suggestive that the expected police transformation and paradigm shift might be possible if the police management could adopt counseling psychological technique like locus of control as a measure of corruption control in the police. Aremu and his colleagues' submission are drawn from a fact that the intervention of locus of control as a psychological tool is efficacious in the reduction of corruption in the police. A cue could be drawn from this by asserting that some psychological models and theories could be employed to enhance governance and curb public corruption.

In light of the above, this chapter, instructively, recommends EI model as a psychological intervention that could be deployed to enhance governance and possibly curb the menace of corruption. EI is a psychological construct rooted in the work of Daniel Goleman (1995). Prior to Goleman's work, David Wechsler had theorized that man is capable of effective functioning in his environment by acting purposefully and rationally. This, he referred to as "nonintellective behavior" (Wechsler, 1940). Thus, if behavior is nonintellective, it should be driven by other factors. These could include: affective, social competencies, trustworthiness, conscientiousness, empathy, and other personal factors that are people-driven. It was on this premise of thoughts that Salovey and Mayer (1990) apt to initiate the term, EI. They described emotional intelligence as a form of social intelligence that involves the ability to monitor one's own and others' feelings and emotions, to discriminate among them, and to use this information to guide one's thinking and action. In the context of the chapter, therefore, EI could become an effective intervention tool to achieve the intended paradigm shift.

Organizations, agencies (including police and paramilitary), and companies have come to appreciate EI as an effective tool for the needed change. Its efficacy has also been reported by scholars (Palmer, Walls, Burgess and Stough, 2001; Aremu and Tejumola, 2008; Bennis, 2011; Aremu et al. 2011; Aremu, 2013). Bennis (2000) affirming the importance of EI, surmised that it is estimated to be responsible for over 85% of outstanding performance in the workplace. Succinctly, Aremu et al. (2011) noted that the emerging view is that in order to be successful in any field that involves frequent social interactions, EI matters. In effect, the art of governance requires multi- and frequent interaction. Hence, EI would come into play in ensuring productivity. Drawing an inference from the work of Aremu et al. (2011), it is incumbent to assert that EI is effective in the reduction of corruption albeit among police personnel. It stands to therefore reason that the interplay of EI in mitigating corruption in governance could also pass a stringent test if it is used as a psychological intervention. In sum, EI is regarded as the most potent psychological intervention that could be fittingly used in organizations, and by extension, in government.

As explained and reasoned from literature, there has been some strong arguments in favor of the efficacy of EI as an intervention tool through which accountability could be enhanced in governance and organizations.

The contention of Gray and Villa (2011) is that more often, it is always difficult to make people accountable in organizations and *perhaps in public governance* (emphasis mine) through externally mediated interventions unlike EI, which is a form of internal principles. Thus, it is explicit that EI could play the expected role in ensuring self-accountability; and by extension, corrupt behavior could become mitigated.

Conclusion

This chapter has advocated a psychological approach through which corruption could be mitigated and quality of governance enhanced. This chapter, therefore, exclusively discussed the problem of governance in Nigeria and the problem of corruption that is always associated with it. The novelty in this chapter is the instructive argument that EI as a behavioral psychological construct could be utilized to stem the tide of increasing corruption in public governance in Nigeria. While this has not been empirically proved, the success stories of EI intervention in corrupt-ridden agencies like police could be motivating enough to affirm its potency as well in public governance. This theoretical strength is drawn from the fact that corruption is a behavioral problem as shown in the chapter. And as a behavioral challenge, a behavioral intervention could as well be deployed to stem the tide. This is to infer that EI as a behavioral intervention having being successfully used in organizations could also have a therapeutic place in governance.

From thence, the inferential thoughts are that physical and punitive measures that stem from the criminal justice system have not always mitigated corruption in Nigeria; and perhaps in other crimes. It is safe then to aver that criminal justice interventions that are in different measures are no longer efficacious and therefore, require a comprehensive review. In light of this, the interplay of EI could be given attention in national life as the country seeks for a new lease of image in the current political dispensation of the administration of President Muahamadu Buhari that advocates change as a mantra.

References

Abdullahi, H. (2010). The Challenges of Corruption in Nigeria: The Role of EFCC and ICPC, in History and Structure of the Nigerian Economy: Pre: Colonial Period to 2007 and Beyond. KadunaMinna, Nigeria: Halygraph Publications, pp. 316–331.

Ademolekun, L. (2002). *Public Administration in Africa*. Ibadan, Nigeria: Spectrum Books Limited.

Adeseyoju A. (2006). Gatekeepers as Money Launderers, *The Guardian*, September 8, pp. 24–26.

Agbu, O. (2003). Corruption and Human Trafficking: The Nigerian Case. *West African Review* 4(1), 1–13.

Aiyede R.E. (2006). The Role of INEC, ICPC and EFCC in Combating Political Corruption. In: A.O. Victor Adetula (ed.), *Money, Politics and Corruption in Nigeria*. Abuja, Nigeria: A Publication of IFES, pp. 37–54.

Aremu, A.O. (2013). The Impact of Emotional Intelligence on Community Policing in Democratic Nigeria: Agenda Setting for National Development. In: A. Verma, D.K. Das, and M. Abraham (eds.), *Global Community Policing: Problems and Challenges*. Boca Raton, FL: CRC Press Taylor & Francis, pp. 25–40.

Aremu, A.O. (2014). *Policing and Terrorism: Challenges and Issues in Intelligence.* Ibadan, Nigeria: Stirling-Horden Publishers.

Aremu, A.O., Pakes, F., and Johnston, L. (2009). The Effect of Locus of Control in the Reduction of Corruption in the Nigerian Police. *Policing: An International Journal of Police Strategies & Management*, 32(1), 144–156.

Aremu, A.O., Pakes, F., and Johnston, L. (2011). The moderating effect of emotional intelligence on the reduction of corruption in the Nigerian Police. *Police Practice and Research: An International Journal*, 12(3), 195–2008.

Aremu, A.O., and Tejumola, T.O. (2008). Assessment of Emotional Intelligence among Nigerian Police. *Journal of Social Science*, 16(3), 221–226.

Ashforth, B.E., and Anand, V. (2003). The Normalisation of Corruption in Organisations. *Research in Organisational Behaviour*, 25, 1–52.

Awuudu, D. (2012). The Challenges of Democratic Consolidation in Nigeria KUBA NNI. *Journal of Arts and Social Sciences*, 5, 33–45, Federal College of Education Zaria, Nigeria.

Bennis, W. (2000). Leadership of change. In: M. Beer and N. Nohira (eds.), *Breaking the Code of Change*, Boston, MA: Harvard Business School Press, pp. 113–121.

Bennis, W. (2001). Corporate Boards Executive Excellence. *Harper and Row*, New York, pp. 7–8.

Brytting, T., Minogue, R., and Morino, V. (2015). The Anatomy of Fraud and Corruption: Organisational Causes and Remedies. Retrieved from http://www. gowerpublishing.com/isbn/9780566091537 on October 16, 2015.

Darley, J.M. (2005). The Cognitive and Social Psychology of Contagious Organisational Corruption. *Brooklyn Law Review*, 70, 1177–1194.

Denis, V. (2006). Democracy, Good Governance and Leadership. In: Oguejiofor J. Obi, (ed.), *Studies in African Philosophy*, Vol. 1, pp. 67–76.

Egbue, N.G. (2007). Africa: Cultural Dimensions of Corruption and Possibilities for Change. *Journal of Social Sciences*, 12(2), 83–91.

Ekei, J.C. (2003). Governance in Traditional Africa: Implications for a Nascent Modern African Polity. In: Oguejiofor J. Obi (ed.), *Philosophy, Democracy and Responsible Governance in Africa*, Transaction Publishers, New Brunswickand, London, pp. 445–456.

Gambo, A.N. (2006). Godfatherism and Electoral Politics. In: A.O. Victor Adetula (ed.), *Nigeria in Money, Politics and Corruption in Nigeria*. Abuja, Nigeria: A Publication of IFES, pp. 88–104.

Gray, A., and Villa, D. (2011). The Loss of Governance through Corruption. *Governance: An International Journal of Policy, Adminstration and Institutions*, 24(3), 419–438.

Goleman, D. (1995). *Emotional Intelligence*. New York: Bantam.

The Guardian, (2011). Navy Raises Fight Against Crude Oil Theft. Retrieved from http://www.guardian-ngr on October 17, 2016.

Lipset, S.M., and Lenz, G.S. (2000). Corruption, Culture, and Market. In: L. Harrison and S. P. Huntington (eds.), *Culture Matters*, New York: Basic Books.

Moore, D.A., Tetlock, P.E., Tanku, L., and Bazerman, M.H. (2006). Conflicts of Interest and the Case of Auditor Independence: Moral Seduction and Strategic Issue Cycling. *Academy of Management Review*, 31, 10–29.

Myint, U. (2000). Corruption: Causes, Consequences And Cures. *Asia-Pacific Development Journal*, Vol. 7(2): 33–58.

National Planning Commission. (2005). *National Economic Empowerment and Development Strategy (NEEDS)*, Abuja, Nigeria.

Ocheje, P.D. (2001). Law and Social Change: A Socio-Legal Analysis of Nigeria's Corrupt Practices and Other Related Offences Act 2000. *Journal of Africa Law*, 45(2), 174–177.

Ogundiya, I.F. (2010a). Democracy and Good Governance: Nigeria's Dilemma. *African Journal of Political Science and International Relations*, 4(6), 201–208.

Ogundiya, O.A. (2010b). Corruption the Bane of Democratic Stability in Nigeria. *Journal of Social Sciences*, 2(4), 233–241.

Ogunsanwo, A. (2015). Slaying of the Supreme Commander: A Sine Qua Non for Nigeria's Development and Progress? *Splash FM 105.5*, Nigeria.

Ojameruaye, E. (2011). Reflection on Nigeria's Social and Political Development: Nigeria's Unfinished Agenda at 51. Retrieved from www.waado.org/Nigerdelta/essays/politics/Nigeria at51.htm on March 18, 2014.

Palmer, B., Walls, M., Burgess, Z., and Stough, C. (2001). Emotional Intelligence effective leadership. *Leadership and Organisational Development Journal*, 22(1), 5–10.

Ribadu, N. (2006). Corruption: The Trouble with Nigeria. Retrieved from http://www.gamji.com/articl 5000/NEWS 5530.htm on April 23, 2015.

Salovey, P., and Mayer, J. (1990). Emotional Intelligence. *Imagination, Cognition and Personality*, 9(3), 185–211.

Soludo, C. (2007). From a Pariah, Failed State to an Emerging Market Economy: The Obasanjo Legacy and Challenges Ahead, Retrieved from http://www.cenbank.org/out/speeches/- 2007/govadd14-5-07.pdf on April 20, 2009.

The Daily Trust. (2013). Newspaper, July 9.

This Day Sunday Online. (2014). May 26.

Transparency International. (2010). Corruption Perception Index.

Transparency International. (2014). Corruption Perception Index.

Ukaegbu, C. (2010). Nigeria; Beyond Good Governance at 50. Retrieved from http://www.allafrica.com/stories/20100628063.html.

Wechsler, D. (1940). Non-intellective Factors in Intelligence. *Psychological Bulletin*, 37, 444–445.

World Bank. (2000). Anti-Corruption in Transition. A contribution to the Policy Debate. World Bank, Washington, D.C.

Supply Chain and Procurement Corruption in Local Government

10

The South African Experience

EVANGELOS MANTZARIS
PREGALA PILLAY

Contents

Introduction

There are serious problems in the South Africa's municipalities. The latter is principally, but not exclusively, one of the key element that brands corruption as both petty and *grand* among the state entities. The importance of supply chain management (SCM) systems in the fight against corruption cannot be overemphasized. Should a middle manager miss a number, or another misuses the ICT database system by default, or on purpose during the adjudication and evaluation process, the tender could be awarded to the wrong bidder. Heggstad et al. (2010:14) revealed in their research that public-sector SCM is in many ways more complicated when compared to that of the private sector. This is primarily because SCM in the public sector plays the role of a strategic planner that is determined by the success of its processes. Successful strategic planning in this instance, benefits the citizens and not capital accumulation, or the maximization of profits. SCM systems and processes are rooted in a number of laws, regulations, procedures, rules, and steps undertaken by professional personnel involved in accomplishing the task or tasks that need to be fulfilled. The regulatory significance in this sense cannot ensure the effectiveness of the systems in any environment. These are examined in the context of this article, in relation to corruption in SCM, and procurement among South African municipalities.

The South African Local Government Setting

South African local municipalities are constitutionally the *third layer* of governance (the other two being the national and the provincial) governed by a set of comprehensive laws, rules, and regulations that determine the parameters of the fundamentals of *good governance* (RSA 1996). Key among these dictates is the *political oversight* of the elected political leadership (municipal councillors) of all financial management and supply chain and procurement functions as well as the administrative leaders, managers, and employees obligation to act honestly and transparently (RSA 2000a). The South African Constitution (Chapter 7 section 52) dictates the establishment of the local sphere of government, whereas Chapter 10 (section 195) outlines fundamental principles that determine the foundations of good governance including the highest standards of ethics, efficiency, transparency, accountability, and effectiveness as a foundation of local development; impartial, honest, fair, equitable and unbiased services, and active public participation in all aspects of service delivery (RSA 1996). The key law related to municipal functions, that is, The Municipal Systems Act (sections 95 and 96) dictates to the elected municipal leadership to oversee the development of aspects of budgeting, rates as well as the collection of money (RSA 2003b) is another key function that must be adhered to, in order for a municipal budget to serve as a guide for the effective management of funds through setting norms and standards that are followed according to the constitutional principles of transparency, community participation, and accountability (RSA 2003b). A financially, socially implementable, and sound budget is required to adhere to a fiscal strategy so that the municipality can proceed toward a foreseeable future without any fundamental changes, especially in terms of irregular, wasteful, or fraudulent spending that can lead to a substantial deterioration in the fiscal position (European Union 2010: 21; WHO 2011:12–13). It is understood that despite having adequate and equally comprehensive legislative and regulatory instruments, transparent, ethical, and corrupt free financial, and supply chain management cannot be guaranteed in state entities because of a number of internal and external factors that will be briefly outlined below.

SCM in South Africa: The Legislative Framework

Wan Weele (2009:11) has shown that today's SCM systems are crucial in ensuring that a public organization is run effectively, efficiently, and decisively based on ethics, solid technology as well as advanced and competently monitored performance management systems. It is only when these prerequisites exist that advanced organizational good governance can be realized. The anticorruption imperatives underline the key significance of good and ethical governance because there is always the possibility and/or probability that the work environment will abound of administrative and/or elected officials who are intent on indulging in corrupt activities. This reality underlines the significance of well-designed, planned and implemented financial, systemic, and functional controls that need to be tested regularly for risks so that existing gaps and weaknesses are rectified. The fundamental principles of the country's constitution states "When an organ of state in the national, provincial or local sphere of government, or any other institution identified in national legislation, contracts for goods or services, it must do so in accordance with a system which is fair, equitable, transparent, competitive and cost-effective." It needs to be understood that government procurement should be based on clear-cut, financially viable choices. The state should be frugal and calculative when obtaining goods and services. This implies that goods and services need to be obtained at reasonable cost.

The key principles of South Africa's SCM system is included in the Constitution of 1996, which was later supplemented by other legislative measures such as the Preferential Procurement Policy Framework Act (PPPFA), 2000 (Act 5 of 2000) (RSA 2000b), and a number of other regulations that were promulgated in order to provide an adequate and comprehensive framework for a preferential procurement system. In essence, the Act adequately supplemented the letter of the sections 217(2) and 217(3) of the constitution. A number of the outlined aims of the latter Act encourages the support of the historically disadvantaged who suffered political, financial, economical, and social discrimination under the apartheid regime. The Broad-Based Black Economic Empowerment Act (BBBEEA), 2003 (Act 53 of 2003) (RSA 2003a) was intended to provide a concrete basis for South Africa's equivalent of *affirmative action*. The latter Act outlines in detail the objectives of the concrete application of the government's legislative and regulatory instruments to achieve Black Economic Empowerment. Moreover, provision is made for government institutions and entities to establish a contract allocation framework for prospective service providers that had been discriminated against in the past, but now form an integral element of the BBBEE group. BBBEE is determined by a *balanced scorecard* devised with the aim to identify individuals and categories of persons/companies for support through the proposed BEE initiatives according to the Act. Empowerment of the historically disadvantaged is an important vehicle for broadening the horizons of an enhanced economic base that could lead to continuous growth and development (RSA Department of Trade and Industry 2003 Strategy for Black Economic Empowerment, 2003). In 2003 the government adopted the "Policy to Guide Uniformity in Procurement Reform Processes in Government" (RSA 2003c) that identified the SCM systems *blueprint* for procurement imperatives within its ranks. The adopted strategy was aimed at guiding an essentially uniform SCM system reform initiative and regulations in accordance to the prescribed stipulation: "The National Treasury may make regulations or issue instructions applicable to all institutions to which this Act applies concerning the determination of a framework for an appropriate procurement and provisioning system that is fair, equitable, transparent, competitive, and cost-effective." Treasury released an accompanying Regulation that determined a uniform strategic policy framework for SCM. Section 38 of the Public Financial Management Act (PFMA), confers general responsibilities on the accounting officer. Section 38 1(a) (iii) of the PFMA states that "the accounting officer for a department, trading entity, or constitutional institution must ensure that he/she has and maintains an appropriate procurement and provisioning system that is fair, equitable, transparent, competitive, and cost-effective ..." Both Section 76(4) (c) and 38 (1) (a) (iii) of the PFMA imposes an obligation on the National Treasury and the accounting officers to realize a procurement and provisioning system that would comply with the requirements of the Act. The Green Paper on Public Sector Procurement Reform (RSA 1997) states that the South African Governments commitment to good governance and the elevation of previously disadvantaged communities is a fundamental issue. This noble intention can only be achieved through an effective and corruption free SCM system. Such a system demands a new set of thoughts and actions regarding the evolution of procurement dynamics, and their historical development, especially in the public sector. The reason for the latter is that the SCM system is not simply a *purchasing tool*, but a fairly complex chain of systems and activities, based carefully on planned processes that are of strategic importance. These need to be driven by persons with appropriate, even advanced skills that are critical for future success (Steyn 2012).

The Dilemma: Centralized or Decentralized Systems

The debate on the significance and usefulness of the centralized and decentralized SCM system has importance, both internationally and in South Africa given the latest developments in the country. In a centralized SCM system, the section engaged in purchasing, controls all such decisions.

Hence, the systems and functions based on a standardized source, process, and technology are final. This is thought to result primarily in economies of scale that are considered important for the process of improving spending power and enhancing organizational/institutional efficiencies. It is believed that such an organization leads to a process of streamlining efficiency, effective purchasing, expertise advancement, and a continuous renewal of the supplier base. It has been revealed that centralized SCM systems are functionally more appropriate in public entities than those that are organizationally/institutionally complex, especially in the private sector. In South African municipalities, where the regulatory and legal directives are unambiguous with emphasis on the local, especially in the case of BBBEE procurement, one would think that centralized procurement (even in its decentralized form) would be ideal. However, as research has revealed that centralized procurement groups often report high incidences of corrupt and fraudulent activities in terms of adjudication, spending, process violations, and policy circumvention that ultimately lead to distorted supply measurement and performance (Lee and Kim 2007:234–5). The centralized SCM system is established in many organizations because all processes associated with it are basically performed by the SCM-based officials. This implies that such officials can be led and managed, assessed, and monitored adequately in their efforts to buy centrally and cheaply through negotiations with prospective service providers without interference. Such a system is deemed ideal because the employees and the concentration of the locality is closer, errors easily detectable, and perhaps collective decision-making (Lee and Kim 2007:235). In a decentralized supply chain organization, all the decisions in terms of sourcing, processes, and procurement are executed at the business unit or local level. This implies that a locally based business unit headed by a manager who most likely reports directly to a Chief Financial Officer (as in the case of South African municipalities). Such an organization empowers SCM systems offices/units and sites to operate with a sense of autonomy, and control over supply processes technology decisions as well as abide by the current legal and regulatory administrations. It has been said that under these circumstances, the process is swift compared to the bureaucracy and red tape with centralized procurement. Such models are often considered to be best suited for organizations that operate in a relative mode. However, this cannot be considered as the optimum system for a number of organizations, especially when the levels of knowledge and understanding of staff is limited. It is understood that as technological changes have advanced significantly over the recent years, the challenges in terms of optimization of functions and structures is instrumental in safeguarding an organization against corruption. Hence, it is the ethical behavior of both decision-makers and implementation agents that ensures the SCM system networks function ethically (Stadtler 2005:578–9). Certain literature suggests that there cannot be a completely centralised or decentralised system. Empirical findings have indicated that both systems share strengths and weaknesses given the combination of strategic and tactical imperatives, decision-making responsibilities, power relations in terms of operational and institutional realities found in particularities, diverse leadership responsibilities as well as institutional environments, and dynamics (Chang and Harrington 2000; Chen and Chen 2005:3194). A centralized SCM system process is usually led by a senior manager who has negotiating skills, delegates tasks according to the needs of the entity, and leads the assessment and monitoring functions effectively (Lee and Kim 2007). However, such a system needs to be closely monitored because it can provide opportunities for corrupt activities (Duan and Liao 2013:195–6).

The New Broom: The Centralized Procurement Office

More than R500 million was spent by the government in the 2015 financial year for goods and services. In 2016, it will spend R800 billion on big-ticket infrastructure, including roads, dams and schools as well as various municipal services (RSA 2016). South Africa's Auditor-General has over several years painstakingly pointed out that the allocated funds for services is not spent properly (RSA 2015). Bearing in mind the latter realities, the National Development Plan called for a centralized procurement office led by a chief procurement officer. The plan was to stop corruption and fraud in the supply chain and procurement process, safeguard financial integrity, and save billions of Rand for the National Treasury, and the people of the country. This step was seen as inevitable because of the different levels and values of SCM transactions found in the South African procurement system. The system accommodates middle to high-range values, quotations, and potential competitors/bidders that inevitably leads to competitive tenders in a *normal* state entity environment, that is, one that is not *polluted* by external forces and dynamics such as *political capture* and *administrative greed* (Woods and Mantzaris 2012). Because of this problem the Procurement Officer was established, in order to manage the SCM governance framework. The operation includes SCM design, development and implementation, monitoring, and evaluation of compliance. Following this process, the incumbent is obligated to pinpoint malpractices that could lead to bid cancellations, disciplinary initiatives against corrupt officials and black-list corrupt business practice (RSA 2015:8–9). The Office of the Chief Procurement Officer (OCPO), which was established in 2013, has been collaborating and cooperating with every government institution on all spheres of government. Its ultimate aim as exemplified in the National Development Plan is to modernize on the one hand, and oversee the South African public sector SCM system with the ultimate objective to ensure that the procurement of goods and services in all sectors is in accordance with the constitutional principles of fairness, equity, transparency, competitiveness, and cost effectiveness (OCPO 2013). One of the many objectives of the office is to increase state savings by using a new centralized procurement system that has been in place for several months, which was made compulsory for the national and provincial government departments from April 1, 2015 (RSA 2015:2). It was hoped that the municipalities would also be able to use the system by July 1, 2015 together with all government entities. Such a centralized system would hopefully save over R1 billion used in advertising tenders. The central database would operate as businesses, and no longer need to simultaneously apply to many departments. Consequently, government would save printing and advertising costs. Suppliers can find tenders by province, sector, and commodity type. It has been revealed that approximately 12% of the hits on the site emanate from Kenya, the Netherlands, the United States, and several other countries. This is an indication that international businesses are exploring trade with government. The transparent system enables everyone to perceive the process and its outcomes on the screen. All the prerequisites for a legally bound application (a tax certificate, a BEE certificate, and confirmation of company registration) is open for scrutiny, and according to internationally-recognized rules, regulations, and benchmarks (RSA 2015:3). There is a strong belief that the new system will be beneficial for both the public and the business sector since it lessens red tape and administrative effort, when undertake business with government and in addition ensure that the payment period for small businesses, or organizations that tender for government is reduced. There is strong evidence of simplification, standardization, and automation of the procurement process and the estimated R30bn-R40bn that was lost to corruption, would be reduced (Maswanganyi 2015:9). It has been assumed that because the South African Revenue Service and other state agencies, including the Companies and Intellectual Property Commission will have access to the database will ensure tax compliance and payment (CPO 2013:3). The CPO has been hailed as a major success by the former Finance Minister (Nhlanhla Nene) as a first step toward decreasing the cost of undertaking business with the state, since funds saved through the process would enable it to accelerate future reforms in SCM. The funds that were saved were due to the reduction in administrative cost for transacting suppliers and departments, through the central supplier database, the commerce centre, and the implementation of an e-procurement system. Funds were also saved through negotiating competitive prices for goods and services required by a number of units, sections, and entities at all spheres of government. The key issue that would guarantee the success of the system would be an improved understanding of the commodities and markets by all the departments and entities of the state. This would be instrumental in reducing costs, since the price of commodities is fully understood (Ensor 2015:4).

Financial Viability and the Threat/s of Corruption in South African Local Government SCM

The foundations of South Africa's SCM system is based on the constitution, and must follow a set of legal and regulatory principles, and guidelines. SCM and procurement is one of the most important systemic and functional pre-requisites for a municipality's financial viability. In many ways it is a vital cog in the regulatory performance imperatives of good governance and sustain-ability that allows the municipality to develop the capacity that will meet its financial obligations, and be in the forefront for service delivery to the citizens (Heggstad et al., 2010:8–9). One of the key determinants for a suc-cessful SCM and procurement system among the South African municipali-ties has been the significant mismanagement of resources. In most instances, human resources and financial management is poorly managed, there is political interference and the lack of a clear mission, vision, and leadership in the public institutions (Mantzaris 2013). This can be realized through the regulatory implementation of International Accounting Standards related to the application of the Generally Recognized Accounting Practices (GRAP) (Swanevelder, 2005). It is the responsibility of the provincial governments to oversee effectiveness and good governance in the municipalities that fall under their jurisdiction. However, there is strong empirical evidence that during the past decade, the municipalities have performed poorly and many were placed under administration because of corruption, irregular and wasteful expenditure and violation of laws, rules and regulations (Mantzaris 2014b). The key laws on which the country's SCM system is based, stipulates a highly decentralized system that *allows managers to manage*. This creates serious problems because the system is highly fragmented; a reality that not only has given impetus to fraud and corruption, but also creates difficulties for government departments to obtain maximum value when purchasing, and making use of goods and services (Mantzaris 2014a). It has been empirically revealed elsewhere (Mantzaris 2014b) that the significance of financial man-agement is fundamental to good and corruption-free governance. This cannot ever be underestimated as a key to efficient, effective, and corrupt-free SCM. Although the CPO has been lauded as a corruption-busting innovation—because the tender system is often where graft ensues—its CEO's philosophy is that there will always be a leak. However, if the procurement system is driven by technology, and is efficient and transparent, this could limit the risk. International benchmarks reveal that ranking efficiency higher than anti-corruption measures as an outcome is best international practice. In reality on the ground, however, the circumstances differ. The first level departments and other public institutions usually do not need to invite tenders to purchase goods and services below a particular sum, for example, in South Africa, it is R100,000. Below this tender cut-off spending sum are numerous day-to-day purchase transactions that are operational in nature. These transactions add up to a considerable sum of money—sometimes more than that spent through the existing tender system that includes the routine SCM system cycle operated by officials, and the relevant financial and distribution sections. These are instances where corruption can be rampant if strict rules and regulations are not adhered to (Woods and Mantzaris 2012:113–14). This is necessary because an essential sequence of actions is not followed and an environment in which risks are minimized does not exist. This implies that, control principles are violated and monitoring systems either do not exist or are ignored. Since 2009, middle value tenders, that is, purchases of R500,000, is subjected to additional regulations such as: more than one quotation (usually three quotations) be obtained from competing suppliers—from which a supplier will be selected. This requirement primarily favors the best price bid. The purchases would often be of a capital nature, for example, office furniture or computer equipment, and is subject to the registration of assets and related accounting practices (Woods and Mantzaris 2012:118). Under competitive tendering, would-be suppliers offer to settle payment for such supplies. The intention is for bidders to respond to the competitive nature of the process by offering optimum value-for-money within the specifications and conditions of the tender documents. Procurement through tendering has various interesting characteristics. These include the following:

- All things being equal, the lowest tender wins the contract. This ensures economy.
- Because the process selects primarily on the basis of price, bids are kept secret up to the point the tender closes. This ensures maximum competition. Arrangements between bidders, that is, collusion, is strictly forbidden.
- Negotiating with bidders after the closing date and before awarding the contract is prohibited. Therefore, the tender documentation contains the stipulations of the contract. The bidder must understand that his or her offer is binding, once accepted by a government institution. Tender processes ensure practices that favor transparency, fairness, and adherence to regulations, rules, and policies as well as comparative assessment of competitive bids (Woods and Mantzaris 2012:120–1).

The intertwined relationship between SCM systems with costing, budgeting, accounting, financial information, cash and stock control, asset management, and internal controls is a reality that has over the years developed (or underdeveloped) through collective and local experience. This is more significant within the context of local government, whose key objective is efficient and effective service delivery (Mantzaris 2014b). One of the key problems facing South African municipalities and the public service in general, in terms of SCM systems regulations, is that it is shaped by more than 80 different regulatory instruments, that is, a framework underpinned by multiple fragmentations. This reality constitutes a serious obstacle to a national or provincial oversight, monitoring process and evaluation, a factor that has, over the years, become a serious hurdle to maintaining high standards of service delivery (Mantzaris 2014a). The Treasury and the Auditor-General have over the past few years attempted to *streamline* the existing regulatory environment, overblown by a multiplicity of independent statutory instruments to no avail. Such realities include divisions of sectors and suppliers that are underpinned by serious fragmentation and duplication in differentiated documentations found in sectors such as water, infrastructure, human settlements/housing, public-private partnerships, and Black Economic Empowerment standards (RSA 2015:12–13). Industrial specificand general standards are prescribed in defense related armament and technologically-based supply chain regulations. Such guidelines are underlined by different rules and regulations that on many occasions result in a variety of legal and statutory uncertainties, especially in terms of interpretation (Mantzaris 2014b). These realities were laid bare in the latest Auditor-General's report who indicated that the quality of the financial statements submitted for auditing during the previous financial year *remained poor at between 92% and 97% of the auditees in five provinces* (Auditor General 2015:4). Such findings pose questions regarding the key reasons behind a poor internal control system and process at the majority of the municipalities. This is coupled with the realities of existing key vacancies in important positions that have a direct and indirect negative effect on outputs and outcomes. The Auditor-General highlighted that the position of head of the supply chain management unit had a vacancy rate in excess of 50%, which implied that a large number of the entities used consultants at a significant cost for financial and performance reporting. However, this did not improve the audit outcomes due to poor controls within the organizational environment (Auditor General 2015:5). These relations and realities are clearly outlined in the South African Auditor-General's latest Annual Report, which revealed that, although in the 2007–2008 financial year there were seven municipalities with a clean audit, the total number of municipalities and municipal entities with clean audits increased from 30 in the 2012–2013 financial year to 58 in 2013–2014. This is equal to 940 (14%) of the municipalities, and 18 (32%) of the municipal entities in the country. This was basically due to the efforts of the auditees to cement strong and efficient financial management with discipline and sustainable oversight. The Auditor-General declared that such results and outcomes are inadequate, whereas acts of corruption continues unabatedly despite the existing efforts. The minor achievements were realized through well-prepared budgets, accompanied by adequate and detailed financial statements, credible and reliable performance reports, and systematic follow-up of the objectives in the respective integrated development plans (IDP), appropriate financial internal controls, and oversight of senior management. All these steps were based on a carefully planned process that was implemented under the guidance of the senior management that provided the oversight and assurance of the credibility of the systems through both routine and substantial realities such as record-keeping and document control as well as employee discipline (Auditor General 2015:7). However, the Auditor-General cautioned that the satisfactory number of clean audits was due to the utilization of overpaid consultants and the correction of errors identified by auditors during the audit process. On the other hand, there were many transgressions in the SCM processes and functions as revealed in the findings. It was reported that irregular expenditure across the local government spectrum was R11.6-billion. Moreover, it was revealed that only R8-billion thereof utilized to procure goods and services was accounted for. The incorrect use and abuse of the SCM procedures and processes was the root cause. The report also revealed that irregular expenditure was reported at 83% of the organizations under review (i.e., 265 out of 268 of the municipalities and entities audited). The key finding highlighted the lack of basic financial and internal audit functions, poor financial performance of sections and a range of transgressions (RSA Auditor General 2015). SCM was singled out by the Auditor-General as the key cause for corruption in three provinces. Irregular expenditure amounted to R3, 651 billion in Free State, North West, and Limpopo. Free State accounted for irregular expenditure to the value of R934 million; North West R1, 899 billion whereas Limpopo, R818 million. It was noted that there was a serious lack of steps undertaken against the transgressors of such acts and these realities have led to continuous noncompliance and corruption. This was a serious oversight by the political leadership that ought to have taken action after completing the assessment process. A number of municipalities recorded irregular expenditure of approximately R3, 643 billion, of which R3, 3 billion was incurred by municipalities that received qualified audits in this category. Such expenditure among the Gauteng municipalities reached R1, 1 billion; KwaZulu-Natal R2, 3 billion whereas the Western Cape R162 million. The inability by leadership and senior management to act has been the root cause of corruption. Certain individuals have expressed the opinion that the centralization of public sector procurement could lead to *centralized corruption*, pointing out that centralizing procurement would not be a panacea in the struggle for the eradication of corruption. Such fear could be close to the heart of the problem since the existence of a completely *corrupt environment on the ground*, shaped by both social, economic, financial, and political relations of state and the private sector, as willing or unwilling participants in corruption has been evident long before the establishment of the institution (Marrian 2015). The government has been forced to improve the SCM and procurement system because of the substantial losses as a result of fraudulent and corrupt tender awards by both public servants and politicians, to increase both patronage and personal wealth. The Public Sector SCM Review (RSA 2015:5–6) highlighted one of the reasons for poor performance as a lack of a clear understanding of the vitality of SCM systems, especially by significant number of personnel as well as organizational and institutional weaknesses. This is evident since a significant number of SCM system practitioners have been unable to comprehend the consequence and power of purchasing decisions that they make. This reality in conjunction with the fact that on many occasions the systems and structures of procurement units, and sections have either substantial weaknesses, and are filled with unmotivated, weak, inexperienced, and unskilled managers and staff leads to failure. The lack of motivation at various organizational levels, high staff turnover, and the lack of essential equipment such as computers, databases, and internet connections does not determine the success of the SCM systems by technical/organizational realities alone. Political and clientist relations with the private sector/principal service providers have been a serious problem internationally with South Africa being no exception. The interface between political and administrative leadership has been a serious foundation of corruption as exemplified in the analysis of political interference, the frontiers of New Public Management (NPM) merit bureaucracy, and the weaknesses created by the *mixing* of political and administrative actions. Huberts et al. (2008), identified such relations in the existence of a mismatch between governance and governing in the international arena, whereas Matheson et al. (2007), pointed out the dangers of direct and/or indirect political involvement in the appointment of senior administrators that leads to confusing responsibility relations. Internationally, the common thread in existing relations among elected officials and administrators is that politicians are basically involved in policy development and oversight, and the administrators' primary responsibility is the corrupt-free, and appropriate implementation of such policies.

Such a relationship demands a transparent, accountable, citizen-driven, and honest relationship based on mutual trust. According to the existing South African laws, the political leader and head of a municipality is the Mayor who oversees the solid performance of the organization. The laws, rules, and regulations demand that the Mayor and/or other elected officials or politicians may not manipulate the administrative offices in government

(Cameron 2010). However, empirical research has revealed that political interference in administrative affairs, the dominance of political parties over municipal councils, interference by politicians in the administrative duties, and the lack of adequate accountability measures and support systems lead to corruption (Department of Cooperative Governance and Traditional Affairs 2009). Such realities have been evident since the dawn of the country's democracy in 1994. Mafunisa (2003) states that without a clear separation of the duties and responsibilities of the sectors and the *de-politicization* of the relationship, the future of state reform is doubtful. Maserumule (2007:147–64), who supports this notion, empirically identified the effects of existing *conflicts* among senior public servants (directors-general) and cabinet ministers. The key role of what has been called *partisan control of the bureaucracy* pinpoints the effects of the great influence of politics in the functions of the public sector, thus inevitably, creating a serious shift in the political/administrative relationships in the country. Direct meddling by politicians in administrative functions and duties, especially in SCM systems poses a serious threat leading to increased corruption as well as a direct negation of the *developmental state* (Cameron 2010:676–701). Such empirical work follows on the footsteps of previous research in relation to the implementation and processes of NPM, which highlights that interference by politicians in issues of staffing could have a detrimental effect on effective service delivery. Such realities point to the significance of meritocracy in employee selection and promotion (Cameron 2003:51–66, 2007:345–71, 2009:910–42). The public sector SCM Review (2015:4) clearly stated that "The lack of clarity about the roles and responsibilities of technical staff and of political officer bearers creates scope for interference, and this gives rise to allegations or instances of corruption." It has been recorded that political interference, weaknesses, and abuse of the SCM system provides opportunities for the municipalities and its personnel, elected municipal councillors, their relatives, and a number of other public service employees to benefit from municipal contracts worth over R800-million between 2013 and 2014. In addition, the largest percentage of the corruption-related financial gains estimated to be R781-million went to close relatives of employees and councillors at 100 of the municipalities and entities (RSA Auditor General 2015:4). It has also been established that R31-million fraud took place, of which the municipal staff or councillors were aware of the existing conflict of interest, but failed to declare the theft. This is not only corrupt, but also an illegal act. More than half of the municipalities—168 in total—engaged in uncompetitive or unfair procurement processes, whereas another 103 had inadequate contract management processes, and a further 37 could not provide auditors with relevant documentation to show which contracts had been to be entered into.

Conclusions

The key challenges in respect of finding the best balance between the two major objectives of Section 217 of the South African Constitution of 1996 as well as the PPPFA lies in the elimination of corruption that exists at present and the transformation of procurement as a developmental tool. The existing situation is a painful reality of fraud, corruption, and avarice at all functional and structural levels of the South African local government terrains and is based on both historical and contemporary reasons. It is hoped that the Central Procurement Office that deals with a vast scope of government procurement will be able to address the major problems in procurement, ranging from corruption to a dearth of skills, legislation and the fact that public procurement has a *political element* to it. State procurement is a bureaucratic process that needs to be strengthened with enforced rules and no political interference.

References

Auditor General. 2015. Municipal Finance Management Act (MFMA), 2014–2015.

Cameron, R. 2003. Politics-administration interface: The case of the city of Cape Town. *International Review of Administrative Sciences*, 69(1): 51–66.

Cameron, R. 2007. Metropolitan government in South Africa: The limits of formal reorganisation. In: Collin, J.P. and Robertson, M. (eds.). *Governing Metropolises: Profiles of Issues and Experiments on Four Continents*. Quebec City: Presses de l'Université Laval, 345–371.

Cameron, R. 2009. New Public Management reforms in the South African public service: 1999–2009. *Journal of Public Administration*, 44(4.1): 910–942.

Cameron, R. 2010. Redefining political-administrative relationships in South Africa. *International Review of Administrative Sciences*, 76(4): 676–701.

Chang, M.H. and Harrington, J.E., Jr. 2000. Centralization vs. Decentralization in a multi-unit organization: A computational model of a retail chain as a multi-agent adaptive system. *Management Science*, 46, 1427–1440.

Chen, J.M. and Chen, T.H. 2005. The multi-item replenishment problem in a two-echelon supply chain: the effect of centralization versus decentralization. *Computers & Operations Research*, 32, 3191–3207.

Chief Procurement Officer (CPO). 2013. Annual Report, Pretoria: Government Printers.

Department of Cooperative Governance and Traditional Affairs. 2009. Report on State of Local Government in South Africa. Pretoria, South Africa: Government Printer.

Duan, Q. and Warren Liao, T. 2013. Optimization of replenishment policies for decentralized and centralized capacitated supply chains under various demands. *International Journal of Production Economics*, 142, 194–204.

Ensor, L. 2015. Treasury's central procurement office saving billions, says Nene, CITY PRESS, November 2.

European Union. 2010. The Contract Committee of the Supreme Audit Institutions of the European Union published guidelines on public procurement audit in 2010. Brussels, Belgium.

Heggstad, K., Froystad, M. and Isaksen, J. 2010. The basics of integrity in procurement—A guidebook. Bergen, Norway: Christian Michelsen Institute.

Huberts, W.J.C., Maesschalck, J. and Jurkiewicz, C.L. 2008. *Ethics and Integrity of Governance: Perspectives Across Frontiers*. Northampton, MA: Edward Elgar.

Lee, J.H. and Kim, C.O. 2007. Multi-agent systems applications in manufacturing systems and supply chain management: a review paper. *International Journal of Production Research*, 46, 233–265.

Mafunisa, J. 2003. Separation of politics from the South African public service: Rhetoric or reality? *Journal of Public Administration*, 38(2): 85–101.

Mantzaris, E. 2013. Corruption is sickness, but a curable one ACCERUS Newsletter, No. 3.

Mantzaris, E.A. 2014a. Public Procurement, Tendering and Corruption: Realities, Challenges and Tangible Solutions. *African Journal of African Affairs*, 7(2): 67–79.

Mantzaris, E.A. 2014b. Supply Chain Management Systems and Corruption: The South African Case. Keynote Address, International Anti-Corruption Conference, Montecasino, Johannesburg, November.

Marrian, N. 2005. Better links with business promised, CITY PRESS, June 26.

Maserumule, M.H. 2008. Framework for strengthening the capacity of municipalities in South Africa: A developmental local government perspective. *Journal of Public Administration*, 43(3): 436–451.

Maswanganyi, N. 2015. New e-tender portal to simplify procurement process, CITY PRESS, April 9.

Matheson, A., Weber, B., Manning, N. and Arnould, E. 2007. Study on the political involvement in senior staffing and on the delineation of responsibilities between ministers and senior civil servants. *OECD Working Papers on Public Governance*. Paris, France: OECD.

Office of the Chief Procurement Officer (OCPO). 2013. Pretoria, South Africa: Government Printers.

Republic of South Africa (RSA). 1996. Constitution of the Republic of South Africa, of 1996. Pretoria, South Africa: Government Printer.

Republic of South Africa (RSA). 1997. The Green Paper on Public Sector Procurement Reform. Pretoria, South Africa: Government Printer.

Republic of South Africa (RSA). 1999. Public Finance Management Act, 1 of 1999. (PFMA) (Act 1 of 1999). Pretoria, South Africa: Government Printer.

Republic of South Africa (RSA). 2000a. Local Government: Municipal Systems Act, 2000 (Act 32 of 2000). Pretoria, South Africa: Government Printer.

Republic of South Africa (RSA). 2000b. Preferential Procurement Policy Framework Act (PPPFA), 2000 (Act 5 of 2000). Pretoria, South Africa: Government Printer.

Republic of South Africa (RSA). 2003a. The Broad-Based Black Economic Empowerment Act (BBBEEA), (Act 53 of 2003). Pretoria, South Africa: Government Printer.

Republic of South Africa (RSA). 2003b. Local Government: Municipal Finance Management Act, 2003 (Act 56 of 2003). Pretoria, South Africa: Government Printer.

Republic of South Africa (RSA). 2003c. Policy to Guide Uniformity in Procurement Reform Processes in Government. Pretoria, South Africa: Government Printer.

Republic of South Africa (RSA). 2004. Financial reporting by municipalities in South Africa in terms of GAMAP/GRAP 23 SA Government Gazette. 2004. No. 26511. Pretoria, South Africa: Government Printer.

Republic of South Africa (RSA). 2015. Public Sector Supply Chain Management Review, Treasury. Pretoria, South Africa: Government Printers.

Republic of South Africa (RSA). 2016. RSA National Budget 2016. http://www.fin24/budgetspeech2016 (accessed March 12, 2016).

Stadtler, H. 2005. Supply chain management and advanced planning—basics, overview and challenges. *European Journal of Operational Research*, 163, 575–588.

Steyn, P.G. 2012. Sustainable Strategic Supply Chain Leadership & Management, *PM World Journal*, December, Vol. I.

Swanevelder, J.J. 2005. Performance measures (ratios) in the evaluation of financial and other results of municipalities: revisited. *Southern African Business Review*, 9(1): 66–77.

Wan Weele, A. 2009. *Purchasing and Supply Chain Analysis, Strategy and Practice.* 5th Edition. Cengage Learning EMEA.

WHO. 2011. Harmonized monitoring and evaluation indicators for procurement and supply management systems. Geneva, Switzerland.

Woods, G. and Mantzaris, E. 2012. Anti-Corruption Reader, ACCERUS. Stellenbosch, South Africa: University of Stellenbosch.

Corruption and Public Procurement Fraud in the English- Speaking Caribbean

11

PERRY STANISLAS
KAREN LANCASTER-ELLIS

Contents

Introduction

In most emergent nations the lack of political leadership role in support of major administrative and management change can be traced to their own concerns for maintaining their elite status and authority-an elite status and authority so crisply controlled that it is difficult for society to penetrate (Hope 1983: 52).

This chapter explores public procurement fraud in the English-speaking Caribbean, in the context of how many of these new countries have emerged, and how their historical legacies have contributed to practices that adversely impact on the development of these postcolonial societies. It explores the key features that have shaped the administrative cultures in various Caribbean countries and how this has resulted in weak institutions of governance that have created the conditions for corruption and public procurement concerns. The chapter is informed by the views of a leading forensic accountant and expert on public sector fraud, and procurement matters, in the English-speaking

Caribbean. These views were obtained via an extensive interview held in a Southern Caribbean country in 2015. The chapter also draws on unpublished data from interviews with senior Caribbean crime journalists, from several countries, on criminal justice matters (see Stanislas 2016a).

The chapter will first explore the administrative culture of many Caribbean countries and how they contribute to forms of abuse, inefficiencies, and poor performance. Second, it will explore the role of political leaders and governments, and how their practices in the area of public procurement in construction and public works contribute to suboptimal performance in the context of national development. Third, the chapter will examine the history of anticorruption legislation, policy, and practice in various Caribbean countries. Fourth, the chapter interrogates controversies and suspected cases of procurement fraud, and what policies and changes have been introduced in their wake to prevent these offences from recurring. Finally, the chapter will conclude by addressing the role of law enforcement in preventing public procurement fraud and their effectiveness in a number of English-speaking Caribbean countries.

The antecedents of most English-speaking post-war independent governments have their roots in three sources. First the labor movement that emerged as a powerful force and closely associated with the second factor, the anticolonial movement, and mass politics that sought independence from Britain, and finally the emergence of the indigenous middle class that saw them entering local administration, the police, and other roles in preparation for independence (Legister 1998, Rueschemeyer and Stephens 1992). The administrative culture of most Caribbean countries crystallize practices rooted in the colonial past and the post-independence realities. One of the defining characteristics of colonial administration that was to have a profound effect on how many of these countries developed was nepotism and the view that the powerful had as a matter of right the ability to appoint those favored by them, regardless of their technical abilities, and suitability (Beasley 2005, Kirk-Green 1999). The colonies had always been used by the powerful and well-connected from Metropolitan countries to send their sons, family members, or others, to prove or preoccupy themselves away from home, where they could do little damage (Kirk-Green 1999). Nowhere did this practice have a more profound effect in shaping the workings of important institutions than the colonial police (Stanislas 2016a).

Administrative and Institutional Cultures in the Caribbean

The problems of post-independence administration in the Caribbean has been hampered by the small geographical size of the majority of English-speaking countries, and their populations that has led to many of them being described as micro states (Bishop and Payne 2010, Schotborgh and van Velzen 2013). Of the 24 members of the Caribbean economic and political union CARICOM (not all English-speaking), they range in size from the largest Jamaica with 2.8 million people, and Trinidad and Tobago with 1.31 million people, to the smallest Turks and Caicos with 37,188 people, and Dominica with 73,499 people (World Bank 2013). The small sizes of these countries and lack of resources, in terms of levels of education and training and physical resources, has severely weakened their capabilities (Caribbean Human Development Report 2012). Moreover, one of the distinguishing features of such small countries is a very personalized form of government leadership that contributes to intervention in minutiae, cum-micro management, lack of transparency, and dependency based on personal association that contributes to unhealthy administrative cultures and corruption (Hope 1983: 56, 2015, see Wayne 2010). This has led to debates about whether there is more corruption in smaller countries than their larger counterparts. Schotborgh's (Undated) review of the literature maintains that there is little evidence other than anecdotal to support the view that smaller Caribbean countries have a higher likelihood of corruption than their larger counterparts. One possible explanation for this is smaller countries may be poorer and have less resources, and opportunities to motivate widespread corrupt practices.

The prevailing model of politics and government that emerged in most English-speaking Caribbean countries, was far more committed to liberal democracy and stability, than their counterparts in other former colonial regions, such as black Africa that has seen violence, attempted coups inter alia (Rueschemeyer and Stephens 1992: 226), but share important similarities in the conduct of politicians in office. In Jamaica, the Stone Committee was given the task to look at the behavior of parliamentarians (Stone 1991). Among the recommendations made was a code of ethics for individuals holding parliamentary positions. The code incorporated a declaration of the parliamentarians' assets and finances, and an oath that would require them to conduct themselves in a manner that would generate trust and respect by those whom they serve. The parliamentarians were also to eschew corruption, lies, and violent acts. It did not end there; they were also to declare their intention to refrain from engaging in political victimization or the acquisition of private funds through public office.

Another shared feature of these infant liberal democracies is the narrow and exclusive notion of majority rule, or what some have described as *majoritarianism* (Mazuri and Tidy 1987, Schotborgh 2013). According to this outlook the winner takes all, and those who emerge victorious from elections as the government, and their supporters have the right to monopolise the spoils of government and its largess (Harriot 2008, Hintzen 2006, Meeks 2000). Caribbean politics is largely based on clientelism, which is explored in detail by Meeks (2000) and Harriot (2008) in the Jamaican instance, and Hintzen

(2006) writing on Guyana and Trinidad and Tobago. In the case of the latter two, ethnicity plays an important role in the politics of these countries with politicians seeking to mobilize and consolidate their support with either the East Indian population or those of African descent, where sections of these groups are rewarded accordingly. This has contributed to very divisive ethnic, near tribal politics that has serious societal consequences.

An example of how this political thinking and practice can have detrimental effects on critical institutions and national development can be seen in the controversy surrounding the appointment of an unqualified and junior technician Reshmi Usha Ramnarine, to a very sensitive position within the Trinidad and Tobago Intelligence Service. The appointment took place in the context of the Indian dominance and control of government and most of the key national institutions (Sunday Express 2016). Staying with Trinidad and Tobago, Hintzen details how the military was used by largely African dominated governments, as a defacto employment bureau for its friends, filling the senior ranks with unqualified individuals with no real interest in military affairs who used their positions for personal gain. This created deep tensions with better educated and more motivated junior officers, openly siding with protesters during major disturbances that occurred during the 1970s (Hintzen 2006: 81).

Placed in this context corruption, weak institutional performance and inadequate governance, is synonymous with most Caribbean countries to one degree or another. On the matter of financial governance, St. Lucia provides some exemplary cases. Wayne (2010: 374–377) details the fundamental weaknesses of the Ministry of Finance who flagrantly breached its own policies and was unable to carry out its mandate of regulating other government department or agencies. One of the best examples of lack of financial and legal accountability is the National Conversation Agency where a catalog of appalling abuses occurred, which included managers *borrowing* funds that were not repaid, equipment being purchased that was never received, ghost workers, and non-existent accounts, or any form of financial record keeping. Nobody was held to account for these gross failings (Wayne 2010: 377).

Dakolia (1996) highlights how cultures of patronage and appointments to judicial positions has compromised the integrity and effectiveness of the legal system in Caribbean and Latin American countries, whereas Wayne (2010: 300) details how many in the legal profession have been compromised by their association and involvement in criminal activities, such as assisting major drug criminals dispose of their ill-gotten gains. The consequences of this culture of patronage and corruption, and its impact on important financial institutions, is further illustrated in the Bahamas. The Bahamian Prime Minister Winston Pinder, who received party funding from the notorious American crime boss Meyer Lansky (Bowling 2010: 55), boasted about his ambition of making the Bahamian banking system the *Switzerland of the Caribbean* (Cratton 2002: 258). The Bahamian banking system became a haven for criminal activities, such as money laundering, and was characterized by serious professional, and procedural lapses that contributed to a confrontation with the United States. This resulted in major reforms and a significant improvement of Bahamian systems of governance and administration (Stanislas 2016b).

St. Lucia provides one of the most graphic examples of how many of the weaknesses of state institutions come together at different levels, to facilitate corruption and criminality in these micro states in a very disturbing way, and exemplified by the career of the disgraced politician Richard Fredrick. Fredrick first began to draw attention as a police recruit trainee where his penchant for flashing money around was odd for poorly paid police officers, raising strong suspicions of corruption very early in his career (Unpublished Interview 2010). After several years he begun to study law, and qualified as a lawyer, and left the Royal St. Lucia Police Force (RSLPF) to set up his legal practice, where he specialized in defending high-profile drugs and criminal clients. One of his claims to fame was Fredrick's boast of never losing a criminal case, which given the fundamental deficiencies of the police (Stanislas forthcoming), and widely believed assistance from friends within the RSLPF (i.e., disposing of evidence and crucial documentation) placed his professional claims in a less exemplary light (see Ally 2010).

Using his money, the flamboyant Fredrick was able to gain support in the deprived areas of Castries among poor youth, and entered politics and government where he was given a ministerial position (see Wayne 2010). His appointment caused shock and incredulity, given widespread suspicions surrounding Fredrick's involvement in the drugs trade that forced opposition leader Dr. Kenny Anthony to make very strong comments describing those events as the "most frightening developments in the politics of the country" (Wayne 2010: 549), and an even more vitriolic response was from former Prime Minister John Compton (Wayne 2010: 306). The influence of Housing Minister Fredrick can be seen in his ability to have two young custom officers who arrested him transferred. The customs officers were investigating Fredrick's involvement in customs fraud, involving a large number of vehicles he imported from the United States (Joseph 2011: 171, Unpublished Interviews 2010). Despite the legendary reputation of Prime Minister Compton in his readiness to dismiss ministers and public officials, and his personal enmity toward Fredrick, he was powerless to act against him other than to express his disapproval (Wayne 2010).

It was the intervention of the U.S. law enforcement who brought to light a number of serious criminal offenses including fraud committed by Fredricks in the United States, and its decision to deny him right to enter the country, which eventually led to his political demise (www.stlucianewsonline.com 2014, www.voteslp.com 2014). The integrity and effectiveness of Caribbean institutions has direct security implications for the United States that shapes its interventionist attitudes. What this experience revealed was the reach of individuals such as Fredrick in small countries and his ability to mobilize friends and associates within the key institutions of the state that made him literally untouchable; especially given the delicate political makeup of the government. In this instance like many others, it was the intervention of U.S. law enforcement that was to play an invaluable role in limiting the potential harm that such unscrupulous individuals could cause.

Procurement Fraud

Research carried out in 2009 on world governance indicators, which included many CARICOM countries, found the following: Bahamas scored highest in the area of integrity of procedures and systems, whereas Barbados had the most effective administrative systems (Bennett and Morabito 2006, Schotborgh and van Velzen 2013). Corruption is defined as: "the extent to which public power is exercised for private gain, including both petty and grand forms of corruption, and the 'capture' of the state by elites and private interests" (Schotborgh and van Velzen 2013: 13). Jamaica and Trinidad and Tobago were among the intermediate performers, with Guyana and Haiti amongst the worse.

Very few Caribbean countries have anti-procurement fraud instruments in place, never mind enforcing them with great diligence to prevent corruption. At the time of Schotborgh's writing, the small number of countries included the Bahamas, Barbados, Dominica, Jamaica, St. Lucia, and Trinidad and Tobago, where policies were in place stipulating that Ministers and senior officials declare all private interests or potential conflicts of interest. Citing the 2004 Transparency International study of eight CARICOM countries public procurement systems, Schotborgh highlights its findings that the majority of the countries in question had poor procurement systems that operated largely on partisan clientelist lines. One of the important challenges and obstacles to regional development is the absence of robust practices to tackle procurement fraud, and the difficulties faced by countries attempting to introduce them in a context, where their neighboring countries and partners lag in this area. According to the United Nations (2012), even if one or a few countries adopt anti-corruption policies and practices, their progress will be stymied by the failure of other Caribbean governments to do likewise. The absence of a regional body with responsibility and authority to enforce decisions taken at CARICOM level is failing the Caribbean and its people. This and similar observations have led some to question the need for and efficacy of CARICOM and its role in the region (Bishop and Payne 2010: 5). Procurement fraud legislation enacted in Jamaica for instance if it is to make significant strides would require similar actions elsewhere in the region, as seen in the European Union (Dorn et al. 2008, Ruddock 2011).

The most comprehensive study of public procurement in a Caribbean country is the work of Harriot (2008) on Jamaica. He outlines the high levels of corruption in local government around matters of procurement and construction work, particularly road-building, school construction, and community facilities. Procurement practices are closely related to political party funding, given the high, and increasing costs involved in running modern election campaigns, and politicians paying back their donors by means of access to lucrative contracts. This has led to the de facto entry of criminals into politics, and the capture of many politicians via campaign funding (Dorn et al. 2008: 249), which has enabled them to exercise considerable influence on politicians in the award of contracts. This is important, given the significance of public construction work to the national development of Jamaica and other developing countries. The Honorable Peter Bunting, Jamaica's Minister of National Security, openly admitted that criminal offenders who have lent their support to candidates in the political process have been awarded government contracts as a reward for their support (Daraine 2014).

Joseph (2011: 168) maintains that the construction industry has filled the space created by the decline of the banana industry in St. Lucia, which is illustrated by the clamor for contracts in the lead up to the 2007 Cricket World Cup. Moreover, given the exposure of Jamaica and other Caribbean islands to natural disasters in the form of hurricanes (Harriot 2008: 136, Stanislas 2016b) that creates the need for emergency repair work, and in other areas such as hotel construction, underscores the lucrative nature of procurement matters. However, one of the concerns highlighted in Harriot's study is how work is awarded to contractors that they are unqualified to carry out in terms of quality, which has serious consequences for public safety and public finances (Goldstock 1990: 17).

The depth of corruption and the highly individualistic political culture in Jamaica that results in members of the public desiring personal reward for their support and access to the *gravy train* that public procurement represents, are described by a respondent in Harriot (2008: 133):

> Everybody is a contractor, if you drive a truck you are a contractor, if you have a backhoe you are a contractor, or if you own two machetes you are a contractor because the contractor business can allow you to move from riding a bicycle today to driving a Bimma (Jamaican term for BMW).

Effort to tighten up on the various forms of bad practice that has led to the wide-scale abuse of the public procurement process is detailed by Harriot.

This includes improving transparency in the contract awarding process, by making it mandatory that contracts over a particular dollar value are advertised nationally. In addition, forcing bidders to purchase the relevant bidding documents that contain a range of stipulations that now have to be met. Once bids have been received by the relevant government departments, they are opened in a public forum, and the names of the contractors read out, along with verification that all required mandatory documents have been submitted. Finally, the figure contained within the bid is read out. A report is then produced about the bid evaluation process and the results then forwarded to an external committee responsible for this aspect of the process, along with a letter from the Permanent Secretary of the relevant government ministry that is responsible for the agency in question. Any bid equal to or more than J$ 15 million is sent to the cabinet for approval (Harriot 2008: 134).

Although the process described by Harriot constitutes significant progress from the laissez faire practices that seem to characterize Jamaican procurement procedures of an earlier period, there still exists significant deficiencies that allow abuse of the system. The most common is the compromising of confidential information, such as the estimates of surveyors at the bid preparation stage, which is facilitated by the number of political supporters in managerial and important positions who are privy to it. Another is politician's ability to exploit special provisions to award contracts to their associates. Harriot (2008: 136) notes how negotiated procedures are abused in the Jamaican context of reconstruction, after major hurricane damage by politicians to give contracts to ill-qualified contractors. Further, an example of this can be seen in China, where corruption in the construction industry is rife, and has a notorious track record of dangerous construction practices that has resulted in structures collapsing, and killing and injuring individuals (Foster 2010). This is particularly disconcerting, given the growing role China is playing in Caribbean construction matters (Wayne 2010: 603).

Organized criminals are also able to take advantage of special provisions that enables them to obtain contracts to work in violent areas, or those under their control. This problem is not unique to Jamaica and replicated in mainland Trinidad (Report of the Commission of Enquiry 2010). The rationale given by politicians in both countries is that their preferred choices of contractors were better able to carry out required work in violent communities than their rivals (see ROCE 2010). Many contractors are unable to work in these environments and have been known to withdraw from contracts due to fear for their lives and their workers (ROCE 2010: 35). As elsewhere in the world such as in Northern Ireland, or in the United States, organized crime gangs, terrorist groups, or contractors representing their interest, are instrumental in creating the environment of intimidation that drives out legitimate businesses (Goldstock 1990, House of Common Northern Ireland Affairs Committee 2006).

Concerns about public procurement practices in Trinidad and Tobago has resulted in some high profile controversies surrounding a statutory corporation and private limited company called UDECOTT, which was formed in 1993. UDECOTT's activities and how it managed its affairs led to a public inquiry into the construction sector, which published its report in 2010. The purpose of the inquiry was to examine whether commissioned projects were value for money, standard of work, and the competiveness, transparency, and integrity of procedures and processes used. In particular, the inquiry sought to establish whether the commissioning of projects complied with public procurement procedures (ROCE 2010: xxiv). One of the drivers for the establishment of the inquiry was the widespread belief that the government procurement procedures was not being adhered to, after the Ministry of Finance was charged with implementing them in all government departments and agencies. The commission reviewed a number of different types of construction projects between 2003 and 2009. One of the observations made very early was the disparity of performance where projects of very similar scale and size had significant differences in terms of their completion time and costs (ROCE 2010: 205). Some examples of the projects reviewed included, the International Waterfront Project and the Prime Minister's residence, and relatively simple projects such as Belmont Police Station construction, and the Government Campus Project (ROCE 2010: 26).

The review also included important prestige projects, such as the Brian Lara Cricket Stadium, which was planned to be ready for the 2007 Cricket World Cup (Stanislas 2014) that ended up in a high profile debacle, with disputes between contractors and subcontractors bringing the project to a grinding halt. Attention was also paid to several projects suspected of collusion, involving foreign contractors, particularly Chinese contractors (ROCE 2010: 28). One problem identified earlier by the inquiry was issues around the quality and competence of key managers, especially in the area of project management, with unqualified people occupying important positions within the procurement process (United Nations Office on Drugs and Crime 2013: 10–11). Another area of concern identified was *price gouging* whereby contractors or suppliers bought goods and materials at low prices, and sought to take advantage of price increases to maximize profit. Common examples of this are the pricing of materials such as steel and cement (ROCE 2010: 62). One of the key recommendations of the inquiry was that the Ministry of Finance should renew efforts to develop a uniform set of procurement rules, and all agencies and Ministries involved in its tendering process were required to make clear what rules are applicable to various bids. This is to prevent the practice of increasing the likelihood of a bid being successful by subjecting it to less exacting procurement procedures, designed for other purposes. It also called for transparency and the need to ensure compliance with procurement rules.

Attitudes to Procurement Fraud in the Caribbean

The issue of whether island size had any import for the degree of corruption and procurement problems is a vexed one (Shotborgh 2012). The traditional assumption is given the small size of particular islands, their administrations, and the familiarity of key actors with each other, helps to facilitate corruption and other problems (Hopes 1983, Kincaid 2000). However, the evidence seems to support the conclusions drawn by Shotborgh (2012) in his review of the literature. The forensic accountant reinforces this view:

> It's rampant in the bigger Caribbean countries which is Trinidad, Jamaica, I will put a question mark by Barbados because there is only so much you could do in countries that are not as large. The smaller Caribbean islands there is only so much development they can do. Also they are more focused on tourism, so their infrastructure activity is really geared by private investors, that is building hotels and so.

Commenting on the smaller islands he continues:

> They don't want too much development because it takes away from the tourist impact of the island being so laid back. So you wouldn't really find procurement fraud that prevalent. There have been projects in Grenada that has been controversial, but it's not so common.

As in the literature billing-related fraud is one of the most common forms of crime that takes place in the construction industry (Kankaaranta and Muttilainen 2010). This can take the form of overcharging relatively modest amounts across numerous items, or activities or significant amounts for a few, or a combination of both. Stanislas (2014) highlights one of the ways this issue was tackled in the context of the 2012 Olympic Games construction projects, was by means of Cross Verification Teams, whose role was to check the accuracy of invoices. In some instances, matters around the correct costs and billing for work can encompass all that has been mentioned and more which is explained:

> A lot of projects that have gone over, over-charged, over-priced and you circumstantially look at it [invoices] and it has nothing to do with the actual work or anything like that. We had these issues with the Brian Lara Stadium in Trinidad; we had issues with Piarco Airport.

Some of the figures involved demonstrate, how prevalent and flagrant this type of fraud is in many Caribbean countries. One illustration given by the respondent was a total bill of $30 million for a contract initially priced at $1 million. It is a common practice that construction projects costs can be revised in the light of unforeseen problems (DEFRA 2013, Zayas 2012) by use of what is termed a change order, which is an officially sanctioned procedure. The types of abuses highlighted by the respondent are not sanctioned adjustments of costs, but caused by weak-cost control and lack of monitoring. One of the practices highlighted was politicians using their influence to inflate budgets deliberately to facilitate these fraudulent practices. This is described as follows by the respondent:

> So now what the smart fraudsters are doing is beefing up the budget, including things like oil prices variances in the budget that is contracted.

He continues:

> You will hear most politicians singing the song over the last five years, the project was done within budget, but then they actually significantly bumped up the budget.

The issue of party political funding and its corrupting influence has been explored in the literature in the developed and developing world, particularly as it relates to procurement fraud (Dorn et al. 2008: 249, Harriot 2008, Schotborgh and van Velzen 2013). Political parties have developed very elaborate ways of receiving funding through public procurement. In some instances, political parties receive funding from financiers for election campaigns, and in return reward their benefactor via lucrative contracts. In other instances, party financiers are paid a percentage of the value of contracts awarded to supporters or funders. In Nigeria, as Aremu Reference in his chapter, illustrates most new incumbents to government office see it as their right to use their positions to accrue as much money as possible, and by any means, in part to recoup, or repay the vast amounts spent on modern election campaigns. Commenting on similar Caribbean region-wide practice, the respondent states:

> You have political financiers, financing the parties and when the parties get in power the only way to pay them back is by giving them contracts.

Most commonly the areas more susceptible to this practice are public works, state enterprises, and telecommunications, which are sources of potentially large contracts. The logic underpinning these practices are structured literally around every aspect of the governance surrounding public procurement, such as the lack of legislation, or policy guidelines, and weak enforcement mechanisms in these countries. The general attitude of government and politicians to tackling procurement fraud is summed up:

Those at the top are benefitting so they're not serious about it. They will talk
about it for political gain, but they're not serious about it.

Closely related to the issue of party political funding is weak or nonexistent legislation regarding procurement matters in most English-speaking
Caribbean countries, which is shaped by the interest of politicians, their
funders, and supporters (Schotborgh and van Velzen 2013). One of the few
countries that is beginning to address the issue of corruption, in all spheres
of public service, and has taken a lead in this important area, is Jamaica.
This can be seen by the arrest of police officers for suspected corruption,
including members of the Major Organized Crime and Anti-Corruption
Agency (Jamaican Observer 2011 and 2015). The Jamaican government has
passed the Corruption Prevention Act 2001 that contains numerous provisions that specifically addresses matters relating to procurement, such as not
disclosing conflicts of interests, the compromising of confidential information inter alia.

The legislation was supported by the formation of a number of key law
enforcement agencies that includes the Office of the Contractor General,
which is specifically charged with eliminating procurement related fraud
and corruption, and has monitoring and investigatory powers; whereas the
Commission for the Prevention of Corruption is responsible for regulating
the behavior of public officials (National Integrity Action Undated). Despite
this important development by the Jamaican government on one level,
the Contractor General's office lacks power in very crucial instances. The
Contractor General does not have the authority to stop a procurement process that does not comply with the procurement guidelines. Neither does the
office have the power to stop procurement that display signs of corruption,
impropriety, or which appears irregular (Christie 2014). Passing legislation
in itself, such as the Public Procurement and Disposal of Public Property Act
2015 by the Trinidad and Tobago government, will not effectively eliminate
bad practice. In order to support legislation there is the need for good effective
guidelines, policies, and procedures that reduce the scope for manipulation
and exploitation by skilled and well-resourced offenders (Levy 1987: 141).
This is explained:

If you pass law and keep things too legal what will happen is that the bright
fraudsters are going to beat you on legalities and technicalities. Remember
white collar crime means somebody who is at your level, just as bright, and if
they are part of a team have lawyers and accountants to advise them as well.

Despite the existence of robust legislation, policy guidelines, and procedures
that have significantly improved the procurement process in Jamaica, the
effectiveness of these instruments is still questionable, given the evidence

presented by Harriot (2008) of the power and influence of politicians inter alia to subvert them. This is also reinforced by the remarks of the forensic accountant when commenting about policies and procedures that exist in other English-speaking Caribbean countries:

> Many do have them, but policies and procedures don't move by themselves. So I could tell you I have policies and procedures, but that doesn't mean that they are being used.

He continues:

> Remember many Caribbean countries go for funding from the IMF, the Inter American Bank, and the International Development Bank what have you. When those institutions disburse money you have to have these policies in writing. But these policies are just what they are something in writing to fulfil certain international expectations.

Lack of resourcing can also be a critical factor in the weakness of the implementation of policies. This can be seen in the funding of contract monitoring units or the lack of technology that enables procurement staff to easily police processes and procedures (Organisation for Economic Cooperation and Development Asian Development Bank 2006: 11–12). Jamaica leads in the English-speaking Caribbean in its level of technological development, and resourcing as seen by the establishment of the Jamaica Constabulary Force's Communications, and Forensic Unit (www.cubesolutions.com, undated). This is not necessarily a reflection of the level of technological development throughout central and local government, but a promising sign. Other countries such as the Bahamas and Trinidad and Tobago are among the more advanced countries where technology is concerned, if their police are indicative of broader trends in public administration, whereas smaller islands such as St. Lucia and others are quite underdeveloped in this area by comparison (Stanislas 2014: 224, 2016b).

Problems with Law Enforcement

A story featured in the Trinidad and Tobago Guardian cited Assistant Commissioner of Police (ACP) Glen Hackett who highlighted the many challenges that the police and law enforcement agencies are confronted within tackling procurement fraud and other forms of corruption (Khan 2012). The ACP identified the problems of: "technical complexity, reluctance of victims to seek prosecution, inadequate punishment, trial dynamics, onerous document examination, and forged currency as major challenges faced by

Caribbean law enforcement" in prosecuting white-collar offenders (see Levy 1987). An additional difficulty faced by the police is the attitude of the private sector to procurement and other forms of white-collar crime. The respondent elaborates:

> In the Caribbean we separate the private and public sector, but in developed countries their law enforcement can go after anyone. If you're a private sector organisation and you lose a million dollars in procurement fraud they say it has nothing to do with the police, but it has everything to do with the police. Other countries will say it has everything to do with the police, because it means you are now short one million dollars. That means your profit is down, which means the taxes accrued to government is now short by 25 percent. So it's a law enforcement issue.

Another set of obstacles highlighted by ACP Hackett, already alluded to, is the use of advanced technology by perpetrators that can frustrate the police who lack the requisite technological resources to assist detection (OECD and ADB 2006: 59). This would probably constitute a major challenge for the majority of Caribbean police jurisdictions. Hackett maintains that "the level of sophistication and complexity of white-collar crimes can sometimes be overwhelming for most police prosecutors and limit their scope for effective prosecutions in court" (Levy 1987). Rose (2012) argues that it is necessary to make changes to the ethical standards and also give recognition to professional and organizational cultures of law enforcement agencies that inhibit their capacity to effectively address complex crimes. In order to remedy one dimension of these matters Rose (2012) suggests that there is a need to build important enforcement competence by introducing more advanced forensic procedures in the investigation of white-collar crime. Caribbean police authorities lack the in-depth training in these matters compared to the more advanced jurisdictions (Levy 1987: 141). To its credit, Caribbean policing is increasingly attracting more educated recruits in many countries (Stanislas 2014, 2016a,b) who are also more familiar with technology, which is a promising and potentially important trend, if not a potential course of policy action, in meeting the needs of contemporary policing, and the deficiencies highlighted in tackling white-collar crime.

Some of the deficiencies with legal trials in regards to procurement matters are highlighted by Hart (2008), as it relates to the Piarco Airport construction project. These proceedings involved four former members of the cabinet that included a former Prime Minister, the major contractor for the project, the political party financier, a quantity surveyor, and an attorney-at-law. The court hearings ran concurrently with similar proceedings in the Courts of Florida, U.S. resulting from the same procurement processes. Although the matters were concluded in Florida where the parties involved being jailed, hefty fines imposed, and some multimillion dollar properties confiscated, in Trinidad and Tobago matters are still ongoing due to workings of the law and criminal justice system whereby well-resourced individuals are able to exploit loopholes, and various avenues to either prolong proceedings or stymie them (see Levy 1987).

Law enforcement agencies must be adequately resourced and have the required expertise to investigate procurement fraud matters. Additionally, law enforcement bodies must be autonomous with no political interference in the running of their affairs, which is an ideal that runs contrary to Caribbean governance where the police are an institution government seeks to tightly control and interfere in its internal workings (Harriot 2000, Stanislas 2016b). Consequently, law enforcement bodies should not be reliant on government funding for specific investigations, since government may not be inclined to assist, particularly where one of their own, that is, officials or party financier is being investigated. Law enforcement agencies need to be properly resourced and have robust policies, and mechanisms, that are adhered to which would prevent political interference. The respondent sums up some of the basic issues that contribute to the poor enforcement and prosecution of offenders for procurement fraud and related matters:

> Procurement leads to corruption, so you're looking at your Anti-Corruption Bureau of your Police Force. Procurement could also lead to laundering so you looking at your Financial Intelligence Unit. If you have those units you are supposed to have no political interference in their running. You are also looking at adequately budgeting for these units, because what we do in the Caribbean we say we have these Units, but we give them a budget just for salaries. Something then happens, there is an allegation, and they [the police] need to bring in some expertise and they don't have the budget for that. They have to go back to the same Cabinet that they are going to investigate, to receive a budget approval.

Other forms of political interference in police investigations can be cited. For example, if the police require information from an agency outside of the originating country, it is necessary to make such a request through their central authority, which in the Caribbean falls under the jurisdiction of the Attorney General, who is a political appointee. In such an instance, the Attorney General can use their power to intervene and prevent the request from being fulfilled.*

---

* The Royal St. Lucia Police Force experienced this problem in an investigation into a corrupt former minister who is believed to have stolen international donor funds and fled with his family to the United States. Their request for FBI assistance in detaining the former politician was blocked. One of the reasons advanced for this action, which is not uncommon, was government's fear that the suspect would reveal further compromising cases of corruption involving senior politicians (see Wayne 2010).

Training and Education and Anti-Corruption and Procurement

Similar to law enforcement training (or any other for that matter), some of the issues that arise are what type of training is required to tackle procurement fraud. When the training is received, its regularity, and content? Equally of importance is who is the recipient of the education and training inter alia (Stanislas 2014)? In the context of preventing procurement crime in the Caribbean, there was no shortage of education and training available for officials in terms of general basic courses to increase awareness, and more specialist programs for key occupational groups that are run by several professional bodies. Some of the training agencies that serve the English-speaking Caribbean region and the type of training they provide are elucidated:

> The Caribbean Procurement Institute focuses on drafting of legislation and policy matters, while the Caribbean Institute of Forensic Accounting has a greater focus on specific problems, how they can be detected and investigated, the various phases of the procurement cycles and what can take place at each stage.

Those who are most likely to receive procurement-related training are the key government departments such as Ministry of Public Works, which is a large spending department and relatively well-staffed in terms of numbers compared to other departments. Training may also be important, when combined with improved recruitment procedures aimed at obtaining the best quality personnel in the critical roles associated with procurement matters (ROCE 2010: 43, United Nations Office on Drugs and Crime 2013: 10). Education on procurement matters should not be limited to professionals working in public administration, and must extend to the general public, and funding agencies. Funding bodies, such as the British Academy[*] and others, have placed emphasis on increasing the participation and information available to civil society and the public at large about procurement fraud (OECD and ADB 2006: 59).

The issue of improving education on anticorruption matters and the importance of the public and civil society in that process has been identified as being crucial in shaping societal intolerance to the matter. In the Caribbean and sub-Saharan Africa, although the population has a high level of awareness about suspected levels of corruption that occurs (See Aremu Chapter 9, COE 2010, Harriot 2008, Wayne 2010), they are not informed about much of the details and mechanisms at work. Part of this is explained by journalists

---

[*] British Academy call 2015 funding call for anti-corruption good practice.

as caused by the institutional weaknesses of the Caribbean media, in its general coverage of crime matters. Lack of resources prevents emerging stories to be covered in depth and over time, as in the type of investigative journalism found in more developed countries (Unpublished Interviews, Stanislas 2016a). In this regard, journalists face similar problems to law enforcement and other investigators (see Chapter 8). One journalist elaborates:

> The population of Caribbean islands are generally too small, as is the revenue base, to support powerful well-resourced major newspapers like you have in the U.S. or UK which have global names. We don't have the capacity of the British Guardian to send journalists to investigate MP expenses over long periods of time that led to that controversy.

Moreover, in high-crime societies, stories around violence and homicide in particular, dominate media attention and resources (Stanislas 2016a,b). Even shocking stories have a very limited media life span, before they are surpassed by other headlines. An illustration of this was the case of a young woman who was allegedly raped by a group of police officers, including a female officer, which went from the front page to disappear completely within a short period of time (Ally 2010). In this environment, politicians can avoid sustained media efforts to hold them to account for perceived wrong-doing, especially in less emotionally compelling matters such as everyday procurement fraud, which is further explained by a senior journalist:

> The politicians are not stupid and are veterans in deceit. They know most newspapers only have one or two senior journalists and are small operations. At best all we can do as journalist is to embarrass them or temper their behavior for a short while. All they have to do is to wait us out and go back to business as usual.

One type of important information that can contribute to the education of the public is the damage to society and their economies caused by procurement fraud and other forms of corruption, within the broader context of the economic performance of the Caribbean countries in question. Christie (2014) contends that despite Jamaica being very corrupt and public procurement being a crucial component of this problem, no one really knows the extent of its direct cost to the country. Collier (2001) suggests an important means of improving the fight against corruption by postulating what could occur in Jamaica and Haiti if there was a one percent improvement in the reduction of political corruption. Collier (2001) concluded that reductions in corruption could result in an increase in domestic savings in the sum of U.S. $2.3 billion for Haiti and U.S. $761.6 million for Jamaica. Although it is unclear how these calculations have been made, what is evident is the general point regarding the cost of procurement fraud, and other forms of corruption to the economies of these countries and the region. These revelations provide the potential basis for affirmative action. The forensic accountant highlights the potential damage to Caribbean economies caused by procurement fraud against the background of weak economies:

> If you were to add procurement fraud, I suspect the English-speaking Caribbean has lost about 85 per cent of GDP. Put that in a wider context, you have Barbados on bending knees 3,600 public servants sent home. St. Lucia almost on bending knees and want to cut public sector salaries by five to ten percent. Trinidad, with no diversification from dependency on oil and gas. If the oil price remains the same we are in problems.

An area of good anti-corruption practice that the respondent came across while attending an international conference in Thailand, and indicative of the significant developments that have taken place in many countries in the Asia-Pacific region (see OECD and ADB 2006: 16–18), is the critical matter of collecting data by national Central Statistical Offices, calculating the costs of suspected corrupt practices. The importance of this practice was expressed in the conference keynote address by the Prime Minister of Thailand. Elaborating on his learning:

> I don't think we have caught on in the Caribbean that these things have a dollar value. These things cost tax payers X amount of money and reduces the standard of living by X percentage. People don't really make the connection of what this means in real terms for their day to day lives.

Removing discussions about the cost of corruption from the preserve of academics and technocrats, and broadening it out in the language of civil society, and the public at large is a vital dimension in effectively tackling corruption. This approach has been adopted in Ethiopia (Kabede 2016), and has contributed to reducing procurement fraud, and other forms of dysfunctional administrative practices. The potential political ramification of an informed electorate for politicians seeking to be elected to office is considerable. The issue of prevailing cultural norms in society and how this contributes to procurement fraud, and other forms of corruption is detailed in the rich descriptions of Wayne (2010) and Kincaid (2000) of St. Lucia and Antigua. The image painted by these authors replicates cultural behavior associated with Western feudal society, where scandal among the elite was a source of scorn, gossip, and entertainment for the powerless masses (Bloch 2014). Societal response to corruption often took similar dramaturgical forms that are described by the forensic accountant:

> It's sensationalized news, the allegations are more important in Caribbean culture than the actual solving of the case. You see with allegations you could

talk about it on and on and on which contributes to the drama and controversy, which people seem to love and enjoy. If someone is found guilty of an
offence, the most you could do with that news is just say this person has been
found guilty. There is no news after that (laughs), if you understand.

In this instance, what is being described is a culture, it could be argued,
where controversy has a value of its own in a society with weak legal norms,
where the public feel powerless to act against the powerful. Gossip and ridi-
cule replaces meaningful action to bring those suspected of corruption to
account (see Clarke 1983, Hill 1993). Societal responses in such instances
are akin to viewers of popular TV soap operas that fuel communal discussion and excitement, until usurped by even more dramatic installments of
suspected wrong-doing (Job 2004: 20–21). Popular music has traditionally
been a source of protest about corruption in Caribbean society (Hill 1993,
Stanislas 2013: 12). For example, in 2007, a song by Calypsonian Jaunty called
*Bobol list** became a major hit in St Lucia invoking a hostile response from
many in government. Bobol is a local term for collusion and corruption. The
song described a long list of people believed to be part of the *bobol* and in
benefit of government largess. It posed the rhetorical question why the singer,
a poor man, was unable to get included on the *bobol list*.

Conclusion

This chapter explores the administrative and political cultures of a number of
English-speaking Caribbean countries, which despite their differences share
important features that shapes regulation and governance in these territories. Administrative systems based on political and other forms of patronage,
and clientelism, along with weak police and criminal justice systems create an environment where public procurement abuse, fraud, and corruption
thrive. This chapter highlights, how prevalent procurement crime is in most
English-speaking Caribbean islands and the larger countries in particular
given the greater infrastructural demands, and is increasingly recognized
as an important problem with serious ramification for the health of these
countries and region.

The larger territories, such as Jamaica and Trinidad and Tobago, have
led discussions about tackling procurement fraud in the most recent period,
with countries such as the Bahamas and Barbados having addressed these
matters in earlier periods and in the case of Jamaica, which has taken the
lead in the development and introduction of good anti-corruption practice.
The Caribbean is also developing its expertise in this area, as highlighted by

* https://www.youtube.com/watch?v=LL-cbj5Mz74.

the establishment of professional bodies, such as the Caribbean Procurement Institute. Despite this progress, many of these anti-corruption initiatives are fundamentally weakened by the lack of power and resources of the key agencies and actors responsible for enforcement that are subject to the various agendas of politicians. The political interest of governments is also an obstacle in developing region-wide enforcement mechanisms to tackle public procurement fraud. Given the lack of appetite for reform in this area from government and politicians, increasing the awareness, and understanding of citizens, the media, and other stakeholders becomes even more essential in bringing about change.

References

Ally, A. (2010). Alleged Rape Victim Responds to Missing Case Files "Oh My God," www.stluciastar.com, December 20.

Beasley, E. (2005). *Mid Victorian Imperialists, British Gentlemen and the Empire of the Mind*, Abingdon, UK: Routledge.

Bennett, R., & Morabito, M. (2006). Determinants of Constables Perceptions of Community Support in Three Developing Nations, *Police Quarterly* 9, 2:234–265.

Bishop, M. and Payne, A. (2010). Caribbean Regional Governance and the Sovereignty/Statehood Problem, Paper No: 8. www.cigonlineorg. Retrieved March 8, 2014.

Bloch, M. (2014). *Feudal Society*, London, UK: Routledge.

Bowling, B. (2010). *Policing the Caribbean*, Oxford, UK: Oxford University Press.

The Guardian (2013). Cambridge, Ucill; "$ Billions in Contracts for UNC Financier: US Monitors Suspicious Deals as Cash Sent out of T&T"; Trinidad and Tobago Guardian; July 7, 2013; accessed May 1, 2016; from www.guardian.co.tt/news/2013-07-07/cash-sent-out-tt.

Christie, G. (2014). Uniformed Attack on Office of Contractor General. http://www.jamaica-gleaner.com. Retrieved December 28, 2015.

Clarke, S. (1982). *Jah Music*, London, UK: Ashgate Publishing.

Collier, M.W. (2001). The Effects of Political Corruption on Caribbean Development, Working Paper No. 5, LACC Working Paper Series 2001, Paper prepared for the Caribbean Studies Association Annual Conference, May 27–June 2, 2002, p 15, FIU Digital Commons. www.digitalcommons.fiu.edu/laccwps/7. Retrieved July 4, 2016.

Cratton, M. (2002). *Pindling, The Life and Times Of Lynden Oscar Pindling. First Prime Minister of the Bahamas 1930-2000*, Oxford, UK: Macmillan Education.

Dakolia, M. (1996). The Judicial Sector in Latin America and the Caribbean: Elements of Reform, World Bank, Technical Paper No: 319.

Daraine, L. (2014). Politicians Have a Hand in Jamaica's Crime Problem-Bunting, *The Gleaner*, May 15, 2014. http://jamaica-gleaner.com/gleaner/20140515/lead/lead7.html. Retrieved May 14, 2016.

Dorn, N., Levi, M. and White, S. (2008). Do European Procurement Rules Generate or Prevent Crime? *Journal of Financial Crime*, 15(3):243–260.

Foster, P. (2010). China's Crumbling Bridges: Not Built to Last, www.telegraph.co.uk, November 16. Retrieved March 3, 2016.

Goldstock, R. (1990). Corruption and Racketeering in the New York City Construction Industry, New University Press, New York.

Harriot, A. (2000). *Police and Crime Control in Jamaica: Problems of Reforming Ex-Colonial Constabularies*, Barbados, West Indies: University of West Indies Press.

Harriot, A. (2008). *Organised Crime in Jamaica*, Jamaica, West Indies: Canoe Press.

Hill, D. (1993). Calypso Callaloo: Early Carnival Music in Trinidad.

Hintzen, P. (2006). *The Cost of Regime Survival*, Cambridge University Press, Cambridge.

Honeychurch, L. (1995) *The Dominican Story, A History of the Island*, London, UK: Macmillan Education.

Hope, R.K. (1983). The Administration of Development in Emergent Nations. The Problems in the Caribbean, *Public Administration and Development*, Vol. 3: 44–59.

Hope, R.K. (ed.). (2015). *Police Corruption and Police Reform in Developing Societies*, Boca Raton, FL: CRC Press.

Job, M. (2004). *Police Reform and Performance Management: Crime, The Darby Report and History*, Alkebulan Ind, Port of Spain.

Joseph, D.T. (2011). *Decolonization in St Lucia: Politics of Global Neoliberalism*, University of Mississippi, Jackson.

Kabede, T. (2016). Ethiopia: Open Dialogue with Public to Solve Corruption, www.allafrica.com, April 23. Retrieved June 6, 2016.

Kankaanranta, T. and Muttilainen, V. (2010). Economic Crimes in the Construction Industry: The Case of Finland, *Journal of Financial Crime* 17(4):417–429.

Khan, A. (2012). Police: White-Collar Crimes Mind-Boggling, *Trinidad and Tobago Guardian*, October 25. www.guardian.co.tt/business-guardian/2012-10-24/police-white-collar-crimes-mind-boggling. Retrieved July 10, 2016.

Kincaid, J. (2000). *A Small Place*, Farrar, Straus and Giroux, New York.

Kirk-Green, A. (1999). On Crown Service, A History of HM Colonial Service 1837–1997, London, UK: I. B. Tauris.

Legister, F.J. (1988). *Class Alliances and the Liberal Authoritarian State: The Roots of Postcolonial Democracy in Jamaica, Trinidad and Tobago and Suriname*, Trenton, NJ: Africa World Press.

Levy, M. (1987). *Regulating Fraud: White Collar Crime and the Criminal Process*, Tavistock, Cambridge.

Mazuri, A. and Tidy, M. (1984). *Nationalism and New African States*, London, UK: Heineman.

Meeks, B. (2000). The Political Moment in Jamaica: The Dimensions of Hegemonic Dissolution, in M. Marable (ed.) *Dispatches From the Ivory Tower: Intellectuals Confront the African-American Experience*. New York: Columbia University Press.

Schotborgh, P. (2012). Small Caribbean Islands, Big Corruption Cases? The Impact of "Small County Size" and "Islandness" on Corruption in the Caribbean. www.Sidsgg.webs.com. Retrieved December 17, 2015.

Schotborgh, P. and van Velzen, S. (2013). National Integrity System Assessment: Curacao, Transparency International, Curacao.

Stanislas, P. (2013). Policing Violent Homophobia in the Caribbean and the British Caribbean Disaspora, *Interventions: An International Journal of Postcolonial Studies*, May 5, DOI:10.1080/1369801X.2013.798134.

Stanislas, P. (2014). Police Leadership and the Management of Mega-Events: Policing the London 2012 Olympics and Paralympic Games, in D. Das and D. Plecas (eds.) *International Perspectives on Policing Major Events*. Boca Raton, FL: CRC Press.

Stanislas, P. (2016a). Caribbean Police Commissioners' Perspectives on Policing, Organisational Challenges, and Change, *Caribbean Journal of Public Safety and Criminology*, August.

Stanislas, P. (2016b). Interview with Commissioner Ellison Greenslade of the Royal Bahamas Police, In B. Baker (ed.) *Trends in Policing Interviews with Police Leaders Across the Globe*. Vol. 5. Boca Raton, FL: CRC Press.

Stanislas, P. (2016c). The Challenge of Postcolonial Political and Social Leadership: Building Inclusive Citizenship, Safety and Security in East Africa, in Ruttere, L. and Mkutu, K. (eds.) *East African Policing*, Suffolk, VA: James Currey.

Stone, C. and Bustamante Institute of Public and International Affairs (1991). Report of the Stone Committee Appointed to Advise the Jamaican Government On the Performance, Accountability and Responsibilities of Elected Parliamentarians, Kingston, Jamaica: The Institute.

Rueschemeyer, D. and Stephens, J. (1992). *Capitalist Development and Democracy*, Oxford, UK: Polity Press.

Ruddock, G. (2011). London 2012 Olympics: The Olympic Stadium Made in Britain, www.telegraph.co.uk, July 16. Retrieved January 19, 2016.

Wayne, R. (2010). *Lapses and Infelicities: An Insider's Perspective of Politics in the Caribbean*, St. Lucia: Star Publishing.

Zayas, D. (2012). Delivering London 2012: Managing the Construction of Olympic Park, www.p2sl.berkerly.edu. Retrieved December 15, 2015.

Newspaper Article

Anti-Corruption Cop Caught Soliciting Money, www.jamaicanobserver.com, September 1, 2015. Retrieved March 6, 2016.

44 Cops Among 64 Arrested for Corruption, www.jamaicanobserver.com, October 18, 2011. Retrieved March 6, 2016.

Spy Lies, Reshmi's Appointment No Misstep, www.trinidadexpress.com, February 5, 2011. Retrieved November 12, 2015.

UWP to Expel Richard Fredrick, www.stlucinewsonline.com, August 18, 2014. Retrieved August 12, 2014.

What the US Told Sir John about Richard Fredrick, www.voteslp.com 2014. Retrieved August 25, 2014.

Government and Agency Report

Caribbean Development Report (2012). www.latinamerica.undp.org. Retrieved June 2, 2016.

Department of Environment Food and Rural Affairs (2013). London 2012 Olympic and Paralympic Games: The Legacy: Sustainable Procurement for Construction Projects, A Guide. Department of Environment Food and Rural Affairs.

House of Commons Northern Ireland Affairs Committee, Third Report of Session 2005–2006, Volume 1.

Organisation for Economic Cooperation and Development Asian Development Bank (2006). Anti-Corruption Policies in Asia and the Pacific, Progress in Legal and Institutional Reform in 25 Countries.

Report of the Commission of Enquiry into the Construction Sector in Trinidad and Tobago, Government of Trinidad and Tobago 2010, http://www.ttparliament. org. Retrieved December 28, 2015.

Transparency International; Caribbean Composite Study 2004; Berlin, Germany: National Integrity Systems, Transparency International Country Reports; 2005; accessed July 6, 2016 from www.transparency.org/news_room/latest_news/ press_releases/2005/2005_01_31_caribbean_nis.

United Nations Convention Against Corruption (2013). A Strategy for Safeguarding against Corruption in Major Public Events, United Nations Office on Drugs and Crime.

World Bank (2013). World Development Indicators, www.worldbank.org. Retrieved June 2, 2016.

Website

National Integrity Action, www.niajamaica.org.

Corruption and Anticorruption Strategies in Pakistan

12

FASIHUDDIN
IMRAN AHMAD SAJID
FARHAT ULLAH

Contents

Introduction

Public sector corruption is a global issue today. Pakistan is no exception. No department in Pakistan is free from corruption. Police, nonetheless, is seen as the flagship department of corruption, as portrayed in many perceptual surveys on corruption. The public, however, cannot understand all forms of corruption. There are at least three types of corruption in police: (1) administrative corruption, (2) legal corruption, and (3) financial corruption. Administratively, there is strong grouping/fraternities in police officers. The merit-based work has very little recognition, if any. Personal considerations are there when the matters of posting/transfer are discussed. On the legal side, the police usually twist the law to give benefit to criminals. The law is manipulated and interpreted in such a way that leads to hampering of investigation and prosecution. The posting/transfer at the desired place, and the twisting of law and rules, is not done for heaven's sack. The ultimate objective of the above two corrupt practices is the financial benefit.

At the global level, scholars are asking the question "why nations fail?" One of the answers to this question is extractive, political, and economic system that is based on corruption. The state has given ample consideration to curtail corruption in public sector. Since 1947, state had been concerned about corruption. The Prevention of Corruption Act, 1947 and the subsequent amendment acts were a step in this direction. In 1999, the National Accountability Bureau (NAB) was established to curtail the problem at federal level. Since then, many provincial administrative efforts have been made in the province of Khyber Pakhtunkhwa and Punjab. In Khyber Pakhtunkhwa (KP), the recent political administration has portrayed itself as a symbol of corruption fight. Many steps have been taken in this regard: an anticorruption department has been established; complaint cells have been established in police stations and other police offices; a complaint cell has been established in the Chief Minister's Secretariat; and a huge media campaign is launched for public awareness on the menace of corruption.

This chapter portrays the historical anticorruption efforts in Pakistan. Its particular focus is on forms of police corruption in Pakistan.

History of public sector corruption is as old as the history of human civilization itself. Public servants have been bribed, since times unknown. Public officials also used their office for public gains. Providing a legal or illegal benefit to a person for personal gratification is not a new phenomenon. It existed and exists in all society at all times with varying intensity. Modern day Pakistan is no exception. In fact, many see corruption as part of the normative structure of Pakistan since her genesis (Fida, 2010). Curtailing corruption has been one of the top priorities of Pakistan since its independence. The Quaid-e-Azam M. Ali Jinnah, Father of the Nation (1876–1948) in his address to the Constituent Assembly on August 11, 1947 said:

> "One of the biggest curse from which India[1] is suffering, I do not say that other countries are free from it, but I think our condition is much worse, is bribery and corruption. That really is a poison. We must put it down with an iron hand" (Allana, 1969)

Keeping in view the priorities set by the Quaid-e-Azam on August 11, 1947, Pakistan established its first anticorruption legislation immediately within a few months. The Prevention of Corruption Act (1947) was the 1st legislation to curtail corruption in Pakistan. The purpose of the act was prevention of bribery and corruption, as mentioned in the preamble of the act (Prevention of Corruption Act, 1947). From its purpose, it is no herculean task to discover that the governments have been concerned about corruption for a long time. The Act does not define corruption in itself nor does it define a public servant. Nonetheless, it uses the colonial definition of corruption and public servant as given in Sections 21[2] and 161 of Pakistan Penal Code (1860)[3]. The Penal Code uses the term *gratification* instead of *corruption*. The Code does not limit gratification only to monetary items and money. It can be in many forms. In sum, corruption as defined in the Code and the Act, can be understood to mean extending legal or illegal favor or disfavor to a person by a public servant for personal gratification.

The Anti-Corruption Act of 1947 failed to curtail corruption, as there were many lacunae in the law. First, the Act was enforced through special police that was part of district police force. Special police did not have any specific resources to deal with the menace of corruption. In most cases, it has to rely on district police for offices and personnel. This police were like a special branch of police that was under the routine police hierarchy. It did not create any specific agency for operational purposes. It was short in scope and independence. Later on, this special police was merged into Federal Investigation Agency (FIA) in 1975.

Second, this Act was limited only to preventing public sector corruption. Private sector was not mentioned in this legislation. The Act adopted definition of misconduct by public servants from Section 161 of Pakistan Penal Code (PPC) 1860. The definition of PPC was very limited in scope as it defined misconduct as "obtaining of any gratification as a motive for doing or forbearing to do any official act." Later on, the scope of the definition was broadened with subsequent amendments to bring possession of resources disproportionate to one's known sources of income. However, its enforcement was still dependent on special police that worked under district police.

Third, the procedural aspects of this law were mostly criticized. According to the law, the anticorruption establishment had to take permission from the respective heads of departments (HODs) before taking action against any public servant. The HODs rarely if ever granted such permissions as it would bring bad name and reputation for his department. According to Qureshi (2013), this provision has its own advantages and disadvantages. On one hand, this provision was intended as a kind of check on misuse of power by anticorruption establishment, as the officials of anticorruption establishment themselves were no more credible than the alleged corrupt. On the other hand, from the point of view of anticorruption establishment, it meant asking the corrupt officials themselves for permission to prosecute them. Besides, this provision meant that only low-level functionaries were perceived as corrupt, although the high-ups remained exception from corruption.

Fourth, the Act considered corruption as any other crime. It was not made a special crime. It was just like any other crime and the same procedural law, PPC, was applicable to corruption cases. The prosecuting agency was responsible for the burden of proof.

Fifth, the Act was against prevention of corruption. Ironically, there was no provision for prevention of corruption. Corruption was seen as an individual behavioral problem. Therefore, anticorruption was primarily seen as a matter of enforcement of law on some miscreant individuals. The legislation was to punish mostly lower subordinate on petty corrupt practices. Big high-ups were mostly ignored.

Despite its shortcomings, the legislation was the first of its nature in Pakistan.

Two more legislations were enacted during General Ayub Khan's era (1958–1969). However, those legislations are severely criticized for their political nature. These legislations targeted only politicians who were found nonconformists in the period of first military dictatorship in the country.[4] These legislations were meant to disqualify prominent politicians of the time, as any politician could avoid prosecution by agreeing to not-take-part in politics for 15 years. In this manner, according to Qureshi (2013), almost 7,000 politicians were banned from politics.

After General Ayub Khan, no significant efforts were made to curtail corruption during 1970s and 1980s. The next prominent anticorruption move was made by Nawaz Sharif government in 1996 by enacting Ehtesab[5] Commission. The Commission was supplemented by an Ehtesab Bureau in 1997. The function of this bureau was to investigate cases of corruption, although the Commission conducted the prosecution of cases. This Commission was also extended to the President and the Prime Minister as even they could be prosecuted as per law. These clauses had significant symbolic value. However, no one dared to initiate investigation against the incumbent Prime Minister or President. Under this law, special benches were created that comprised of the High Court judges. Such benches were to complete a trial within 30 days maximum. Nonetheless, Ehtesab Commission also fell to political victimization. It became a tool to repress political rivals.

Another agency to fight corruption at Federal level is the Federal Investigation Agency (FIA) that was established in 1975 under the FIA Act, 1974. The act repealed the previously enacted two laws namely the Pakistan Special Police Establishment, 1948 (VII of 1948), and the Special Police and Provincial Police (Amalgamation) Order, 1962 (P.O. No. 1 of 1962). Till 2004, FIA's scope was limited to anticorruption and white-collar crimes. Cyber crime, counter-terrorism and human trafficking are now also scheduled crimes for FIA. Fighting mega corruption, however, has been taken over by the National Accountability Bureau (NAB), as explained subsequently.

Soon after taking over the government, former Chief Executive General (R)Pervaiz Musharraf promulgated the National Accountability Ordinance 1999. It repealed Nawaz Sharif's Ehtesab Bureau Act of 1996. It established a completely new agency, the NAB, which has become the major agency to counter high-profile corruption in Pakistan. NAB was established on the lines of anticorruption agencies that are prevalent in Hong Kong and Singapore. NAB was established on the pattern of anticorruption agencies in countries like Hong Kong and Singapore. NAB Ordinance brought significant changes in anticorruption efforts. First, it broadened definition of corruption. Section 9 of the NAB Ordinance includes "persons who maintain a living standard not commensurate with their known sources of income." Its purpose was "to eradicate corruption and corrupt practices and hold accountable all those persons accused of such practices and matters ancillary thereto. NAB was established with the goal to provide for effective measures for the detection, investigation, prosecution, and speedy disposal of cases involving corruption, corrupt practices, misuse/abuse of power, misappropriation of property, kickbacks, commissions, and for matters connected and ancillary or incidental thereto" (National Accountability Ordinance, 1999). The Ordinance also broadened the scope of the agency and included private sector. NAB can initiate proceedings against highest to lowest public or private sector officials. It can even initiate proceedings against the FIA officials. In previous laws, it was the prosecutor's responsibility to provide evidence of corruption. It was based on the legal doctrine of *being innocent unless proven guilty*. However, NAB changed the legal doctrine. It is now the accused's responsibility to prove his/her innocence. Further, remand period was also extended by this Ordinance. Normally, the law allows for a 14-day police custody for investigation. This Ordinance extended this period to 90 days. NAB adopted a three-pronged approach for eradication of corruption: enforcement, prosecution, and awareness & prevention (NAB Annual Report, 2014). NAB works with complete independence. Once appointed to the post, Chairman of the NAB can only be removed by a Supreme Judicial Council, which is the highest constitutional authority for initiation of an action against the judges of the apex courts as given in the Constitution of Pakistan, 1973. Initially, NAB was run by military generals, mostly close colleagues of General Musharraf. Soon after its genesis, NAB started arresting corrupt politicians and bureaucrats. Its transparent and bold moves made it a very popular agency at the time. It arrested and prosecuted many corrupt politicians. Some escaped the country. However, when Musharraf's priorities shifted from fighting corruption to staying in power, the role of NAB was also restricted (Fida, 2010). It is one of the reasons that despite this wider scope, advantages, power and resources, NAB has yet to effectively curb corruption in Pakistan. Critics argue that like its predecessors, NAB has also become a tool for punishing those who oppose the political regime in power. Even at times, NAB is criticized for being active and selective in small and poor provinces as remarked by a judge of the Peshawar High Court (NAB dy khpala karawai sama kai, 2015).

Anticorruption has become synonymous with political victimization (Fida, 2010; Khan, Kakakhel and Dubnick, 2004; Samad, 2008).

Besides these organized agencies, each of the line departments has its own Departmental Misconduct Committee. Such committees initiate inquiries against any misconduct or misuse of power by respective official.

Police and Corruption

Police are much known in public for its rampant corruption. It is even more popularized by the media. Police corruption is not only the problem of a few third world countries, rather it is an international problem (Bayley and Perito, 2011). For example, two officers of Detroit police were charged with stealing money and selling drugs (Lambertz, 2015). An FBI investigation team reported a Miami cop helped drug ring. Known as *The Milk Man*, Lt. Ralph Mata also helped New Jersey cocaine dealers move around hundreds of thousands of dollars (Anderson, 2014). Some police, particularly males, have been found to have let the female criminals go for sexual favors. Police have also been charged with taking bribes from anyone and from anywhere possible. For example, a YouTube video shows a Nigerian police taking $155 from a driver (The Huffington Post, 2013; Jauregui, 2014). This scene is not uncommon in Pakistan.

> A policeman stops a vehicle and starts writing something on his pad. The driver comes out of his vehicle and "shakes" hand with the policeman with a smiling face. With this, the policeman tells the driver to be careful and go now. The driver sits in his vehicle and goes on his way.

Corruption in police has been called *endemic* (emphasis added) by many researchers (Chattha and Ivkovic, 2004). However, it is not something new in police. Corruption has been pervasive in police and was pointed out earlier in 1902–1903 in Fraser Commission Report (Chaudhry, 1997):

> The forms of this corruption area [are] very numerous. It manifests itself in every stage of the work of the police station. The police officer may levy a fee or receive a present for every duty he performs. The complainant has often to pay a fee for having his complaint recorded. He is to give the investigating officer a present to secure his prompt and earnest attention to the case. More money is extorted as the investigation proceeds. When the officer goes down to the spot to make his investigation, he is a burden not only to the complainant, but to his witnesses. (p.70).

Nature and Forms of Police Corruption

The nature of police corruption in Pakistan is no different from the police corruption anywhere else in the world. Generally, there are three major forms of police corruption:

1. Legal corruption
2. Administrative corruption
3. Financial corruption

Legal Corruption

Legal corruption occurs in at least three forms, including: (1) twisting or mis-interpretation of law, (2) nonregistration of First Information Report (FIR), and (3) wrongful accusation and implication of innocents or acquittal of accused persons.

Twisting of law is one major area for police legal corruption. The legal codes for criminal charges vary from soft to hard. Police have the discretion to apply any legal codes or apply section of law over certain criminal conducts. If a crime is committed and police arrest the person who has committed the crime, and if the accused bribes the police station officials, he may be dealt with soft criminal codes. On the other hand, if the opposition party bribes the police, the police station officials may use hard codes for criminal behavior. This depends on police discretion. The severity of the offence is generally attenuated bringing minor punishment, being bailable and compoundable. Here is a short case study,

> Mr. Zahoor[6] and his three brothers were intercepted and severely beaten by Mr. Dilawar and his gang at village PirSabaq, Nowshera. They were beaten so severely that they fell unconscious. They were brought to home by some other village-men who happened to be passing through and found them unconscious. Mr. Zahoor and his brothers were taken to DHQ hospital by their cousins. In hospital, the police recorded the narrative of Mr. Zahoor and brothers. They remained in hospital for 12 days. When they returned home, they waited for the police to arrest Dilawar and his gang who were running freely in the village. The wait lasted for a month but Zahoor and brothers knew nothing of the progress on the case. The author was contacted by one of the brothers. When the author investigated into the matter, it was found that the police have applied the soft codes to the offender that said that Zahoor and brothers have very minor injuries. Those codes were bailable.

Registering a crime on being reported is a legal obligation for police under Section 154 of the PPC (1860). However, the police have the discretion whether to launch an FIR or to record the reported offence in Daily Diary. Launching an FIR means that the case has entered into formal criminal justice system. It shall pass through all the stages of the system now. On the other hand, recording an incident in Daily Diary does not imply any such obligation. It involves an enquiry, not an investigation. FIR is registered on commission of a cognizable offence, whereas a Daily Dairy report is limited to an ordinary complaint, rarely culminating into an FIR after a proper enquiry, or by an order of a magistrate, or any other superior police officer. Now when a case is brought to the police station, the police have the luxury of including case in Daily Diary or launching an FIR. Here, too, bribery plays significant role. If bribery plays its role in favor of the offender, the case is written down in Daily Diary. On the other hand, if bribery plays its role in favor of the complainant, a proper FIR with hard codes is launched against the offender. In Pakistani culture, it is also encouraged to include the names of as many names as they want to the list of suspects. The reason being the joint and extended family system, where damage to the maximum number of family members is a value, particularly those family members who have some power or money. There is a saying, *da sarkaspakyragyrka. Arrest the prominent member of the family.* This wrongful implication leads to a third form of legal corruption.

Police station investigation officer has the discretion to accuse any innocent or acquit any offender at any stage of investigation. It is a usual practice for the police to acquit any offender in investigation. They generally draw their powers from Section 169 of the Code of Criminal Procedure (CrPC) (1898) in this context. The investigating officer writes "there is enough evidence that Mr. X has no connection to the offence committed." Or "there are enough evidences that Mr. Y has also committed the offence."

Administrative Corruption

Administrative corruption is committed in at least three forms: (1) illegal recruitment, (2) maneuvered posting transfer, and (3) undue promotions.

Past year, the Deputy Commandant, Frontier Reserve Police (FRP) was accused of illegal recruitments of 378 police constables. The recruitments were made in 2013. The inquiry committee found Mr. Younus Javaid to be guilty of irregularities in recruitment. He was accused along with six more officers. In order to put veil on irregularities, the recruitment record of August 2013 was burnt in an incident of short-circuit (Sama News, 2014). Likewise, in 2010, the ex-Inspector General of KP police was charged with illegal recruitment of 713 people during his time as commandant Frontier Constabulary (FC) back in 2006. NAB launched an investigation into the matter and found enough evidence regarding illegal recruitments. The case was put forward to NAB court (Dastageer, 2010).

Such illegal recruitments are a norm for police higher-ups. The reason is many fold. First and foremost is the cultural structure of Pakistani society. In Pakistan, if one person succeeds in reaching a powerful position of authority in government structure, it is expected of him to provide jobs to as many people of his family and village as possible. An officer who does not provide illegal jobs to his extended family, village men or tribe, is not respected back in his hometown. Sometimes, political pressure is also involved for such recruitments. Political parties gain votes over jobs. A job to one police recruit means a vote of the entire extended family. In such a political environment, providing jobs become the topmost priority. Besides, many such recruitments are done for the sake of making money. Each recruitee pays a healthy sum of money for being recruited easily.

Undue promotions are another kind of departmental form of corruption. It is a routine matter in police to promote junior officers to higher posts who fulfill certain promotion criteria like necessary training and certain length of service, and so on. However, at times, junior officers are given promotion over their seniors. For example, Mushtaq Sukhera (Police Service of Pakistan [PSP]) was posted IG Balochistan while Ghalib Bandesha (PSP) was still serving there. Bandesha (PSP) was senior to Sukhera. On this posting, Bandesha refused to work under Sukhera as it was considered an insult by him. Sukhera was followed by Muhammad Amlesh as the IG Balochistan while Ahsan Mehboob was still serving there. Ahsan Mehboob was two years senior to Amlesh. Later on, he was appointed as Federal Ombudsman. In short, there is no functional criteria for promotion in police. The criteria for promotion as given in police rules is not followed. Recently, the Central Selection Board (CSB) made 400 recommendations for promotion in May 2015. However, almost 60 officers challenged the decision of CSB and launched a complaint in the High Court against the CSB. On July 27, 2015, the Court decided the case and nullified the CSB selections (Rao, 2015). This was a major blow to the corrupt practices at such a higher level, though not motivated by financial consideration, but personal likes and dislikes played havoc with the service and career of more than 100 officers.

Besides higher-ups' promotion, the promotion of district level police is also used very unduly. The police hierarchy usually granted out of turn promotions to certain officials on the recommendation of some influential figures within the government (for details see Karachi, 2004).

Posting/transfer is another gray area of police in Pakistan. It seems as if there is no criteria for posting/transfer in police. The posting of station house officer (SHO) is usually based on political grounds. Politicians, when they come in power, want their own breed of SHOs and other officers to be appointed in their area. In some instances, posting/transfer is used as a means of punishment. For example, Mr. Fasihuddin (PSP), one of the authors of this discussion, was appointed as Director, Federal Investigation Agency (FIA), Khyber Pakhtunkhwa. The author took some bold steps during his four months tenure and annoyed a few superiors (FIA director replaced, 2010, November 26). An anonymous letter was issued against him and a newspaper made a news story out of that letter. He was removed from his position right the same day. As a punishment, he was sent to Balochistan province to perform normal police duties (for details see Cheema, 2010; Dawn, 2010; The Nation, 2010). He then lodged a defamation suit of 50 million rupees against the news reporter, Mr. Umar Cheema, for slanderous story against him, and the case is still under trial in the session courts of Peshawar.

Financial Corruption

In public opinion, police is the most corrupt government department in Pakistan (Transparency International, 2013). The word corruption is usually associated with financial corruption. The ultimate objective of the previous two forms of corruption prevalent in police is financial corruption. One of the ex-police chief of KP has been arrested by NAB for receiving kickbacks in multibillion procurement of weapons and vehicles for police department. He has been alleged to have procured locally made weapons (made in Darra Adam Khel) instead of purchasing weapons from China. A Chinese AK-47 cost was 80,000 rupees whereas the locally made AK-47 costs only 20,000 rupees. In this manner, billions of rupees were received in extra money. Besides such mega scams, financial corruption is spread throughout the police processes. Recently, the KP police started registration of all the residents in Peshawar. The registration form was available in all the police stations in the provincial capital. One of the authors, Imran Ahmad Sajid, went to get the form from the Pakha Ghulam police station. He was given the form with an instruction, "take 10 copies of this form and bring the original and 10 copies back to us. We do not have budget for copies." This is not uncommon or unusual in police stations. During PhD field study, the author Imran Ahmad Sajid was informed by police station staff that they do not have budget for traveling, food, refreshments, fuel, and so on. When they have to take the accused or the evidence to Forensic Services Laboratory, the one in charge of carrying it has to bear all the traveling cost by himself. Further, no stationery is provided to the police station. The SHO has to manage it through his own expenses. Owing to this budgetary constraint, the system forces the low ranks to ask for minor financial contributions (see also, Fasihuddin, 2008).

New Anticorruption Initiative in Khyber Pakhtunkhwa

Imran Khan's political party, Pakistan Tehrik-e-Insaf (PTI) entered into power with a slogan of *Naya Pakistan* (New Pakistan) in Khyber Pakhtunkhwa.[7] On its coronation to provincial assembly, the PTI led government initiated numerous steps to fight corruption. One of these steps was establishment of Ehtesab Commission in 2014. The purpose of Ehtesab Commission is to fight public sector corruption. The commission is wider in scope and it is applicable to all the public office holders. Soon after its establishment, the commission has taken vigorous steps to bring corrupt bureaucrats and politicians to prosecution. For example, on July 9, 2015, the commission arrested provincial minister for minerals, Mr. Ziaullah and associated bureaucrats of the provincial ministry of mines and minerals against strong evidence that suggests misappropriation of funds and misuse of authority. On June 8, 2015, the commission arrested a senior officer of Accountant General (AG) office on account of accumulating assets through illegal means (News and Updates, 2015).

Besides Ehtesab Commission, the sitting Inspector General of the KP police also started taking rigorous operations against corrupt police officials. In this connection an online service has been initiated to launch complaints against any police official. As of September 20, 2014, more than 400 police officials were suspended or terminated by the KP police chief (Wardag, 2014).

Conclusion

The corruption history in Pakistan is rich with corruption stories and anticorruption movements. From Prevention of Corruption Act of 1947 to Ehtesab Commission of 2014, the history is rich with anticorruption efforts. Intensity of corruption also goes up and down throughout the history. The variation in corruption intensity depends on the commitment of the incumbent governments of the time. Corruption has a negative association with government's commitment against corruption. Overall, nonetheless, Pakistan has yet to make significant efforts to become a *least corrupt nation*.

Police corruption does not happen in vacuum. Police is part of the larger government with many departments. It is influenced by the larger government structure. Commitment of the police to fight internal corruption also depends on the larger government's commitment against corruption. The existing efforts against corruption in police are commendable. However, KP police has to consistently carry-on these efforts for a few years in order to be considered one of the top police agencies around the world.

Notes

1. Pakistan was still part of India on August 11, 1947, as it got its independence on August 14 the same year.
2. "*Public servant.*"

    The words *public servant* denotes a person falling under any of the descriptions herein after following, namely:

    First: Every Commissioned Officer in the military, naval, or air forces of Pakistan while serving under the federal government or any provincial government.

    Second: Every judge.

    Third: Every officer of a court of justice whose duty it is, as such officer, to investigate or report on any matter of law or fact, or to make, authenticate, or keep any document, or to take charge or dispose of any property, or to execute any judicial process, or to administer any oath, or to interpret, or to preserve order in the court; and every person specially authorized by a court of justice to perform any of such duties.

    Fourth: Every juryman, assessor, or member of a panchayat assisting a court of justice or public servant.

    Fifth: Every arbitrator or other person to whom any cause or matter has been referred for decision or report by any court of justice, or by any other competent public authority.

    Sixth: Every person who holds any office by virtue of which he is empowered to place or keep any person in confinement.

Seventh: Every officer of the government whose duty it is, as such officer, to prevent offences, to give information of offences, to bring offenders to justice, or to protect the public health, safety, or convenience.

Eighth: Every officer whose duty it is, as such officer, to take, receive, keep, or expend any property on behalf of the government, or to make any survey, assessment, or contract on behalf of the government, or to execute any revenue process, or to investigate, or to report, or any matter affecting the pecuniary interests of the government, or to make, authenticate, or keep any document relating to the pecuniary interests of the government, or to prevent the infraction of any law for the protection of the pecuniary interests of the government, and every officer in the service or pay of the government, or remunerated by fees or commission for the performance of any public duty.

Ninth: Every officer whose duty it is, as such officer, to take, receive, keep, or expend any property, to make any survey or assessment, or to levy any rate or tax for any secular common purpose of any village, town or district, or to make, authenticate, or keep any document for the ascertaining of the rights of the people of any village, town, or district.

Tenth: Every person who holds any office in virtue of which he is empowered to prepare, publish, maintain, or revise an electoral roll, or to conduct an election or part of an election.

3. Public servant taking gratification other than legal remuneration in respect to an official act:

Whoever, being or expecting to be a public servant, accepts or obtains, agrees to accept, or attempts to obtain from any person, for himself or for any other person, any gratification whatever, other than legal remuneration, as a motive or reward for doing or forbearing to do any official act or for showing or forbearing to show, in the exercise of his official functions, favor or disfavor to any person, or for rendering or attempting to render any service or disservice to any person, with the federal, or any provincial government or legislature or with any public servant, as such, shall be punished with imprisonment of either description for a term that may extend to three years or with fine or with both.

4. The Public Representatives Disqualifying Act and Elected Bodies Disqualification Ordinance.

5. Ehtesab is Urdu language alternative for *Accountability*.

6. Names used are not original names.

7. Now its Naya Pakhtunkhwa (New Pakhtunkhwa).

References

Allana, G. (1969). Pakistan Movement Historical Documents. Karachi: Department of International Relations, University of Karachi. pp. 407–411. Retrieved November 02, 2016 from http://www.columbia.edu/itc/mealac/pritchett/00islamlinks/txt_jinnah_assembly_1947.html.

Anderson, C. (2014). Miami Cop Known As "The Milk Man" Helped Drug Ring, Plotted Murders, FBI Says. *The Huffington Post*, April 15.

Bayley, D., and Perito, R. (2011). *Police Corruption: What Past Scandals Teach about Current Challenges*. [Special Report 294]. United States Institute of Peace.

Chattha, Z.N., and Ivkovic, S.K. (2004). Police Misconduct: The Pakistani Paradigm. In C.B. Klockars, S.K. Ivkovic and M.R. Haberfeld. (eds). *The Contours of Police Integrity*. Thousand Oaks, CA: Sage Publication, pp. 175–194.

Chaudhry, M.A.K. (1997). *Policing in Pakistan*. New York: Vanguard.

Cheema, U. (2010). FIA official denies allegations, seeks SC intervention. *Daily The News International*, November 30. http://www.thenews.com.pk/ Todays-News-13-2393-FIA-official-denies-allegations-seeks-SC-intervention.

Dastageer, G. (2010). Illegal recruitment in Frontier Constabulary. *Daily The News International*, November 25.

Dawn (2010). Transfer of FIA director exposes multi-billion-rupee scam. *Daily Dawn*, November 29. www.dawn.com/news/586890/transfer-of-fia-director-exposes-multi-billion-rupee-scam.

Fasihuddin (2008). *Expanding Criminology to Pakistan*. Peshawar: Pakistan Society of Criminology.

FIA director replaced. (2010). *Daily The News International*, November 26. Retrieved October 05, 2016 from https://www.thenews.com.pk/archive/ print/271696-fia-director-replaced.

Fida, M. (2010). The Logic of Corruption in Pakistan: A Journey from NAB to NRO. *Pakistan Journal of Criminology*, 2(4), 43–53.

Government of Pakistan. (1898). *Code of Criminal Procedure: Act No V of 1898*. Retrieved October 05, 2016 from http://pakistancode.gov.pk/english/ UY2FqaJw1-apaUY2Fqa-apea-sg-jjjjjjjjjjjjjj#1999F.

The Huffington Post (2013). Nigeria's Police Corruption Problem Highlighted By YouTube Clip Of Cop Soliciting Bribe (VIDEO), September 8. Retrieved July 26, 2015 from http://www.huffingtonpost.com/2013/08/09/nigeria-police-corruption_n_3730947.html.

Jauregui, A. (2014). Crooked Cop Let Woman Off In Exchange For Oral Sex: Police. *The Huffington Post*, October 14.

Karachi (2004). Promotions in police upset deserving officers. *Daily Dawn*, September 10.

Khan, M., Kakakhel, N.A., and Dubnick, M. (2004). Prosecuting Corruption: The Case of Pakistan. Working Paper QU/GOV/11/2004. Institute of Governance, Policy and Social Research, Queen's University, Belfast. www.qub.ie/schools/ SchoolofLaw/Research/InstituteofGovernance/Publications/briefingpapers/ Filetoupload,47644,en.pdf.

Lambertz, K.A. (2015). Indicted Detroit Police Officers Allegedly Used Authority To Steal And Sell Drugs. *The Huffington Post*, April 9.

NAB Annual Report (2014). Retrieved July 28, 2015 from http://www.nab.gov.pk/ Downloads/Annual-Report-2014.pdf.

NAB dy khpala karawai sama kai (Pashto). (2015). *In Daily Khpalwaak*.

The Nation. (2010). FIA director being repatriated for saying "no." *Daily The Nation*, December 01. http://nation.com.pk/national/01-Dec-2010/ FIA-director-being-repatriated-for-saying-no.

National Accountability Ordinance (XVIII of 1999). Retrieved October 05, 2016 from http://www.nab.gov.pk/Downloads/nao.asp.

News and Updates. (2015). Ehtesaab Commission. Government of Khyber Pakhtunkwha. www.ehtesabcommissionkp.gov.pk.

Pakistan Penal Code (1860).

Prevention of Corruption Act (1947).

Qureshi, Z. (2013). A Review of Anti-Corruption Laws in Pakistan. *Hamari Web*. Retrieved July 27, 2015 from http://www.hamariweb.com/articles/article. aspx?id=31063.

Rao, S. (2015). IHC rules in favour of 300 bureaucrats' promotion. *In Daily The Nation*. Retrieved October 05, 2016 from http://nation.com.pk/newspaper-picks/09-Jun-2016/ihc-rules-in-favour-of-300-bureaucrats-promotion.

Sama News. (2014). September 11: 3:44 pm.

Samad, S. (2008). Combating corruption: The case of the National Accountability Bureau, Pakistan. *Journal of Administration and Governance*, 3(1). joaag.com/uploads/9_SamadFinal.pdf.

Transparency International (2013). Annual Report 2012. Transparency International Pakistan. Retrieved July 27, 2015 from http://www.transparency.org.pk/documents/annual_report12.pdf.

Wardag, T. (2014). I have fired more than 400 corrupt officers and officials from police force. IGP Nasar Khan Durrani. *Dir News*, September 10. Retrieved July 27, 2015 from http://www.dirnews.net/fired-400-curropt-officers-officials-police-force-igp-nasar-khan-durrani/.

Government Corruption and Authoritarian Rule in Turkey

13

HASAN T. ARSLAN
AYDOĞAN VATANDAŞ

Contents

Introduction

Corruption and government are two interrelated concepts, which are part of the human history almost dating back to the origins of the statehood. Both concepts intercept at the juncture of the power and authority. The institution of government was established as part of the need for security and maintenance of order in a society, however, the behavior of corruption is a learned one that emerged as the result of power poisoning. Corruption in government is mostly a product of the existing societal, political, and economical diseases in a society. The main problem of corruption is the mindset of people, most likely as the result of human inhibition on choosing the path of the least resistance on a daily basis in the face of getting things done. Corruption is usually only a matter of smoothing one's path. Thus, "in the political field, the traditional concept of corruption was strictly related to the morality of societies, rather than to actions of individuals" (Terracino, 2012, p. 8). When it comes to government, however, corruption appears in the form of a side effect of the political power. Corruption is mostly the first signal of power poisoning and collapse of moral authority. The famous quote of "Power tends to corrupt, and absolute power corrupts absolutely. Great men are almost always bad men" By an English historian, politician, and writer Lord Acton, should be great reminder of this situation. Therefore, in this context, corruption results when politics use the state structure as a mean to gain wealth and absolute power, which later finds itself in denial of the legal principle of *no one is above the law*. Understandably, "political parties need money to run their electoral machines and keep their militants deployed wherever needed" (Taheri, 2008). Furthermore, more scarier than the former, sometimes society view the commission of *violence* by any government either as a reflection of, or necessary auxiliary tool for an effective state authority. President Recep Tayyip Erdogan's leadership style fits the textbook profile of this assertion. It has been seen throughout history that some politicians have a superlative piece of skill that is very subtle (Freedman, 2013). According to Human Rights Watch report (2016), "Turkey jailed journalists and closed media groups that showed themselves willing to scrutinize government policy and corruption, or report evidence of arms transfers to Syrian opposition groups" (p. 17).

The Justice and Development Party (Adalet ve Kalkinma Partisi—AKP) was born out of Welfare Party (Refah Partisi—RP) in the summer of 2001 and moderated its vision around the lessons learned after the postmodern military intervention in 1997, which led the closure of the RP, and banned its leaders from politics for the next five years. Although RP was more Islamist and anti-Western in its' rhetoric and its' both domestic and international policies, AKP adopted more western oriented policies building a broader conservative coalition with support from liberals, which emphasized a market economy and fighting injustice, corruption, and inequality. The AKP's platform crucially promoted religious freedom, economic liberalization, and democratization (Dalay and Friedman, 2013). The beginning of the twenty-first century started with the new hopes, both for the AKP and Turkish people. In the mid of political pessimism, Recep Tayyip Erdogan emerged as the new leader with a full spectrum of inclusive political agenda for Turkish people. When Erdogan came to power, during the first years of his rule, he honored democracy by advancing judicial independence and the rule of law by a series of amendments. "To all these groups, Erdogan promised honest government, democratic reforms, civilian-led rule, the restoration of the proper role of Islam within the state, and economic prosperity" (Fradkin and Libby, 2014). This success was the initial result of the AKP's strict loyalty to its own party program that gained the respect of people from variety of cultural and ideological backgrounds in Turkey. This initial prediction has failed due to several historical and structural constraints that undermine democracy in Turkey, and the high level of government corruption is one of those chains. What started, as a dream and optimism, became one of the most corruptive and abusive administrations in Turkish political history. "And it is the AKP's leader, Recep Tayyip Erdogan, that is destroying the world's hope. And it is utilizing this authoritarianism, with a great brazenness, to cover up corruption" (Oran, 2014).

The first two terms (2003–2011) of the AKP ruling were very promising, in fact, as late as 2012, 16 EU foreign ministers drooled that Turkey was "an inspirational example of a secular and democratic country" (Ellis, 2016). However, since then, the Turkish democracy has been a subject of contention. Indeed, "Turkey is now an ideal worldwide observation post for being a textbook case of absolutist behavior of a political leader for the eyes of political scientists and the gentlemen of the long robe" (Arslan, 2015, p. 40). More particularly, since the mid-December 2013, the discovery of a historic scale of corruption, a political cover-up has been put in action. The lack of accountability in the current Turkish political system, demonstrates the weakness of the existing institutions and internal constitutional devices. Indeed, systematic corruption in any political system is an important socio-political indicator, which undermines democracy and transparency in a society.

This chapter examines the government corruption in Turkey by mostly scrutinizing on the AKP's third term policies between 2011 and 2015 along with President Erdogan's leadership style. First, a brief history of relationship between power and politics in Turkey will be described, followed by the revelations of the corruption operations of December 17 and 25, 2013. Finally, the authors presented an argument whether Turkey has been on a road to more authoritarian rule as a result of the existing grand-scale corruption in government offices than a participatory democracy in the light of AKP's retaliatory political maneuvers in the past few years.

History of Government Corruption and Scandals in Turkey

In a world of politics, deception, and trickery are natural and seen very often (Freedman, 2013). The political corruptions are universal occurrences in almost every society and state. Turkey is not immune to this disease. There are many corruption scandals in Turkish history and a few of the most notable and damaging ones will be mentioned below.

There was a military coup on September 12, 1980 in Turkey and until December 13, 1983, the country was ruled under the shadow of the National Security Council (Milli Guvenlik Kurulu—MGK), which was constituted by the head of each military branch. By 1984, slowly but surely a democratic progression began under Turgut Ozal administrations. Consequently, the 1980s have been marked as *Ozal era* that actually opened Turkey to market economy, integration process to global world, and Turkish capitalism. In 1985, it was discovered that Ismail Ozdaglar, a deputy Prime Minister of 45th government of Turkey, involved in a corruption case, where he was accepting bribe from the petroleum ship owner. Prime Minister Ozal asked his immediate resignation, which resulted in Ozdaglar's trial at Turkish Supreme Criminal Tribunal. Ismail Ozdaglar was sentenced two years in prison and banned from public employment for two years after the end of his punishment.

The 1990s can also be called the *lost decade* for Turkey in Turkish politics as well as counter-terrorism policies. On one side of the medallion were the short-lived coalition governments, and the other side was the escalating Kurdistan Worker's Party (PKK) terrorism. According to Turkish Union of Chambers in 2001, the Turkish politicians have squandered $195 billion between 1990 and 2000, and 13 private banks were forced to be taken over by the state due to corruption related bankruptcies (Koch and Chaudhary, 2002). The era began with a scandal at Istanbul Water and Sewerage Administration of Istanbul (Istanbul Su ve Kanalizasyon Idaresi—ISKI). Ergun Goknel, the chief of this municipal water company, had ditched his second wife to marry a young secretary. Despite the fact that Mr. Goknel paid her ex-wife £500,000 in cash along with a house and car, she still went to media by pointing out that there could be no legitimate source for the money and accused him of accepting all kinds of kickbacks. The later government investigation discovered "the systematic extortion from municipal contractors and regular 'salaries' for a Social Democrat minister and 29 journalists" (Pope, 1993). The long-term impact of this scandal resulted very serious political consequences for the Socialist parties in Turkey.

On November 3, 1996, a black Mercedes full of passengers crashed into a truck full of load. This accident, which happened near the small town of Susurluk, Balikesir province, in Western Turkey, has also come to be known as the *Susurluk Scandal*. The notorious black Mercedes contained four different characters that seemed to have been extracted from a movie scene: a police chief (Huseyin Kocadag), a wanted right-wing hitman (Abdullah Catli), and his beauty queen girlfriend, who all died in the accident (Anthony, 2007). "The single survivor was an MP, who was left to explain the presence in the car of false passports and guns fitted with silencers. The Minister of the Interior was obliged to resign when his signature was found on the passports" (Paterson, 1997). The Susurluk accident simply exposed the links of the deep state in Turkey, and went beyond its name by becoming the symbol of corruption, and dark relations between state, gangs, and politics in Turkey since then.

Another political scandal in 1998 exposed the dirty relationship between the government, the private sector, and underground world. The *Turkbank scandal* ensued the full investigation by the Grand National Assembly of Turkey (Turkiye Buyuk Millet Meclisi—TBMM), which resulted the fall by motion of no confidence of the Prime Minister Mesut Yilmaz and his cabinet in January 1999. Yilmaz was the first Turkish prime minister to stand trial for alleged abuse of power in Turkey. Basically, he was accused of rigging the sale of the bank to "establish a media order under their control for political gains" (Hurriyet Daily, 2004).

Finally, the 1990s closed with a scandal called *Operation Hurricane* in which, involved a young nephew of the former President Suleyman Demirel.

Yahya Murat Demirel was charged with embezzling money through a complex network of front companies and offshore banks. Initially, nephew "Demirel and other bank officials had used the institution to obtain tens of millions of dollars in fraudulent loans that contributed to the bank's demise" (Moore, 2000). After a very long investigation and judicial process, Yahya M. Demirel was sentenced to 30 years for two crimes, but was able to escape Turkey for Belize in 2012.

By 2000, Turkish public were frustrated of the slow and unfinished government policies as well as many political and economical scandals of the 1990s. Furthermore, the coalition governments were one of the reasons for newly established AKP's elections victory in its first general election on November 2002, which was "a drastic response to the old, statist, clientalist, corruption producing, and crisis-ridden system by the Turkish electorate" (Keyman and Koyuncu, 2005).

During his first general election campaign in 2002, Recep Tayyip Erdogan made several political promises; one of them was the lifting parliamentary immunity in the investigation of corruption cases. With every consecutive successful election results since 2002, Erdogan has been implicating himself as the *political boss* (Reis) of the government in Turkey. However, Erdogan defended the retention of the immunity when he became prime minister. Moreover, the ruling AKP introduced the Tax Reconciliation Law in 2003 to provide some legislative cover for the corruptive actions (Sami, 2006, p. 70). There is a similar story from the American politics during late 1800s and early 1900s. Like the Tammany Hall political machine in New York City, George Washington Plunkitt, made his name as a corrupted politician. At the time of his death, according to the New York Times obituary, Plunkitt was worth "considerably more than $1,000,000," about (pounds) 5 million today (O'Toole, 1999). Furthermore, Plunkitt has become famous for his description of the term *honest graft* as described by him below:

> Just let me explain by examples. My party's in power in the city, and it's goin' to undertake a lot of public improvements. Well, I'm tipped off, say, that they're going to lay out a new park at a certain place. I see my opportunity and I take it. I go to that place and I buy up all the land I can in the neighborhood. Then the board of this or that makes its plan public, and there is a rush to get my land, which nobody cared particular for before. Ain't it perfectly honest to charge a good price and make a profit on my investment and foresight? Of course it is. Well, that's honest graft (Nolan, 1986).

To understand the mechanics of this alleged *honest graft operations* in Turkey, one must look at the social network system within the local government structures in Turkey. Particularly, construction business stands alone in a unique way to make many rich in short period of time in Turkey. However, this industrial sector heavily relies on the help of friends in local politics to win contracts. "Part of the blame must be apportioned to a social system in which everything is negotiable and friends always help each other. If a mayor or other public official has a friend or relative who owns a construction company, tradition dictates that they make some arrangement so both can prosper" (Kinzer, 1999). The *honest graft* appeared a little bit differently in AKP ranks. Truly, as Prime Minister, Erdogan made promises on vast construction projects during every general election campaigns. Initially, he had come from local politics and served as the mayor of a large metropolitan city, Istanbul. During his entire premiership he still continued to run Turkey like a city, *where he controlled local projects as if he is playing in his own private Legoland* (Hansen, 2014). Erdogan Bayraktar was a minister, who was in charge of the massive Public Housing Project Administration (TOKI) in Erdogan's third administration and is seen as the *black box* for dealings in that context. Bayraktar revealed that Erdogan had given the final *go ahead* to all the key decisions associated with the big construction biddings (Baydar, 2013). In exchange, the AKP received a certain percentage of gratitude.

The Mother of All Corruption Scandals

On July 12, 2011, AKP claimed victory for a third time by receiving 49.9% of the vote, and 326 seats out of the 550 in Turkish parliament. As part of the election campaign, "the AKP focused on launching grand projects in line with its '2023 vision' for the Turkish Republic's centennial, such as building the multibillion-dollar Istanbul Canal and establishing new cities in Istanbul and in Ankara" (Demirtas, 2011). By describing this term as their *period of mastery*, then Prime Minister Erdogan raised the bar with promises like drafting a new civilian constitution, settling the Kurdish issue, the purging of the military tutelage with all of its traces, and expanding the process of purging all institutions and organizations of corruption (Kenes, 2012). Unfortunately, "that the AKP's third term is mired in systemic corruption is discouraging for Turkey's democracy. Even more worrisome, though, is the fact that corruption has led to an authoritarian trend in which those who refuse political obedience are profiled and discriminated against" (Aslandogan, 2014).

On December 17, 2013, officers from the financial crimes and battle against criminal incomes unit within the Istanbul police department raided several houses of prominent government officials, businessmen, and mayors. Among the detainees, the three sons of Turkish ministers: *Baris Guler,* son of Minister of the Interior, *Kaan Caglayan,* son of Minister of Economy, and *Oguz Bayraktar,* son of Minister of Environment and Urban Planning were also included. During operation, $4.5 million in cash was packed in shoe boxes in the home of the chief executive of a state-run bank, Halkbank was seized, another $750,000 along with a money-counting machine in the bedroom of a government minister's son. "In a way, police operations caught them in the form of 'in flagrante delicto'" (Arslan, 2015, p. 37). All of the 52 people detained that day were connected in various ways with the ruling AKP (Orucoglu, 2015).

A week later, on December 25, 2013, in the early hours, a second wave of graft operation aiming people, who were in primarily Prime Minister Erdogan's inner circle including his son, took place, but was not able to be carried out. The newly appointed police chief of Istanbul by Erdogan's administration after the first wave, refused to continue on the operation. In addition, the Deputy Director of Public Prosecutions dismissed the Prosecutor leading the investigation by nighttime. The details of both the operations were later leaked to the media in the following days. One of the interesting discoveries is the link between the Turkish officials and the Iran via a businessman Reza Zarrab. "Sales from Iran were silently facilitated by the Turkish bank through the purchasing of gold that was given to Tehran as payment, instead of a currency, after Tehran was blocked from using the SWIFT international money-transfer system in March 2012" (Nazemroaya, 2014).

Many other voice recordings linked to the corruption probe, apparently from wiretaps, have shown up on YouTube, Vimeo, Twitter, and other social media sites (Arango and Yeginsu, 2014). Furthermore, to prevent the future damages of the similar *seismic waves* of the corruption scandal in the cyberspace, AKP passed a new law, which allowed the authorities, without a court order, to block web pages under the guise of protecting personal privacy. This was clearly a transparent effort to prevent social media and other sites from reporting on a corruption scandal that might embarrass the party officials. Basically, Erdogan and his inner circle started a propaganda war purely targeting the party's image among Turkish citizens. In fact, this should be considered as one of the most intensive perception games in politics at work. As a matter of fact, the Turkish media outlets also became more biased and began to favor the reporters allied to Erdogan, thus undermining the opinions of the opposition (Akser and Baybars-Hawks, 2012).

AKP's Brand is "Perception"

The Erdogan administration has done nothing to pursue the corruption allegations by letting the judiciary reviewing the facts, which is a routine procedure in a democratic state with a principle of rule of law. "The AKP and Erdogan were quite clear in deciding whom to blame for these problems: a U.S.-based Islamic cleric who held deep sway in Turkey" (Taylor, 2014). Erdogan called the probe a sinister *coup attempt* by the members of an alleged secret organization within the judiciary, and police directed by

Fethullah Gulen, a mainstream Turkish–Sunni scholar who has been living a self imposed exile in the United States since 1999. The AKP leadership
alleged that Gulen attempted to overthrow the government through its followers in the state apparatus. They even further contended that members of
the Hizmet movement (*in English: Service*) are "traitors and terrorists allied
with foreign interests" (Sterling, 2014, December 10). In reality, Erdogan had
previously viewed the Hizmet movement as a close ally during AKP reign
for a long time. With the support from the movement under the pretense of
fighting for more democratic reforms in Turkey, Erdogan was able to extend
AKP's influence, both over the people and the military-bureaucratic structures. Indeed, even though the Turkish military was partly sidelined in the
Turkish politics during AKP rule, what replaced it was not a consolidated
democracy, but Erdogan's autocracy. Simply, the AKP led-government pursued a systematic trio-perception campaign primarily in the following areas:
empowering the executive power, seizing the control over the judiciary, and
suppressing the media.

"The AKP leadership empowered the executive branch over other
Turkish institutions, which was done knowingly and maliciously, violating the
principles of the rule of law" (Arslan, 2015, p. 37). By Spring of 2015, thousands
of high-ranked police chiefs were forced to retire from their positions followed by the government's closure of the prestigious institutions of Police
Academy and Police College. All of these were looked to be an attempt to
pave the way for promoting pro-government police officers. The perception
game also continued on the officers and prosecutors, who were also portrayed in the service of foreign powers like the United States and Israel by
Erdogan himself (Baydar, 2013). Such defamation is the cliché of Turkish
politics, more specifically for the conservative and nationalist politicians.
According to Mehmet Baransu, a journalist in Daily Taraf newspaper, who
was also imprisoned in 2015, "Erdogan wants to show that this is a conspiracy, that the United States and Israel are behind it. Under no circumstances
does he want to talk about corruption." (Arango, 2014). The AKP government
also alleged that the millions of dollars seized in the operations along with
the money counting machines were staged by those police officers to frame
the AKP government. One should note that throughout history, there has
not been any recorded coup d'état, where the plotters brought their own
millions and counting machines, to the scene with the intention to frame
the existing authority. Yet, the amount of millions of dollars seized in the
operation would be so hard to be accumulated by the accused coup plotters.
This absurdity itself defeats its own argument. "Obsessed with his enemies,
increasingly erratic and dictatorial, and seeming to have little to no interest
in further structural reform" (Hullsman, 2014); thus, the ruling AKP leadership continues to blame for all the shady elements on Hizmet Movement
without showing any single evidence.

The second part of the campaign specifically aimed at the judiciary. First, in mid–June 2014, the AKP introduced the creation of *special criminal judges* with extensive powers, which empowered them making all decisions on detention, arrest, and release of the individuals along with the seizure of property. The most shocking part of this is that anybody who would seek appeal against these judge's decisions could only go before another special criminal judge. This itself is a clear violation of natural judge principle. "Both the Turkish legal doctrine and the constitutional court rulings confirm that this clause prohibits the creation of courts with competence to try cases of violations of law that took place before their creation" (Ozbudun, 2015, p. 5). Second, on October 26, 2014, President Erdogan appointed AKP-linked lawyers to fulfill the four seats out of the 22-member judicial body at the High Council of Prosecutors and Judges (Hakimler ve Savcilar Yuksek Kurulu–HSYK) (Benli, 2014). Furthermore, the *special criminal judges* were appointed by proAKP members of the First Chamber of HSYK. Third, in early December 2014, a 35-article judiciary package was passed, which extended the police power based on a concept called *reasonable search*. Finally, the HSYK suspended all the prosecutors of the graft operations a day before the New Years Eve of 2014. As of early 2016, a total of 69 people including Gulen are on trial, facing possible jail terms ranging from seven years to 330 years if convicted (The Guardian, 2016).

In the third phase of the perception game the government-orchestrated crackdown on independent critical media outlets in Turkey. According to Human Rights Watch report of 2016, "government-led restrictions on media freedom and freedom of expression in Turkey in 2015 went hand-in-hand with efforts to discredit the political opposition and prevent scrutiny of government policies in the run-up to the two general elections" (p. 580). Besides, journalists are not the only individuals suffering from the authoritarian nature of Erdogan's government. Through suctioning, sacking, and imprisoning of government critics, Erdogan has managed to control the Turkey's business leaders and the military officials as well. In addition, other tactics include disseminating spurious news and slandering those media outlets, which provided any information about the details of the graft. This was done in order to discredit the sources. Nevertheless, in the eye of law, the evidence discovered during corruption probe should not have been subjected to political criterion, but the legal doctrines. The political motivations neither determine nor judge the admissibility of the evidence in any investigation; for evidence to be admissible depends solely on its relevancy and reliability to the facts and its methods of collection within the existing legal framework. Sadly, many intriguing questions remained unanswered due to abrupt government interruption in the corruption graft probe.

It should also be mentioned here that political corruption is only the tip of the iceberg in Turkish society. There are many other unspoken problems that have significantly augmented during the entire AKP administrations such as drug and alcohol addiction, prostitution, and suicide rates. According to a recent study done by Professor Hakan Yilmaz, there have been critical levels of increase in cocaine use (572%), marijuana (140%), prostitution cases (700%), and suicide rate (36%) between 2009 and 2014 in Turkey. The substance abuse among the high school students has also been significantly rocketed (Unal, 2014). Basically, the AKP's brand is perception, which is also like a paint to cover-up many dents on a car. The majority of the society has not even been aware of the aforementioned problems in the country.

Turkey Toward the Authoritarian State

Mustafa Kemal Ataturk founded the modern Turkey in 1923. By gaining the invaded territories from the Greek, French, and British forces, he appeared as the savior of the nation as a semigod and tried to create a new Turkish nation. Ataturk devised the legal system as the protector of his revolution—rather than citizens' rights. His politically motivated *Independence Courts* executed or imprisoned many dissidents. In the following years, Republican elites passionately continued this bad tradition (Akyol, 2014). Historically, even though Ataturk attempted to create a modern nation on secular basis, the new Turkish Republic failed to create a democratic political environment. Truly, the Turkish system of governance has been formulated on a framework of a strong state and a weak society. The government and the governed have one-dimensioned relationship that oppressed the governed. As a result of this historical practice, the Turkish society has never been able to establish an autonomous sphere that free from the state.

The necessary political will, which is needed to transform Turkey into a fully functioning democracy has been always lacking. Therefore, AKP has been controlling overwhelming majority in the Turkish Parliament. Such a strong presence with the lack of strong opposition trigger the fears to not only the old Kemalist center state establishment, and secular segments of the society, but also the liberals and moderate religious circles as well. Although AKP receives a huge approval from the society, the great majority of the Turkish society has become suspicious of the real intentions of the Islamist periphery and the President Erdogan, suggesting that they want slowly to change the regime on nonsecular basis, and turn the country into a dictatorship. One primary obstacle for the AKP is the current Turkish Constitution of 1980. Despite a landslide victory on the 2010 referendum, the AKP administrations failed to keep their promise on the adaptation of a new democratic constitution, due to the deepening of the existing internal divisions in the country.

Andrew arato is a professor of political and social theory in the department of sociology at The New School in New York and one of the authors of the book *Civil Society and Political Theory*. Arato was one of the few voices in American academia who repeatedly warned Turkish liberal intellectuals about the authoritarian direction that Erdogan's leadership was inclined to. He asserts that Turkey is experiencing some type of a hard democracy, *democradura* (a term used in Latin America to call authoritarian rule or low-intensity democracy), that bordered a soft dictatorship in the past few years of Erdogan's authoritarian rule. Arato further explains:

> The 2010 referenda, to me, represented an attempt to conquer yet another branch of the separation of powers, the judiciary. I saw more attractive provisions of the package as window dressing for a monolithic project. It was already clear to me that this project aimed at a version of hyper-presidentialism, and sought to remove all impediments in its way, especially the judiciary that established its jurisdiction over constitutional amendments (Vatandas, 2015b).

As of 2016, the political system in Turkey was raped through the unequal distribution of the power among the government branches. Evidently, the AKP leadership empowered the executive branch over other Turkish institutions, which was done knowingly and maliciously, violating the principles of the rule of law. It is very clear from Turkish experience that justice can only be served when the right people—AKP affiliated people—control the judiciary. For example, people who are closely affiliated with the AKP took control over the High Council of Judges and Prosecutors, which is responsible for judicial functions, including appointments. Currently, the justice minister has a greater authority over legal discipline, judicial investigations, and the appointment of judges and prosecutors. This act itself severely undermines the separation between the executive and judiciary branches (Bilefsky and Arsu, 2014). To establish full control over, Erdogan also heavily relies on the use of the National Intelligence Service (Milli Istihbarat Teskilati—MIT) to spy on and profile citizens and civil servants (Aslandogan, 2014).

The leadership style of President Recep Tayyip Erdogan must also be mentioned in here. In their *Leadership Trait Analysis* work, Margaret Hermann, Gorener, and Ucal examined the leadership style of Recep Tayyip Erdogan, and his prospective impact on Turkish Foreign policy. They conclude that that Erdogan's convictions are so tightly held and preferences fixed, and that he tends to see only what he wants to see, renders him incapable of deciphering the nuances of diplomacy, and successfully navigating the tricky waters of international affairs. The research reveals that his dichotomizing tendency predisposes him to view politics as a struggle between right and wrong, just and unjust, and villains and victims (2011). It is also asserted that Erdogan has the qualities of a charismatic leader (Arik and Yavuz, 2015). However, not all the charismatic leaders tend to be democratic. If they are authoritarian in nature, authoritarian charismatic leaders most likely are determined to turn into dictators. Erdogan's authoritarian charisma and narcissistic personality organization provide evidences that he would be willing to rule Turkey as an autocrat, but not a democratic leader, which prevents transparency and accountability, and institutional struggle against corruption. In short, the only enemy for the President is now himself.

Conclusion

Turkey's unique position on the world map puts the country in the juncture of the world's geographic and political crossroads, while keeping it in the virtual epicenter of Bermuda Triangle, Balkans, Caucuses, and Middle East regions. It is this unique position that makes Turkey a pivotal state for preserving the peace in a hot zone, where in each corner is prone to religiously, ethnically, and politically motivated conflicts. Alas! An efficient leadership is a hard commodity to find in that geography as the recent 100 years have demonstrated to us. Simply, corruption and institutionalized greed have been serving as powerful engine pushing any government over the edge into absolutism for a long time (Finkel, 2013) in this edge of the worlds.

Historically, although the Turkish political system seemed democratic, the state has continuously denied the legitimacy of certain groups that threaten the centralized authority from the social stratification that give the elites control over the state (Caylak, 2008). The initial method of suppression as a government authority also reduced the advocacy for democracy in the country, thus favoring autocratic governance. Therefore, the conquest of the existing civil organizations in Turkey has prevented citizens from exercising their freedom of speech and right to protest for democracy (McLaren and Cop, 2011). In other words, according to Mustafa Akyol, a Turkish columnist in the New York Times, the AKP did not abolish the old logic of the Republican ideology, which was protecting the state's interests rather than the rights of citizens; they just adopted it for their advantage (2014).

The Barometer Survey conducted in 2004 revealed that Turkish respondents have trust problems with all the institutions in public and private domain. The survey demonstrated that from personal to political life, from family domain to business environment, there is no area that was considered free of corruption's influence (Yasar, 2005). The recent developments in Turkey have provided evidences that a conservative political party, which claims to have an ontological link to Islam, was not free of corruption's influence either.

Evidently, AKP's success story depends on favorable economic conditions or the favorable economic performance of the AKP governments. According to investigative journalist Aydogan Vatandas:

> Due to the lack of a powerful political opposition in Turkey, Gulen movement was considered, as the only civil society that can challenge Erdogan's autocratic ruling. However, unless the needs and demands of the masses still exist and economy is stable, the masses tend to support the AKP because there was no other party around that can respond to their demands. Likewise Gulen movement is not a political party and not capable of responding the needs of the masses, either. This is pure and simple money driven politics of Turkey. Therefore, the only legitimate way to change Erdogan's power play in Turkey relies primarily on the failures of the Erdogan's economic policies as well as the emergence of a new party in the center right (2015a).

As of 2016, Turkey can now be "described as being on the borderline between illiberal (or electoral) democracies and *competitive authoritarian* regimes, increasingly approaching the latter" (Ozbudun, 2015, p. 7). Indeed, the AKP policies have been shaking the foundations of state control daily, since December 17 with near-absolute power-oriented decisions, which are only observed in authoritarian regimes and not in democracies. The only way out is to restructure the Turkish judiciary to make it both independent and non-partisan, so that it protects the rights of all citizens and rule of law. Finally, it should be noted that "corruption in Turkey is not as pervasive as it is in many nearby countries...This reflects a culture in which murderers are sometimes esteemed because they are presumed to have acted in defense of family honor, whereas thieves are despised for violating one of God's most elemental laws" (Kinzer, 1999). For the sake of covering this mother of all scandals, there are many other crimes that have been committed in many levels whether against people or institutions. Indeed, the Transparency International report of 2016 indicated the marked deterioration in Turkey where the organization had observed more corruption and less space for democracy in the country. According to Anne Koch, Director for Europe and Central Asia, "Corruption won't be tackled until laws and regulations are put into action and civil society and the media are genuinely free" (Transparency International, 2016).

References

Akser, M. and Baybars-Hawks, B. (2012). Media and Democracy in Turkey: Toward a Model of Neoliberal Media Autocracy. *Middle East Journal of Culture and Communication,* 5(3), 302–321.

Akyol, M. (2014). Turkey Needs Justice for All. *The New York Times,* January 11. New York City. Retrieved from www.lexisnexis.com/hottopics/lnacademic.

Public Corruption

Anthony, A. (2007). A Fight for the Soul of the New Turkey. *The Guardian*, May 19. London, UK. Retrieved from http://www.theguardian.com/world/2007/may/20/turkey.andrewanthony.

Arango, T. (2014). In Scandal, Turkey's Leaders May Be Losing Their Tight Grip on News Media. *The New York Times*, January, 11. Retrieved on November 30, 2015 from http://www.nytimes.com/2014/01/12/world/europe/in-scandal-turkeys-leaders-may-be-losing-their-tight-grip-on-news-media.html?_r=3.

Arango, T. and Yeginsu, C. (2014). Amid Flow of Leaks, Turkey Moves to Crimp Internet. *The New York Times*, February 6. Retrieved on November 30, 2015 from http://www.nytimes.com/2014/02/07/world/europe/amid-flow-of-leaks-turkey-moves-to-crimp-internet.html?_r=0.

Arik, I. and Yavuz, C. (2015). The Importance of Leadership in International Relation-Recep Tayyip Erdogan Sample. *International Journal of Research in Social Sciences*, *4*(9), 142–148.

Arslan, H. T. (2015). A Never Ending Story in the Country of Zigzags. *Wyno Academic Journal of Societal Sciences*, *3*(4), 31–44.

Aslandogan, A. (2014). Turkey's Fading Democracy. *Huffington Post*, February 10. Retrieved on January 21, 2016 from http://www.huffingtonpost.com/alp-aslandogan/turkeys-fading-democracy_b_4733996.html.

Baydar, Y. (2013). Erdogan's Dream Turns into a Nightmare. *Al Monitor*, December 26. Retrieved on November 30, 2015 from http://www.al-monitor.com/pulse/originals/2013/12/turkey-erdogan-resignation-ministers-akp-power-corruption.html#.

Benli, H. (2014). Turkish President Sends AKP-Linked Lawyers to Key Judges and Prosecutors Council. *Hurriyet Daily*, October 27. Retrieved from http://www.hurriyetdailynews.com/turkish-president-sends-akp-linked-lawyers-to-key-judges-and-prosecutors-council.aspx?pageID=238&nID=73513&NewsCatID=338.

Bilefsky, D. and Arsu, S. (2014). Turkish Government, Shaking Up Police, Now Seeks More Power Over Judiciary. *The New York Times*, January 9. Retrieved on November 16, 2015 from www.lexisnexis.com/hottopics/lnacademic.

Caylak, A. (2008). Autocratic or Democratic? A Critical Approach to Civil Society Movements In Turkey. *Journal of Economic and Social Research*, *10*(1), 115–151.

Dalay, G. and Friedman, D. (2013). The AK Party and the Evolution of Turkish Political Islam's Foreign Policy. *Insight Turkey*, *15*(2), 123–139.

Demirtas, S. (2011). Turkey's 2011 Election Campaign: A Tale of Crazy Projects and Cassette Scandals. *Hurriyet Daily*, June 6. Istanbul, TR. Retrieved on January 21, 2016 from http://www.hurriyetdailynews.com/default.aspx?pageid=438&n=a-tale-of-campaign-hitting-crazy-projects-cassettes-projects8230-2011-06-10.

Ellis, R. (2016). Erdogan is on the Brink of Ultimate Power, But Turkey is Falling Apart. *The Independent*, February 4. Retrieved on February 8, 2016 from http://www.independent.co.uk/voices/erdogan-is-on-the-brink-of-ultimate-power-but-turkey-is-falling-apart-a6853416.html.

Finkel, A. (2013). The Filth in Erdogan's Closet. *The New York Times*, December 28. Retrieved from www.lexisnexis.com/hottopics/lnacademic.

Fradkin, H. and Libby, L. (2014). Turkey on the Brink. *World Affairs*, *177*(1), 58–66.

Freedman, L. (2013). *Strategy: A History* (1st Edition). New York: Oxford University Press.

Gorener, A. S. and Ucal, M. S. (2011). The Personality and Leadership Style of Recep Tayyip Erdoğan: Implications for Turkish Foreign Policy. *Turkish Studies, 12*(3), 357–381.

The Guardian. (2016). Erdoğan Critic and Ex-Police Chiefs Go on Trial Over Corruption Inquiries. *The Guardian*, January 6. Retrieved on January 10, 2015 from http://www.theguardian.com/world/2016/jan/06/recep-tayyip-erdogan-critic-fethullah-gulen-turkey-police-chiefs-corruption-trial.

Hansen, S. (2014). Whose Turkey Is It? *The New York Times*, February 9. Retrieved from www.lexisnexis.com/hottopics/lnacademic.

Hullsman, J. (2014). Why Politics Will Dominate 2015: Losers and Winners in this Maddening New Era. *The Forum*, December 22. City A.M., Retrieved from www.lexisnexis.com/hottopics/lnacademic.

Human Rights Watch. (2016). World Report 2016. *Human Rights Watch*. Retrieved on January 29, 2016 from https://www.hrw.org/sites/default/files/world_report_download/wr2016_web.pdf.

Hurriyet Daily. (2004). Yilmaz, Former Ministers Face Ten Years If Convicted of Graft. Hurriyet Daily, July 15. Retrieved on February 8, 2016 from http://www.hurriyetdailynews.com/yilmaz-former-ministers-face-ten-years-if-convictedof-graft.aspx?pageID=438&n=yilmaz-former-ministers-face-ten-years-if-convicted-of-graft-2004-07-15.

Kenes, B. (2012). First Year of AKP's Third Term. *Today's Zaman Online*, June 12. Retrieved on January 21, 2016 from http://www.todayszaman.com/columnists_first-year-of-akps-third-term_283316.html.

Keyman, E. F. and Koyuncu, B. (2005). Globalization, Alternative Modernities and the Political Economy of Turkey. *Review Of International Economy, 12*, 107–130.

Kinzer, S. (1999). The World; The Turkish Quake's Secret Accomplice: Corruption. *The New York Times*, August 29. Retrieved on January 12, 2016, from www.lexisnexis.com/hottopics/lnacademic.

Koch, L. and Chaudhary, M. A. (2002). February 2001 Crises in Turkey: Causes and Consequences. *The Pakistan Development Review, 40*(4), 467–486.

McLaren, L. and Cop, B. (2011). The Failure of Democracy in Turkey: A Comparative Analysis. *Government & Opposition, 46*(4), 485–516.

Moore, M. (2000). Turkish Economy Shaken by Corruption Revelations; Privatization, Globalization Open Door to Malfeasance. *The Washington Post*, December 30. Retrieved from www.lexisnexis.com/hottopics/lnacademic.

Nazemroaya, M. D. (2014). Turkey & Iran: More than Meets the Eye. *RT News*, January 20. Retrieved on November 30, 2015 from https://www.rt.com/op-edge/turkey-iran-sanctions-corruption-scandal-883/.

Nolan, M. F. (1986). Deaver's "Honest Graft." *Boston Globe (Pre-1997 Fulltext)*, May 19. Retrieved from http://search.proquest.com/docview/294356316?accountid=13044.

Oran, B. (2014). What Will The End Of The Erdogan Regime Be? *Radikal Newspaper*. Retrieved on March 18, 2016 from http://www.radikal.com.tr/yazarlar/baskin-oran/erdogan-rejiminin-sonu-ne-olacak-1249446/.

Orucoglu, B. (2015). Why Turkey's Mother of all Corruption Scandals Refuses to Go Away. *Foreign Policy*. Retrieved on January 10, 2016 from http://foreignpolicy.com/2015/01/06/why-turkeys-mother-of-all-corruption-scandals-refuses-to-go-away/.

O'Toole, F. (1999). Tammany Hall is Real Spiritual Home of Fianna Fail. *Irish Times*, July 2. Retrieved from http://search.proquest.com/docview/310554960?accountid=13044.

Ozbudun, E. (2015). Pending Challenges in Turkey's Judiciary. *Global Turkey in Europe*, **20**, 1–8.

Paterson, P. (1997). A splitting headache: Television. *Daily Mail*, November 20. Retrieved on January 12, 2016 from www.lexisnexis.com/hottopics/lnacademic.

Pope, H. (1993). Slighted Wife Spills Beans on Husband's Kickbacks. *The Irish Times*, August 24. Retrieved on January 12, 2016 from www.lexisnexis.com/hottopics/lnacademic.

Sami, S. (2006). Silent Capitulations: The Kemalist Republic Under Assault. Bloomington, IN: iUniverse.

Sterling, H. (2014). Turkish Leader's Words Disclose His Darker Side; Erdogan's Extremism a Clear Danger, Writes Harry Sterling. *The Calgary Herald*, December 10. Retrieved from www.lexisnexis.com/hottopics/lnacademic.

Taheri, A. (2008). Turkey: Trouble at Home, Gains Abroad. *Gulf News (United Arab Emirates)*, October 22. Retrieved on January 12, 2016 from ww.lexisnexis.com/hottopics/lnacademic.

Taylor, A. (2014). This Single Tweet Got a Turkish Journalist Detained. *The Washington Post*, December 30. Retrieved on November 30, 2015 from http://www.washingtonpost.com/blogs/worldviews/wp/2014/12/30/this-single-tweet-got-a-turkish-journalist-detained/.

Terracino, J. B. (2012). *The International Legal Framework against Corruption: States' Obligations to Prevent and Repress Corruption*. Oxford, UK: Intersentia.

Transparency International. (2016). Corruption Perceptions Index 2015. *Transparency International*. Retrieved on January 29, 2016 from https://www.transparency.org/cpi2015.

Unal, A. (2014). Caliyor ama Calisiyor (In English: It Steals while Serving-to People). *Zaman Daily*, May 12. Retrieved on November 30, 2015 from http://www.zaman.com.tr/ali-unal/caliyor-ama-calisiyor_2216670.html.

Vatandas, A. (2015a). Money-Driven Politics of Turkey: Winners Take All!. *Today's Zaman Online*, November 29. Retrieved on January 21, 2016 from http://www.todayszaman.com/op-ed_money-driven-politics-of-turkey-winners-take-all_405631.html.

Vatandas, A. (2015b). What we have in Turkey is a hard democracy, A "demokra-dura." *Today's Zaman Online*, November 7. Retrieved on January 11, 2016 from http://www.todayszaman.com/interviews_what-we-have-in-turkey-is-a-hard-democracy-a-demokradura_403505.html.

Yasar, M. M. (2005). *A Complex Systems Model for Understanding the Causes of Corruption: Case Study—Turkey*. (Unpublished doctoral dissertation). Denton, TX: University of Texas.

Index

For Product Safety Concerns and Information please contact our EU representative GPSR@taylorandfrancis.com Taylor & Francis Verlag GmbH, Kaufingerstraße 24, 80331 München, Germany

Printed and bound by CPI Group (UK) Ltd, Croydon, CR0 4YY
01/05/2025
01858450-0005